THE METHODS AND SKILLS OF HISTORY

A Practical Guide

THE METHODS AND SKILLS OF HISTORY

A Practical Guide

THIRD EDITION

Conal Furay

Michael J. Salevouris

Webster University

WILEY Blackwell

Registered Office
John Wiley & Sons, Ltd, The Atrium, Southern Gate, Chichester, West Sussex,
PO19 8SQ, UK
Editorial Offices
350 Main Street, Malden, MA 02148-5020, USA
9600 Garsington Road, Oxford, OX4 2DQ, UK
The Atrium, Southern Gate, Chichester, West Sussex, PO19 8SQ, UK

For details of our global editorial offices, for customer services, and for
information about how to apply for permission to reuse the copyright material
in this book please see our website at www.wiley.com/wiley-blackwell.

Library of Congress Cataloging in-Publication Data

Furay, Conal.

Furay, Conal.
The methods and skills of history: a practical guide / Conal Furay,
Michael J. Salevouris. — 3rd ed.
    p. cm.
Includes bibliographical references and index.
ISBN 978-0-88295-272-7
1. History—Examinations, questions, etc. 2. History—Methodology. I. Salevouris,
Michael J. II. Title.

D21.F947 2010
907.6—dc22

                                                            2009036480

For Clare Conall Furay of happy memory.—C. F.

For Peggy, the best part of the best part of my life.—M. S.

CONTENTS

PREFACE

This book first saw the light of day in 1979 under the title *History: A Workbook of Skill Development*. The first revision came almost a decade later (1988), with a new title (the present one) and a new publisher, Harlan Davidson. Over the years the book attracted a loyal group of users, making it more successful than we had any reason to expect, prompting a second revised edition in 2000, and this one, the third, in 2010. It is tempting to let well enough alone. "Don't fix it if it ain't broke," goes the common wisdom. But no work can remain fresh and challenging without the rethinking that is spurred by continual reuse as well as student comments and criticisms, not to mention the dramatic developments in computer technology and electronic research techniques. Still, it would be folly to jettison too much of what made the book successful in the first place. The most dramatic changes (new chapters, significant reorganization, and the use of introductory vignettes for individual chapters) came in 2000. In this third edition the changes are more subtle, but the aim remains the same: to improve the book while keeping the essence unchanged. Regular users will find much that is familiar, along with additions and alterations that (we hope) have enhanced rather than transformed the previous editions.

Two trends in American higher education prompted us to write this book in the first place—trends that, even in the twenty-first century, are still very much in evidence. First, there has been a drift away from traditional forms of history in many high schools and colleges in favor of what are seen as more "relevant" topic courses in the social sciences. Valuable though they may be, such courses often make students aware of many contemporary problems but leave them uninformed of the relevant historical background. Further, these courses do little to encourage students to develop the conceptual tools to think historically. Second, there continues to be an exodus from "liberal arts" curricula to professional and pre-professional programs of study. The assumption, explicit or not, is that courses in the liberal arts—especially those in the humanities—do little to prepare one for a career in the "real world."

Both trends are deeply disturbing, for we are convinced—and there is evidence to support the conviction—that a good liberal arts education often can provide better all-around career preparation than many narrowly focused professional or vocational programs. Further, we firmly believe that, within the context of a liberal arts education, the development of basic historical literacy is essential. Not only can history give a perspective on the world that no other discipline can provide, but the serious study of history will help develop skills that one can use in any career or field of work.

The purpose of the book is thus twofold:

1. To provide a general introduction to the nature and methods of history that will help students think historically and better appreciate the importance of historical literacy.

2. To help students develop the intellectual and communication skills applicable not only to the study of history, but also to many other academic disciplines and to a wide variety of professional pursuits.

To accomplish these goals we combine theory and practice, with slightly more emphasis on the latter. Each chapter provides a brief introductory overview of a topic followed by a number of exercises. The aim of the essays and exercises is not to teach sophisticated research skills to prospective graduate students, but to make the study of history more meaningful for students whether they are majoring in history, taking a history course as an elective, or simply reading history on their own. It is our hope that this book will enhance students' appreciation of history on a purely intellectual level and at the same time help them develop skills useful in other academic disciplines and in their post-college lives—the "real world," if you will.

The exercises in this book range from the relatively simple to the complex. Most of them have two sets of questions—Set A and Set B. Few instructors will want to assign both sets, and some may not assign every exercise in a given set. But should the instructor feel that the repetition of an exercise might help a particular student, a second set of materials is provided. Although most of the exercises call for written responses, ideally students should have the opportunity to discuss their answers in a classroom setting. History, obviously, is not a subject in which only one answer is "correct," and the value of many of the exercises will be greatly enhanced by general debate and discussion. It might be worth noting here that we have deliberately included exercises or sections of exercises for which there are no universally acceptable "right" answers. In using this book in our own classes, we find that ambiguous questions or passages are often quite useful educationally because they force students to define terms and present their arguments clearly and carefully.

Another important point: Although we have ordered the chapters in a way we think makes sense, both students and instructors should feel free to use the chapters in whatever order seems most appropriate to their immediate purposes. For example, students beginning to collect information for research papers might want to skip ahead to the section on taking research notes in Chapter 6 or to the section on how to write the history paper in Chapter 12.

If circumstances so dictate, individual students can use this book as a program for self-directed learning. The programmed approach may be especially valuable for students with family and work responsibilities who find it difficult to conform to class schedules designed for resident nonworking students. It is also quite conceivable that a teacher might wish to assign certain exercises to individual students in "content" courses so that they might strengthen their skills in a particular area—e.g., writing book reviews, reading secondary sources, etc.

We might note here that many of the quoted extracts from historical literature reveal a bias toward the more traditional narrative varieties of history. This may seem old-fashioned at a time when so many researchers have abandoned the narrative approach to history in favor of analyses with a distinctly sociological flavor. Nonetheless, we believe that when history is true to its intellectual heritage it does tell a story. Historical literacy implies the ability to see events as part of an organic continuum linking past ages and experiences to our own—one of the strengths of narrative story telling. A sense of chronological development is one of the basic characteristics that distinguishes history from other academic pursuits.

The Third Edition: Features Old and New

This third edition retains the essence of its predecessor as well as some of the exercises and their content. But there are changes as well.

From the second edition we have retained the introductory vignettes in each chapter, although we have written new vignettes for chapters 2 and 11. Also carried forward to the third edition are the "Writing Capsules" leading up to the chapter on writing, the self-standing chapters on Oral History and Statistics and History on Film, and the four-part organizational scheme. The chapters progress from a theoretical discussion of the nature of history (Part I), to practical considerations involved in confronting historical accounts (Part II) and then actually "doing" history (Part III). The final section (Part IV) provides a brief overview of how history as a discipline evolved and how it relates to other academic disciplines.

Third edition revisions include:

- An expanded treatment of electronic research in Chapter 6, "Libraries." We could have said much more on this topic, but we wanted to keep all the chapters uniformly brief.
- The replacement of some excerpts within the exercises, and the updating of others.
- The elimination of a few exercises and the slight abbreviation of others in order to "open up" the book for illustrations and a more readable format.
- A new appendix on source references and bibliographies; all students need to know how to write source citations (endnotes or footnotes) and how to format a bibliography.
- Innumerable editorial attempts to make the writing clearer and exercise directions more precise.

We are deeply indebted to a number of people who assisted us along the way. Of most importance was the emotional support of our wives, Jean Furay and Peggy Brockmann. Also helpful was Peggy's careful editorial eye. We also owe our thanks to numerous colleagues at Webster University who have given unselfishly of their advice and classroom materials: to historian John Chappell for his aid in identifying landmark titles in recent American social and cultural history; to political scientist Kelly Kate Pease for allowing us to incorporate her ideas on paper writing; to reference librarians Sue Gold and Kathy Gaynor for their help in preparing the chapter on libraries; and to our departmental associate, April Tate, for her help in preparing the index. Our students over the last decade have been indispensable partners in this enterprise, and this revision reflects their comments, complaints, suggestions, and answers—both brilliant and questionable—in ways that cannot be enumerated. We owe a huge debt to publisher Andrew Davidson, who enthusiastically encouraged us to undertake the current revision, and whose editorial wisdom has been indispensable. Linda Gaio, also at Harlan Davidson, has frequently provided patient counsel on myriad production details and has played a central role in revising this book's design. Finally, who can write a book such as this and fail to thank the many scholars from whose works we have sought counsel? They have been our mentors throughout. Of course, the standard closing line is appropriate: For all errors of commission and omission, we are fully responsible, though we wish we could find someone else to blame.

Conal Furay
Michael Salevouris
Webster University, 2009

A Personal Note

The authors have been a team since the beginning, but Conal Furay is now retired with the well-earned title "Professor Emeritus." Much of the work on this edition, as a result, was done by Michael Salevouris. Still, Furay's influence is very much visible. He originated the idea of writing such a book, and his words and insights are still an integral part of both the narrative and the exercises. I will always be grateful to him for including me as a partner in this enterprise.

Michael Salevouris
Webster University

PART I
HISTORICAL THINKING

CHAPTER 1   THE USES OF HISTORY

"[Since college] I've spent a third of my life exploring Europe—enjoying my 'continuing education' with a curriculum I've tailored specifically for myself. I marvel how my travels stoke my interest in history, and how much fun my interest in history brings."

—Travel writer (and history major) Rick Steves[1]

"When history was no longer an instrument of the [Russian Communist] Party, the Party was doomed to failure."

—David Remnick

In mid-August 1991, Colonel Aleksandr Tretetsky of the Soviet (Russian) Army wondered whether to continue his gruesome task. The word out of Moscow several hundred miles away was that the overthrow of the Gorbachev regime by a hard-line Communist faction was imminent and that "treasonable" projects like the one he was overseeing were to be immediately terminated.

Some months earlier the government had assigned Tretetsky to manage the excavation of mass graves near the Katyn Forest in eastern Poland. The graves contained the remains of thousands of Polish army officers who, in the Russian version of things, had been murdered by the Nazis during their 1941 invasion of eastern Poland and Russia. Hints that the Russian secret police had really been responsible for the massacre had circulated for years, but in Russia such stories had been ruthlessly suppressed by the state. Information control was the centerpiece, perhaps the vital factor, in sustaining the long, seventy-year rule of communism in Russia. Press reports, film productions, and especially history textbooks had to clear censors in the Moscow bureaucracy. The result was that the Russian people received a cliché-ridden, doctored, party-line version of the past that systematically hid from view the criminal viciousness of earlier Soviet regimes. An entire nation, with few exceptions, believed in a vast fairy tale.

Things began to change in the mid-1980s, especially when Mikhail Gorbachev came to power as the leader of the Soviet Union's Communist Party. Gorbachev was a true believer in the Communist system, yet at the same time it was he who took the Soviet Union onto a new path of *glasnost* (openness) that included leanings toward honesty concerning the historical record. Perhaps it is significant that both his grandfathers had suffered imprisonment during the Stalinist era (1924–53). Gorbachev seemed to believe that the course of development of the socialist state

---

[1] Quoted with permission of Rick Steves, author of *Rick Steves' Europe Through the Back Door* (Avalon Travel Publishing, 2009).

would be advanced if it confessed to its earlier sins—a public cleansing that somehow might bring renewed public devotion to the original Marxist ideals. He therefore ordered the "blank spaces"—essentially those ugly episodes of the Communist past previously hidden by party slogans and lies—filled in. Now, as one writer put it, "the lion of history came roaring in."[2]

What followed went far beyond Gorbachev's intent. The "return of history" shook the Soviet regime to its foundations and brought the eventual collapse of the Communist state. After the August 1991 coup by the Communist Party hard-liners against Gorbachev failed, Colonel Tretetsky was able to resume the work of detailing the massacre, in the process confirming that it had indeed been a Soviet secret police operation. But this was only a small part of a much larger movement. Throughout the Soviet Union, historians, researchers, writers, and journalists, with the historical record now open to them, provided elaborate accounts of past Communist crimes. Finally, the Soviet people were informed that since the Russian Revolution in 1917 literally millions of citizens had been systematically exterminated, and that millions more had been imprisoned without trial in Siberian labor camps. In time the "return of history" completely destroyed the Communists' credibility, and with it their power to govern. David Remnick, in his dramatic account of the collapse of the Soviet Union writes:

> [D]espite Gorbachev's hesitation, the return of historical memory would be his most important decision, one that preceded all others, for without a full and ruthless assessment of the past—an admission of murder, repression, and bankruptcy—real change, much less democratic revolution, was impossible. The return of history to personal, intellectual, and political life was the start of the great reform of the twentieth century and, whether Gorbachev liked it or not, the collapse of the last empire on earth."[3]

The foregoing is but one lucid example of how history can be influential in shaping human affairs. But history has other uses as well, giving each of us an informed perspective on the world around us. The twentieth century, with its rapid and far-reaching changes, has made the past seem irrelevant and uninteresting to many. Yet a moment of reflection will show us that in countless areas of life organic connections with the past have not been broken. The legacies and burdens of the past, the long-term continuities, are with us still. In fact, one could argue that precisely because change has been so rapid in our time, the need for good history has actually increased. There is much truth in the aphorism "the more things change, the more they stay the same." Without historical perspective we are in danger of falling into the mistaken and perhaps arrogant notion that the problems we face and the solutions we propose are unprecedented and bear no relationship to past human problems. Just one of the contributions history can make is to serve as a useful antidote to such narrow present-mindedness.

Even the rapid change we see around us should not hide the basic reality that all we do, all we think, indeed all we are is the cumulative result of past experiences. The future is an abstraction, the "present" but a fleeting moment, all else is history.

---

[2] David Remnick, *Lenin's Tomb: The Last Days of the Soviet Empire* (New York: Vintage Books), 1994, 49.
[3] Remnick, *Lenin's Tomb*, 4.

The past, and judgments about the past, are inescapable. Daily we speak and act according to some perception of past events; and though our knowledge of the past may be incomplete or fallacious, we are thinking historically. When we choose to enroll in a particular course because we like the teacher, when we vote Democratic or Republican on the basis of our assessment of each party's record, when we decide not to go to a movie with someone who "isn't our type," we are making judgments based on our analysis of past experience. We are thinking historically.

Not only is it impossible to escape history, it would be catastrophic to try. Imagine for a moment what life would be like if you totally lost your memory. You would, in a very real sense, have no sense of belonging—no family, no friends, no home, no memories to guide your behavior, no identity. In short, you would no longer "be" you. Clearly, your sense of personal identity is not so much a function of what

A silent tribute at the Cenotaph (completed 1920), Britain's World War I memorial dedicated to "The Glorious Dead." Museums, monuments, and memorials help societies remember their past. Cenotaphs around the world are monuments to those whose remains are buried elsewhere. *Image courtesy Roll of Honour.*

History and the Formation of Public Policy

The events discussed in the introduction to this chapter marked the end of the decades-long conflict between the Soviet Union and the West (especially the United States) known as the "Cold War." During that period (roughly 1946–1991) the basis of U.S. foreign policy was known as "containment"—the idea that if the West "contained" Soviet expansionism, eventually the Soviet Empire would collapse under its own weight.

The idea of containment was suggested in 1947 by one of America's most brilliant diplomats and historians, George Kennan. And, it is interesting to note, Kennan's idea owed much to his reading of history. According to a recent reassessment of the Cold War, "This idea of time being on the side of the West came—at least as far as Kennan was concerned—from studying the history of empires. Edward Gibbon had written in *The Decline and Fall of the Roman Empire* that 'there is nothing more contrary to nature than the attempt to hold in obedience distant provinces,' and few things Kennan ever read made a greater or more lasting impression on him. He had concluded during the early days of World War II that Hitler's empire could not last, and in the months after the war he applied similar logic to the empire [Soviet leader Josef] Stalin was setting out to construct in Eastern Europe."

From John Lewis Gaddis, *We Now Know: Rethinking Cold War History* (Oxford: Clarendon Press, 1997), 37.

you are at the moment but of what you have been your entire life. The same can be said of society as a whole. A society's identity is the product of the myriad individuals, forces, and events that constitute its past. History, the study of the past, is society's collective memory. Without that collective memory, society would be as rootless and adrift as an individual with amnesia. Of the many legitimate reasons for studying history, this seems to us to be one of the most compelling. Individually and collectively what we are is the product of what we have been. In the words of philosopher George Santayana, "A country without a memory is a country of madmen."

EXERCISES

Our discussion of the uses of history emphasized the relationship between the past and the present, and the role history plays in defining our own identity. These concepts are summarized below, along with a variety of other reasons why the study of history is a rewarding venture.[4]

A. History provides us a sense of our own identity. This has already been discussed above, but a bit of elaboration may be useful. Each of us is born into a nation, but also into a region, a culture, an ethnic group, a social class, and a family. Each can or does influence us in a number of ways. The life experiences and values of an African American born into a poor rural family in the South are likely to differ greatly from those of a white middle-class Californian. The study of history helps us to get our bearings in such respects—in other words it allows us to achieve a social as well as a personal identity.

B. History helps us better understand the present. The cliché is true that to understand the present one must understand the past. History, of course, cannot provide clear answers to today's problems (past and present events never exactly parallel each other), but knowledge of relevant historical background is essential for a balanced and in-depth understanding of many current world situations.

C. History—good history—is a corrective for misleading analogies and "lessons" of the past. Many who believe the proposition that history is relevant to an understanding of the present often go too far in their claims. Nothing is easier to abuse than the historical analogy or parallel. Time and again politicians, journalists, and sloppy historians can be heard declaring that "history proves" this or "history shows" that. But the historical record is so rich and varied that one can find examples that seem to support any position or opinion. If one reads selectively, historical episodes can be found to support a variety of policies and ideas. Good history, on the other hand, can expose the inapplicability of many inaccurate and misleading analogies, as well as the dishonesty inherent in "cherry-picking" historical episodes in order to bolster a predetermined conclusion.

D. History enables us to understand the tendencies of humankind, of social institutions, and all aspects of the human condition. Given the vast range of its inquiry, history

---

[4] Even this list is but a selection of the "uses" of history proposed by thinkers from ancient times to the present. For an excellent overview of these ideas see Beverley Southgate, *What Is History For?* (London: Routledge, 2005).

is the best "school" for study of many dimensions of human behavior: heroism and degradation, altruism and avarice, martyrdom and evil excess, freedom and tyranny—all part of the record and part of the story that history tells.

E. History can help one develop tolerance and open-mindedness. Most of us have a tendency to regard our own cultural practices, styles, and values as right and proper. Studying the past is like going to a foreign country—they do things differently there. Returning from such a visit to the past, we have, perhaps, rid ourselves of some of our inherent cultural provincialism.

F. History provides the basic background for many other disciplines. Historical knowledge is extremely valuable in the study of other disciplines—literature, art, philosophy, religion, political science, anthropology, sociology, and economics. Further, with regard to the last four, it is fair to argue that the social sciences "are in fact daughter disciplines [to history], for they arose, each of them, out of historical investigation, having long formed part of avowed historical writing."[5]

G. History can be entertainment. This may seem trivial, but it certainly must be counted as one of the central "uses" of history. Much written history is also good literature, and the stories historians relate are often far more engaging and entertaining than those we find in works of fiction.

H. The careful study of history teaches us many critical skills. As noted in the Preface, this is the central message of this book. Educational psychologists use the term *transfer* to describe cases in which something learned in one setting is found to be useful in very different settings. This is the sort of transaction that takes place in connection with the following critical skills: research skills (Chapter 6), the evaluation of evidence (Chapters 9, 10, and 11), writing (Chapter 12 and the Writing Capsules), critical reading and viewing (Chapters 7 and 8), and, of course, historical thinking (Chapters 3, 4 and 5). These analytical and communication skills are highly useful in other academic pursuits—and in almost any career you choose.

SET A *Exercise 1*

Below are a number of statements describing the various uses of history. Using the letters A through H (review the list below), indicate which category best describes each quotation. In each case be prepared to justify your selection. **You may use a category more than once or not at all.** The first item is completed for you.[6]

---

[5] Jacques Barzun and Henry Graff, *The Modern Researcher*, rev. ed. (New York: Harcourt, Brace and World, 1970), 218.

[6] Many of the quotations in this exercise, and the companion exercise in Set B, were drawn from an extensive list compiled by Ferenc M. Szasz, *The History Teacher*, "The Many Meanings of History," Pt. I, 7 (August 1974); Pts. II and III, 8 (November 1974 and February 1975). The quotations in Part IV of the series, 9 (Febraury 1976), were contributed by subscribers.

A. History provides us a sense of our own identity.

B. History helps us better understand the present.

C. History—good history—is a corrective for misleading analogies and "lessons"of the past.

D. History enables us to understand the tendencies of humankind, of social institutions, and all aspects of the human condition.

E. History can help one develop tolerance and open-mindedness.

F. History provides the basic background for many other disciplines.

G. History can be entertainment.

H. The careful study of history teaches us many critical skills.

___A___ 1. "History is a means of access to ourselves." *(Lynn White, Jr.)*

_____ 2. "History presents the pleasantest features of poetry and fiction—the majesty of the epic, the moving accidents of the drama, and the surprises and moral of the romance." *(Robert A. Willmott)*

_____ 3. "The chief lesson to be derived from the study of the past, is that it holds no simple lesson, and . . . the historian's main responsibility is to prevent anyone from claiming that it does." *(Martin Duberman)*

_____ 4. "History can help us shake off the shackles of ethnocentrism and the debilitating bias of cultural and racial purity. . . . History helps us to illuminate the human condition." *(Lester Stephens)*

_____ 5. "Everything is the sum of its past and nothing is comprehensible except through its history." *(Pierre Teihard de Chardin)*

_____ 6. "[History's] chief use is only to discover the constant and universal principles of human nature." *(David Hume)*

_____ 7. "History provides a training ground for development of many valuable intellectual traits." *(Anonymous)*

_____ 8. "The chief practical use of history is to deliver us from plausible historical analogies." *(James Bryce)*

_____ 9. "The study of history is in the truest sense an education and a training for political life. . . ." *(Polybius)*

_____ 10. "In an age when so much of our literature is infused with nihilism, and other social disciplines are driven toward narrow, positivistic inquiry, history may remain the most humanizing of the arts." *(Richard Hofstadter)*

SET A   *Exercise 2*

On a separate sheet of paper, write a short, paragraph-length essay on the following topic: What is the most important reason for studying history? Read Writing Capsule 1 (next page) before you begin.

WRITING CAPSULE 1

Coherent Paragraphs: The Topic Sentence

A strong paragraph requires a meaningful topic sentence. The topic sentence should summarize the central point of the paragraph it begins. For instance, in responding to the question in Exercise 2, write a brief one-sentence answer: "The most important reason for studying history is . . . ." That sentence should serve as your topic sentence. Then, complete the paragraph by indicating *specific reasons or examples* that support your position on the most important reason for studying history.

To summarize, ordering your ideas is a basic task. When you write a paragraph, begin by putting down your basic generalization followed by two, three, or four supporting points that make the generalization plausible.

(For more on this point see Chapter 12, "Writing the History Paper," page 205.)

SET B   *Exercise 1*

Below are a number of statements describing the various uses of history. Using the letters A through H (review the list on pp. 6–7), indicate which category best describes each quotation. In each case be prepared to justify your selection. **You may use a category more than once or not at all.** The first item is completed for you.

___B___ 1. "With the historian it is an article of faith that knowledge of the past is a key to understanding the present." *(Kenneth Stampp)*

_____ 2. "If history teaches any lesson at all, it is that there are no historical lessons." *(Lucien Febvre)*

_____ 3. "What man is, only history tells." *(Wilhelm Dilthy)*

_____ 4. "History has to be rewritten because history is the selection of those threads of causes or antecedents we are interested in." *(Oliver Wendell Holmes, Jr.)*

_____ 5. "History maketh a young man to be old, without either wrinkles or gray hairs; privileging him with the experience of age, without either the infirmities or inconveniences thereof." *(Thomas Fuller)*

_____ 6. "The ultimate reason for studying history is to become conscious of the possibilities of human existence." *(Rudolf Bultman)*

_____ 7. "History is, in its essence, exciting; to present it as dull is, to my mind, a stark and unforgivable misrepresentation. *(Catherine Drinker Bowen)*

_____ 8. "To be ignorant of what happened before you were born is to be ever a child." *(Cicero)*

_____ 9. "History is not only a particular branch of knowledge, but a particular mode and method of knowledge in other disciplines." *(Lord Acton)*

_____ 10. "History enables bewildered bodies of human beings to grasp their relationship with their past, and helps them chart on general lines their immediate forward course." *(Allan Nevins)*

SET B *Exercise 2*

Write a short, paragraph-length essay on the following topic: What is the most important reason for studying history. Before you begin, review the Writing Capsule 1 (on page 9).

CHAPTER 2

THE NATURE OF HISTORY: HISTORY AS RECONSTRUCTION

"God alone knows the future, but only an historian can alter the past."

—Ambrose Bierce

"The past does not influence me; I influence it."

—Willem de Kooning

Historians know, and you should too, that "periods" and "eras" are artificial constructs that help the human mind come to grips with the immensity and complexity of the human past. For instance, some historians have referred to the previous century as the "short" twentieth century, citing the inclusive dates 1914 to 1989. Why only seventy-five years? Because, these historians argue, the years 1914–89 mark a series of interrelated conflicts—World War I (1914–18), World War II (1939–45) and the so-called Cold War (ca. 1945–89)—that finally came to an end in 1989.

From this perspective, then, 1989 marked the end of an era—a major turning point in Western history that deserves considerable attention from scholars. Indeed historians have already begun the process of describing and explaining the events that led to the end of the Cold War, and the literature on the subject grows daily. Given the twenty-four-hour news cycles of the electronic age, one would assume that historians have mountains of information on which to base these accounts. To some degree this is true, but it would be a mistake to assume that we can easily and completely write the history of these world-shaking events. One small example dramatizes this reality.

During the Cold War a number of Eastern European states were closely controlled by communist Russia, or, more accurately, the Soviet Union (USSR). In 1989, as the world watched with astonishment, these states began to break free of Soviet control and set up more democratic, noncommunist governments. In Czechoslovakia this process was called the "Velvet Revolution," a reference to the peaceful, "soft" nature of the transition. Noted British historian and journalist, Timothy Garton Ash, an observer of the events in the capital city of Prague, commented on the difficulties of writing history:

> [T]he evidential basis on which history is written is often extraordinarily thin. Sometimes we have only one witness. During the Velvet Revolution in Prague, in 1989, crucial decisions were taken by a group around Václav Havel [who was to become Czechoslovakia's new president], meeting in a curious glass-walled room in the subterranean Magic Lantern theater. Most of the time, I was the only outsider present, and certainly the only one with a notebook open, trying to record what was being said. I remember thinking: if I don't write

this down, nobody will. It will be lost forever, as most of the past is, like bathwater down the drain. . . . [W]hat a fragile foundation on which to write history.[1]

This story reveals an important truth about the nature of history: a vast gulf separates the actual events of the past from the accounts that journalists record and historians later analyze.

What Is History?

In English the word *history* has two distinct meanings. First, history is the sum total of everything that has actually happened in the past—every thought, every action, every event. In this sense, history is surely one of the broadest concepts conceived by the human intellect. History, broadly defined, encompasses the entire scope of the human experience on this planet. And this meaning of the word—things that happened in the past—is what most people have in mind when they use the term in daily conversation.

But it is the second meaning of the term *history*, that is more central to this book. If history is the past, it is also *an account* of the past—i.e. books, articles, and lectures. It should be clear with just a moment's thought that the past (all of the thoughts and events that actually happened) is lost forever, as Ash noted in the quotation above. Our only contact with the past is through the relatively scant records left by those who lived before us and through the accounts written by historians on the basis of those records. It is this history—created accounts of the past—that we read, think about, and study in school. And, it is history in this sense—history as a creation of human intelligence—that is the subject of this book. As historians James Davidson and Mark Lytle put it, "History is not 'what happened in the past'; rather, it is the act of selecting, analyzing, and writing about the past. It is something that is done, that is constructed, rather than an inert body of data that lies scattered through the archives."[2]

The Nature of History

History, then, is both the past and the study of the past. In order to appreciate better the vast intellectual distance that separates the past-as-it-actually-happened (history in the first sense) from historians' accounts of that past (history in the second sense) we ask you to take a brief journey of the imagination. Try to visualize yourself walking at night amidst a rugged landscape punctuated by dramatic peaks and valleys. As you walk a companion turns on a powerful searchlight that illuminates some of the recesses and promontories that were formerly veiled in darkness. As the light moves, the previously lighted objects disappear from view and new features of the landscape appear. You want to see the entire landscape spread before your eyes, but the beam of light, narrow and imperfect, lets you see only a tiny fraction of the reality before you at any given time. When the light is turned off, you can see nothing at all. The

---

[1] Timothy Garton Ash, "On the Frontier," *New York Review of Books*, November 7, 2002, 60.
[2] James Davidson and Mark Lytle, *After the Fact: The Art of Historical Detection*, 4th ed. (New York: Knopf, 2000), xviii.

peaks and valleys and forests are still there, and remain there, awaiting other beams, projected from other angles, to reveal their features.

In this allegory the peaks and valleys of the landscape represent the "past-as-it-actually-happened"—history in the first sense. The person with the searchlight is the historian who, by using the beam, reveals some of the outlines of the landscape. Essentially, the historian "lights up" some segment of the past that we cannot perceive directly, just as the person carrying the searchlight illuminated a feature of the landscape hidden in darkness. The glimpse of the landscape provided by the beam, as transient and incomplete as it is, is analogous to an account of the past written by a historian.

This analogy is imperfect in that the historian cannot even shine a weak beam of light on the real past as if it were a mountain or a valley. The past, unlike any existing geological feature, is gone forever. To the extent we can know anything about the past-as-it-actually-happened, that knowledge must be based on surviving records. Still, the analogy is useful. Just as a landscape can be real, so, too, is the past that historians study. The actual events of the past are gone forever, but they were just as "real" as all the human activities you see around you every day. Further, as inadequate as the beam of light was in illuminating the totality of the landscape, it did provide useful glimpses of reality. Similarly, historians' accounts can and do provide useful, if partial, glimpses of the past.

To reiterate the central point: Even though a relationship exists between the past-as-it-happened and the historian's account of a segment of the past, the historical account can no more show past events as they actually took place than the narrow beam of light can illuminate an entire landscape. The historian can reveal a tiny piece of the past, can present us with an individual version of a segment of the past, but no one can present the past as it actually was.

This leads us to another point: All historical accounts are reconstructions that contain some degree of subjectivity. Whether written or spoken, every piece of history is an individualized view of a segment of past reality—a particular vision, a personalized version based on incomplete and imperfect evidence. Writing history is an act of creation or, more accurately, an act of *re*-creation in which the mind of the historian is the catalyst. Any piece of history that we read or hear ought to be treated as an individual creation. In fact, one might even say that any history we read is as much a product of the historian who wrote it as of the people who actually lived the events it attempts to describe!

Reconstructing the Past

The subjective, reconstructed, nature of written history becomes clearer if we look more closely at the process whereby the historian bridges the chasm between the past being studied and the historical account that is the product of that study. Actually, the intellectual task of the historian is as challenging as any on earth. Unlike the scientist who can experiment directly with tangible objects, the historian is many times removed from the events under investigation.

The historian, as noted before, cannot study the past directly, but must rely on surviving records. It should be obvious that surviving records, compared to the real

Alfred R. Waud, artist for *Harper's Weekly,* sketching on the battle-field of Gettysburg (July 1863). Historians are not the only ones who seek to "reconstruct" the past. *Library of Congress, Prints & Photographs Division, (LC-DIG-cwpb-00074).*

past they reflect, are like a few drops of water in a large bucket. For instance, most past events left no records at all! Think of the number of events in your own life for which there is no record but your own memory. Multiply those unrecorded events in your own life by the billions of human beings who inhabit the earth and you get some idea of the number of events each day that go unrecorded. That is only the beginning of the problem. In the words of historian Louis Gottschalk:

> Only a part of what was observed in the past was remembered by those who observed it; only a part of what was remembered was recorded; only a part of what was recorded has survived; only a part of what has survived has come to the historians' attention; only a part of what has come to their attention is credible; only a part of what is credible has been grasped; and only a part of what has been grasped can be expounded or narrated by the historian. . . . Before the past is set forth by the historian, it is likely to have gone through eight separate steps at each of which some of it has been lost; and there is no guarantee that what remains is the most important, the largest, the most valuable, the most representative, or the most enduring part. In other words the "object" that the historian studies is not only incomplete, it is markedly variable as records are lost or recovered.[3]

Clearly, then, the historian can never get or present the full truth about a given past. The best the historian can provide, even under ideal conditions, is a partial sketch of a vanished past. "Even the best history," said historian Bruce Catton, "is not much better than a mist through which we see shapes dimly moving." Or, in the words of W. S. Holt, "History is a damn dim candle over a damn dark abyss."

If all this were not enough, the historian is also a factor in the equation. Not only are historians fallible and capable of error, but personal biases, political beliefs, economic status, religious persuasion, and personal idiosyncrasies can subtly and unconsciously influence the way in which they interpret existing sources. We all have a unique "frame of reference"—a set of interlocking values, loyalties, assumptions, interests, and principles of action—that we use to interpret daily experience.

---

[3] Louis Gottschalk, *Understanding History* (New York: Knopf, 1950), 45–46.

Artist Peter Rothermel's rendition of the Battle of Gettysburg (1863) created ca. 1872. Like historians, artists often attempt historical reconstructions long after the original event. *Library of Congress, Prints & Photographs Division, (LC-DIG-pga-03266).*

Suppose a newspaper publishes a photograph of the president of the United States playing golf at a country club on a Sunday morning under the headline "President Relaxes." A variety of reactions would be likely, each of them reflecting a different frame of reference:

- A political opponent: "I wonder if he's as bad on the course as he is in the Oval Office."
- A party loyalist: "Good for him. He deserves a break from the political wars he's been fighting."
- A physical fitness guru: "Why doesn't he spend his free time in a more physically demanding activity?"
- A clergyman: "As a role model for all of us, he shouldn't be playing golf on a Sunday morning."

Same newspaper, same headline, same photograph, and four different responses.

A frame of reference is like a lens through which we view the world around us. It leads us to make certain conjectures, to classify individual items in a certain way, to ask certain kinds of questions, and to develop certain interpretations. Conservative Republicans often read and interpret the political history of the United States in a very different way than do liberal Democrats. Protestants and Catholics frequently disagree when writing about the religious upheavals known as the Reformation. And Northerners and Southerners are notorious in their differences concerning the history of the American Civil War. For example, Hodding Carter III, assistant secretary of state under President Jimmy Carter (1977–81), was aware at a young age that the American history he was taught in the South differed from that taught in the North. "It was easy for me as a youngster growing up in Mississippi to know that my eighth-grade state history textbook taught me a lot which didn't jibe with what my cousins in Maine were being taught. We spoke of the War Between the States. They spoke of the Civil War. . . . But our texts might as well have been written for study on different planets when it came to the status and feelings of the black men and women of the state or nation."[4]

Small wonder that there is an element of subjectivity in historical accounts, inasmuch as we have historians with widely differing ideals, loyalties, interests, motivations, and even biases, each of which are shaped by different ethnic experience, religious allegiance, political leanings, and class interests.

That said, we must express a certain caution. Historians are justified in viewing an event from any perspective they wish, and from that perspective explain how and why that event happened as it did. However, there is a danger involved in allowing one's singular frame of reference to shape completely a historical inquiry. Excessive focus on one's own viewpoint closes the mind to the legitimate insights residing in alternative perspectives and, equally troublesome, to evidence that contradicts one's own view. Some call this tendency *Procrustean*, the term referring to an ancient Greek brigand who strapped his victims to a bed—if their legs were too long, he cut them off till they fit; if too short, he stretched them to the proper length. In the realm of ideas this describes a tendency to make the evidence fit the theory.

The Question of Truth

At this point you might be asking, "Why study history at all if historical accounts are so far removed from the past they attempt to understand?" What happens to the search for "truth" if we acknowledge that historical accounts are by nature subjective and incomplete? How can we justify the pursuit of knowledge that appears so shallow and fleeting?

This entire book addresses this question, but for now it is sufficient to note that an element of subjectivity by no means invalidates the importance or substance of historical studies. First, it is worth reminding ourselves that the past did happen. Even though the records of past events are inadequate and difficult to interpret, they do constitute a tangible link between past and present. And even though historians can never completely escape their personal frames of reference, that does not preclude their writing credible and convincing accounts firmly grounded in the existing evidence. As Stephen Jay Gould, the Harvard paleontologist and historian of science, put it: "We understand that biases, preferences, social values, and psychological attitudes all play a strong role in the process of discovery. However, we should not be driven to the opposite extreme of complete cynicism—the view that objective evidence plays no role, that perceptions of truth are entirely relative, and that scientific [or historical] conclusions are just another form of aesthetic preference."[5]

This is an important point: history is not fiction. Different historians will interpret the past differently for many different reasons. But in all cases their accounts must be based on all the available relevant evidence. A version of the past that cannot be supported by evidence is worthless and will quickly be rejected by other historians. Thus one opinion (no matter how strongly held) is not as good as another, and the student

---

[4] "Viewpoint," *The Wall Street Journal* (September 23, 1982).
[5] Stephen Jay Gould, *Wonderful Life, The Burgess Shale and the Nature of History* (New York: W. W. Norton, 1989), 244.

of history, whether beginner or seasoned professional, must learn to discriminate closely between reasoned claims supported by the available evidence and those that fail this basic test. (Don't panic right now if you don't know how to make this kind of determination; it is something that this book intends to teach you.)

Finally, history is not unique in its subjectivity, nor is it the only discipline in which conclusions are tentative and constantly open to revision. No field of study is ever static. All research is, to some degree, conditioned by the "climate of the times" and the values and attitudes of the researchers themselves, not to mention the discovery of new evidence. Even theories in the so-called "hard sciences" are subject to the vagaries of time, place, and circumstance.

Conclusion

The realization that history involves the study of individual interpretations or versions of the past can be unsettling. Many of us yearn for the security afforded by unchallenged, definitive "answers" to a limited and manageable set of "questions." To find out that historians are always asking new questions, and continually offering new answers to old ones, eliminates the possibility of discovering the absolute and singular truth about the human past. At the same time, this is also what makes history so intellectually exciting. History is not the lifeless study of a dead past; its purpose is not the memorization of dates, names, and places. History is a living and evolving dialogue about the most important subject of all—the human experience. And all of us are capable of taking part in that dialogue.

The remaining question is: How do *you* do this? Simply by learning how historians think and by sharpening the analytical and communication skills essential for success in college and professional life. This is what we mean by the methods of history.

And the methods of history are not especially complicated or confusing. Most of them are based on common sense and can be learned without a great deal of specialized or technical training. Still, "doing" history is not altogether easy. (One historian compared writing intellectual history to trying to nail jelly to the wall.) Nonetheless, with some time, effort, and enthusiasm even beginning students can become historically literate.

EXERCISES

SET A   *Exercise 1*

The following statements use *history* in one or the other of its two meanings: (1) the past itself or (2) an account of the past. (See page 12.) Your task is to decide which meaning of history the author of each statement intended. Use "P" (for "**P**ast") to indicate passages that use the word "history" to mean the past-as-reality, and "A" (for "**A**ccount") to indicate passages that use the word "history" to mean an account or accounts (a reconstruction) of the past. Be prepared to defend your conclusions orally. [6]

---

[6] Many of the quotations in this exercise, and the companion exercise in Set B, were drawn from an extensive list compiled by Ferenc M. Szasz, *The History Teacher*, "The Many Meanings of History," Pt. I, 7(August 1974); Pts. II and III, 8 (November 1974 and February 1975). The quotations in Part IV of the series, 9 (February 1976), were contributed by subscribers.

_____ 1. "Fellow citizens, we cannot escape history. " *(Abraham Lincoln)*

_____ 2. "History, as the study of the past, makes the coherence of what happened comprehensible by reducing events to a dramatic pattern and seeing them in a simple form." *(J. Huizinga)*

_____ 3. "History is baroque [complex]. It smiles at all attempts to force its flow into theoretical patterns or logical grooves; it plays havoc with our generalizations, breaks all our rules." *(Will Durant)*

_____ 4. "A page of history is worth a volume of logic." (Oliver Wendell Holmes)

_____ 5. "History is not the accumulation of facts, but the relation [i.e., recounting] of them." *(Lytton Strachey)*

_____ 6. "Life is not simple, and therefore history, which is past life, is not simple." *(David Shannon)*

SET A *Exercise 2*

A major theme of this chapter is the re-creative nature of historical study. The past is real, but accounts of the past reflect the historian's interests, priorities, values, and abilities. A work of history is never *the* history of a subject, but *a* history of a subject—just one of many possible versions. Another way of saying this is that any history has subjective elements. As a student of history you should try to become alert to the many ways the hand of the historian shapes the account you read. Below are a number of statements drawn from history books, magazines, and newspapers (remember journalists are historians). Some of the statements are predominately factual; that is, they simply describe a person or event. Other statements reflect the writer's judgment or opinion. The opinion might be very much justified in light of the evidence, but it is an opinion nevertheless.

This exercise is designed to sharpen your awareness of how strongly historical writing depends on the interpretations and judgments of the historian. Below, label each passage either "F" for **F**act or "O" for **O**pinion. If a passage contains both Facts and Opinions, write "**FO**" and underline the segment that you think is the opinion or judgment. In all cases assume there is evidence to support the statements. To give you a start, we have completed the first two items.

___F___ l. "Hosts at Last, Cardinals Show Falcons the Door" (Sports Headline)

Comment

In a sense every statement can be categorized as an "opinion," since the choice of each word reflects some individual's judgment. Note how differently this short headline would read if the writer had said that the Arizona football Cardinals had "trounced" or "whipped" the Atlanta Falcons. For the purposes of this exercise, let's ignore this technicality. We labeled this statement "Fact" (F) because it is a straightforward description of the outcome of an event—a 2009 National Football League playoff game.

___FO___ 2. "It had been 61 years since the Cardinals had hosted a playoff game, and almost as long since anyone had seen Edgerrin James, <u>but James emerged Saturday from months in Coach Ken Whisenhunt's doghouse to carry Arizona to a 30–24 victory over the Atlanta Falcons</u> in a National Football Conference wild-card playoff game."

> ### Comment
> There are certainly facts in this passage, but the author, Billy Witz of *The New York Times*, is also offering an explanation (opinion) as to why the Arizona Cardinals won this particular game. The key figure, according to Witz, was running back Edgerrin James, who apparently had been out of favor (in the "doghouse") with his coach. We labeled this passage "Fact" and "Opinion" (FO). The "Opinion" section is underlined.

_____ 3. "The young Peter [the Great of Russia] was almost seven feet tall, and extremely lively."

_____ 4. "At about the same time that Austria issued its declaration [of war] designed to assist Louis XVI, the king, never short on poor ideas, decided to flee the country. Departing at midnight on June 20, 1792, the royal family made an escape that took on aspects of a comic opera."

_____ 5. "*Gunga Din* (1937). This Hollywood film, from the Rudyard Kipling poem of the same name, is not just a sentimental story about the nineteenth-century British Raj. . . . So patronizingly racist that it has to be seen to be believed, this film demonstrates that, on the issues of imperialism and racism, the 1930s mentality is much closer to that of the Victorians than it is to ours."

_____ 6. "[The invasion of Normandy on D-Day, June 6, 1944, marked] the beginning of a new era. The largest military invasion in history laid the foundation for the Marshall plan, the recovery of Europe and the birth of the Atlantic alliance. It confirmed America's rise from wary isolationism to a new role as the world's strongest power." (Magazine story on 40th anniversary of D-Day invasion.)

_____ 7. "Edward III [of England] was fifteen years old when he ascended the throne in 1327, 25 when he embarked on war with France, and 34 at the time of the second attempt in 1346."

_____ 8. "The Arab-Muslim Empire [in the seventh century, CE] spread landward around the Mediterranean. The Iberian peninsula [Spain and Portugal], where the land of Europe came down to meet the land of Africa, was the part of the west European mainland that came under the Muslim sway."

_____ 9. "In August 1936 [Adolf Hitler] had appointed Ribbentrop as German ambassador in London in an effort to explore the possibility of a settlement with England—on his own terms. Incompetent and lazy, vain as a peacock, arrogant and without humor, Ribbentrop was the worst possible choice for such a post. . . ."

_____ 10. "The largest group of these 'orphans' were the children of living single mothers (a group that constituted 9–10 percent of all children in the United States). The low wages and harsh working conditions of the jobs that were available to women—domestic service and sewing most commonly—often made it impossible for lone mothers simultaneously to care for their children and earn enough to support them."

Sources

1. and 2. *The New York Times,* January 4, 2009, Sports 1.
3. Crane Brinton, et al., *A History of Civilization,* Vol. II, 3rd ed. (Englewood Cliffs, NJ: Prentice-Hall, 1967), 222–224.
4. Douglas R. Egerton, et al., *The Atlantic World* (Wheeling, IL: Harlan Davidson, Inc., 2007), 371.
5. Norman F. Cantor, *The American Century* (New York: HarperPerennial, 1998), 513.
6. *Newsweek,* June 11, 1984, 18.
7. Barbara Tuchman, *A Distant Mirror* (New York: Knopf, 1978), 72.
8. Daniel J. Boorstin, *The Discoverers* (New York: Random House, 1983), 181.
9. William L. Shirer, *The Rise and Fall of the Third Reich* (New York: Crest, 1962), 410.
10. Linda Gordon, *The Great Arizona Orphan Abduction* (Cambridge, MA: Harvard University Press, 1999), 8.

SET B   *Exercise 1*

The following statements use *history* in one or the other of its two meanings: (1) the past itself or (2) an account of the past. (See page 12.) Your task is to decide which meaning of history the author of each statement intended. Use "P" (for "**P**ast") to indicate passages that use the word "history" to mean the past-as-reality, and "A" (for "**A**ccount") to indicate passages that use the word "history" to mean an account or accounts (a reconstruction) of the past. Be prepared to defend your conclusions orally.

_____ 1. "History is the witness of the times, the torch of truth, the life of memory, the teacher of life, the messenger of antiquity.s" *(Cicero)*

_____ 2. "History does not usually make real sense until long afterward." *(Bruce Catton)*

_____ 3. "We cannot escape history and neither can we escape a desire to understand it. *(Anonymous)*

_____ 4. "In its amplest meaning History includes every trace and vestige of everything that man has done or thought since first he appeared on the earth. *(James Harvey Robinson)*

_____ 5. "History began to exert its fascination upon me when I was about six. . . ." *(Barbara Tuchman)*[7]

_____ 6. "But history is neither watchmaking nor cabinet construction. It is an endeavor toward better understanding." *(Marc Bloch)*

---

[7] Barbara Tuchman, *Practicing History* (New York: Alfred A. Knopf, 1981), 13. For the source of the other quotations in this set, see footnote 6.

SET B   *Exercise 2*

Below are a number of statements drawn from history books, magazines, and newspapers. Some of the statements are predominantly factual; that is, they simply describe a person or event. Other statements reflect the writer's opinion. The opinion might be justified in light of the evidence, but it is an opinion nevertheless.

This exercise is designed to sharpen your awareness of how strongly historical writing depends on the interpretations and judgments of the historian. Label each passage below either "F" for **F**act or "O" for **O**pinion. If a passage contains both Facts and Opinions, write "**FO**" and underline the segment you think is the opinion. In all cases assume there is evidence to support the statements. For sample answers see Set A, Exercise 2, pages 18–19.

_____ 1. "Unlike World War One, then, the Second War [in Europe]—Hitler's War—was a near universal experience. And it lasted a long time—nearly six years for those countries (Britain and Germany) that were engaged in it from beginning to end. In Czechoslovakia it began earlier still, with the Nazi occupation of the Sudetenland in October 1938."

_____ 2. "In the U.S. armed forces, women gained increasing influence as well. A new, light weapon—the M-16 rifle—made women's participation at the front more feasible, while the Supreme Court ordered the gender integration of the Citadel [a military school] in Charleston, South Carolina. In l990, when President George Bush called for American troops to fight in the Gulf War, women formed part of the battlefield troop movement. "

_____ 3. "On first seeing a portrait of Falkenhayn [a World War I German general], one's immediate reaction is: 'this is a typical Prussian general.' The hair is close-cropped, the nose well-bred, the features vigorous and stern. The eyes have that Prussian turn-down at the corners. . . . But when one comes to the mouth, partly concealed under the aggressive military moustache, the whole picture changes. It is not the mouth of a determined leader, a man of action, but that of an indecisive, introversive man of thought, and the sensitive, dimpled chin confirms the implications of weakness."

_____ 4. "Future historians, therefore, must surely look back on the three decades between August 1914 [beginning of World War I] and May 1945 [end of World War II] as the era when Europe took leave of its senses. The totalitarian horrors of communism and fascism, when added to the horrors of total war, created an unequalled sum of death, misery, and degradation."

_____ 5. "On the afternoon of June 25, l876, with guns blazing and sandy hair shining, Lieut. Colonel George Armstrong Custer, along with some 220 of the troopers under his command, was massacred near Montana's Little Bighorn River."

_____ 6. "[Architect] Eero Saarinen was cut down in his prime when he died, of a brain tumor, in 1961, a mere fifty-one years old. In his all-too-brief heydey, during the expansive Eisenhower years, he was one of America's most lionized architects, a pet of the popular and the professional press."

_____ 7. "Certainly, Vietnam marked a definitive exit point in American history and the l960s, a sharp break with the past. There [at that time], the war story finally lost its ability to mobilize young people under 'freedom's banner' except in opposition to itself, a loss experienced by a generation as both a confusing 'liberation' and a wrenching betrayal. There, the war story's codes were jumbled, its roles redistributed, its certitudes dismantled, and new kinds of potential space opened up that proved, finally, less liberating than frightening."

_____ 8. "Rock [music] itself split into several directions in the seventies. Although the Beatles broke up in 1970, the British invasion continued. British vocalists Elton John and David Bowie proved to be among the decade's most popular performers. A smaller share of the popular music audience patronized American vocalists like Joni Mitchell, who mixed folk and rock. . . . The Carpenters offered a sugary and immensely popular variation of this singing sensitivity. Very much in contrast was 'hard' or 'progressive' rock. Its elaborately orchestrated compositions, performed at full blast encouraged . . . the purchase of still more expensive record and tape players. "

Sources

1. Tony Judt, *Postwar: A History of Europe Since 1945* (New York: Penguin, 2005), 14.
2. Glenda Riley, *Inventing the American Woman*, 2nd ed. (Wheeling, IL.: Harlan Davidson, Inc., 1987), 363.
3. Alistair Horne, *The Price of Glory*, abr. ed. (New York: Penguin Books, 1964), 40.
4. Norman Davies, *Europe: A History* (Oxford: Oxford University Press, 1996), 897.
5. *Time*, May 28, 1984, 49.
6. Martin Filler, "Flying High with Eero Saarinen," *New York Review of Books*, June 12, 2008, 36.
7. Tom Engelhardt, *The End of Victory Culture* (Amherst: University of Massachusetts Press, 1998), 14–15.
8. James L. Baughman, *The Republic of Mass Culture* (Baltimore: The Johns Hopkins University Press, 1997), 196.

CHAPTER 3

HISTORICAL THINKING: CONTINUITY AND CHANGE

"A society in stable equilibrium is—by definition—one that has no history and wants no historians."

—HENRY ADAMS

"All things flow, but they need not necessarily rush down a cataract."

—G. J. RENIER

In June of 1939 Admiral Isoroku Yamamoto was made commander-in-chief of the Combined Fleet of the Empire of Japan. An original thinker and instinctive gambler, Yamamoto was Japan's most distinguished military man, and he knew how vulnerable America was in the western Pacific. He recognized that Japanese power could readily overrun the Philippines, Indo-China, Malaya, the Dutch East Indies, and many island chains to the south and the east. But Yamamoto was also a keen student of history, both of his own country and of the United States. He told his countrymen that easy early victories might prove too costly in the long run, because they would arouse America's "fierce fighting spirit," as shown in so many Civil War battles and in the naval actions of the Spanish-American War. He did not want to see that force, nor the force of American industrial strength, unleashed against Japan. Again and again he urged caution upon his nation's rulers.[1]

By late 1940, however, the Japanese war party had become dominant, and soon Yamamoto was directed to prepare for war, though he told the Japanese premier "If I am told to fight regardless of the consequences, I shall run wild for the first six months or a year, but I have utterly no confidence for the second or third year."[2] It was the reluctant Yamamoto who conceived the bold Pearl Harbor attack plan (based on his historical awareness of the successful surprise attack against Port Arthur in the Russo-Japanese War of 1904), organized it, and brought it to completion on December 7, 1941. Yet so strongly did his sense of history enter into his thinking that even as toasts to his great victory lingered in the air, he remarked that he feared that all they had done was awaken a slumbering giant and fill him with a terrible resolve.

Though he did not survive the war, Yamamoto's vision of what would happen in the Pacific proved prophetic as the Japanese navy began its long slow retreat in June of 1942. Yamamoto was a prophet not because he could look directly into the future, but because he saw that forces active in the past would reassert themselves. He knew that, as they had in the past, the raw industrial power of the United States along with American organizational skills would be decisive in the long run. Clearly, Yamamoto had a sense of history.

---

[1] Edwin P. Hoyt, *Japan's War: The Great Pacific Conflict* (New York: McGraw-Hill, 1986), 187–93.
[2] Nathan Miller, *War At Sea* (New York: Oxford University Press, 1995), 195.

Wreckage of *USS Arizona,* Pearl Harbor, December 7, 1941. *Library of Congress, Prints & Photographs Division, (LC-DIG-fsa-8e09026).*

Yamamoto's well-developed foresight is a good example of something very important about education: There is much more to it than acquiring and memorizing factual information. We learn grammatical rules, geometric axioms, principles of government, how to operate a computer, and other segmented bits of knowledge. These things are worthwhile, and often occupationally relevant, but there is something much more important about education. A computer can be programmed to "learn" all of the above and more, but it is a poor imitation of the educated human mind. This "something more" is a special quality of the mind that develops through years of study—a cultivation, a breadth, an enlargement. This is not the exclusive product of any academic discipline, for it can be learned while pursuing many fields of study. But we believe that the study of history is especially conducive to developing it. In fact, many historians would argue that the development of this quality of mind, which in these chapters we are calling "historical thinking," is far more important than any sterile memorization of facts. It is an outgrowth of serious reflection upon the past and is its longest lasting benefit.

A recent book on the subject entitled *Historical Thinking and Other Unnatural Acts,*[3] shows the unsettling truth that thinking historically is not something that comes naturally. Historical reality is complicated, and becoming historically "literate" can be a challenging enterprise. But it is well worth the effort. To begin, we would emphasize the following three major components as the basis of effective historical thinking:

- **Sensitivity to *multiple causation***

All too often our popular culture favors quick, simplistic answers to the challenges of the day. In 2008 and 2009 a question on the lips of every American was, who or what was responsible for the unprecedented economic collapse that seemed to appear out of nowhere? Many pointed to a *single* culprit out of a long list of contenders:

[3] Sam Wineburg, *Historical Thinking and Other Unnatural Acts* (Philadelphia: Temple University Press, 2001).

greedy CEOs, manipulative investment bankers, President George W. Bush and his administration, the policies of the previous Clinton administration, Congress, lax regulatory institutions, naïve home buyers, the *idea* that one could become rich with no risk, or some other convenient scapegoat. Historians, and students of history, however, know that it is a mistake to look for a single cause. Every situation or event is the product of *multiple* "causes" or factors, some short-term and some long-term. To think like an historian you will need to consider the wide range of factors that have led to the events you are investigating.

- **Sensitivity to *context*, or how other times and places differ from our own**

This component of historical thinking involves a philosophical dilemma of sorts: How can twenty-first-century observers understand cultures from a strange and distant past? Originally historians thought this wasn't a serious problem. Because human nature has been the same from the beginning, they argued, we should have no trouble understanding other human beings, whether they be ancient Greek philosophers or Japanese samurai warriors. The famous British historian, R. G. Collingwood said in the 1940s that we can understand the past by simply getting into the mind of long-dead individuals. To understand the actions of Julius Caesar, for instance, the historian must think "for himself [or herself] what Caesar thought about the situation and the possible ways of dealing with it."[4] More recently, however, historians have emphasized how *different* the past is from the present. As Carlo Ginzburg, a noted Italian historian, said, "The more we discover about these people's mental universes, the more we should be shocked by the cultural distance that separates us from them."[5] Therefore, historians must still make a serious effort to bridge the cultural and temporal gap, but they know it won't be easy. We will say more about context and multiple-causation in separate chapters. For now, we turn to the third component of historical thinking.

- **An awareness of the interplay of *continuity and change* in human affairs**

As implied by the discussion above, every situation is an amalgam of the old (continuity) and the new (change). As historian Alan Bullock put it, "The mixture is never the same; history does not repeat itself; the new is new. But the old persists alongside it and in time the new is grafted on to the old and continuity with the past—continuity, not identity—is not disrupted but restored."[6] The challenge for the historian is to figure out how this balance manifests itself at any particular point in the past.

Change

Someone once said, "The mountain has no history." Neither does the polar ice cap, nor do oceans. Why? Because they never seem to change, at least not to our eyes. Geologists would disagree with this observation, but it serves to bring out a major point: There can be a "history" only when there is change. In essence, history is the story of change.

---

[4] R. G. Collingwood, *The Idea of History* (London: Oxford University Press, 1956; 1974), 215.
[5] From *The Cheese and the Worms* quoted in Wineburg, *Historical Thinking*, 10.
[6] Quoted in John Tosh, ed., *Historians on History* (Harlow, England: Pearson Education Ltd., 2000), 209.

Change is an ever-present part of life, especially for those who live in modern in-dustrialized states. We routinely change our clothes, change courses, change schools, change jobs, change apartments, none of which are of any great significance. But we use the same term to describe developments that are of potentially enormous importance, such as major policy swings after an election, the sudden outbreak of a war, a coup, or a revolution, a decisive shift in public attitude, the advent of a new technology, the effects of a natural disaster. Ideally we would have three or four dif-ferent words to distinguish between minor and major changes. In this case, however, the English language, ordinarily so rich in vocabulary, fails us.

History is concerned with significant change. Sometimes this involves an entirely different state of existence for society, such as that brought on by wars, revolutions, and plagues. At other times, a society remains the same structurally but important social, political, and attitudinal changes have occurred. And then there are the changes that are even more gradual, such as population shifts, which can greatly affect the balance of political power or the economic advance of nations and peoples.

Continuity

When we open a history book, we often find we have entered a world where change is so constant that it is almost overwhelming. Events parade by us in bewildering succession, each representing a change from that which preceded it. We get a sense of perpetual motion and can begin to lose our perspective. (Today the subject is the Ancient Greeks, but tomorrow we discuss the Renaissance!) We know things don't happen that way in our personal lives, and gradually we retreat from that historical world that seems so unreal.

As preoccupied with change as our society is, if we were asked personally whether change or continuity was more dominant in our lives, most of us would probably say "continuity." We would then speak of the monotony of the things we do, including eating, working, sleeping, talking to friends, watching television, making monthly payments—all adding up to continuity. Life, as experienced on the day-to-day level, is inevitably routine and frequently boring, so we hunger for some variety, anything fresh, such as a major news event, some exciting gossip, or even a crisis on our favorite TV show. Yet, almost paradoxically, we also happily return to familiar patterns.

This leads us to qualify an earlier statement: To regard history as a story of change is a half-truth, at best a three-quarters truth. For in human societies, inertia, stability, and tradition are powerful forces. Most changes take place in the overall context of continuance of many of the old ways of doing things, and they are often no more than patchwork alterations of the existing system. Further, social, political, and economic inertia create limits to the extent of change. A few months after his inauguration in 1961, John F. Kennedy remarked to an associate that he had found that despite his impressive constitutional powers there was very little a president could do to bring about substantive change. To cite another example, many revolutions are justified as designed to *preserve* the status quo. For example, in the 1860s the Confederate States of America was created to preserve the traditional southern way of life in the face of encroaching change. The most effective historians remain conscious of the essentially conservative nature of human society and weave their stories with threads

Top: Continuity and Change: Nineteenth-century America was a study in contrasts. "My Cottage Home," a Currier and Ives print (ca. 1866) idealizes a traditional and timeless vision of America's past. *Bottom:* Julian Oliver's 1883 engraving of an electrified New Orleans levee testifies to the dramatic changes that were reshaping the face of the nation. *Library of Congress, Prints & Photographs Division, ("Cottage Home" LC-DIG-pga-00833; "Levee" LC-USZ62-5367).*

of both change and continuity. "Indeed, given human and cultural patterns, it would be most surprising if major changes in public mentality occurred at anything more rapid than a glacial tempo."[7]

_____

[7] Conal Furay, *The Grass-Roots Mind in America: The American Sense of Absolutes* (New York: New Viewpoints, 1977), 136.

Continuity and Change: Striking the Balance

Historians are well aware of the resistance to change represented by the fixed ways of society, even though in telling their story they may not discuss these continuities directly. Their approach is more often to explore emergent factors, which in their combined influence become strong enough to produce change despite resistance. Their discussion might include such themes as newly prominent ideas, dissatisfied interest groups, charismatic leadership, compelling motivations, institutional weaknesses, and significant recent events—with appropriate detail concerning each. To counterbalance a preoccupation with the new, historians will then consider existing elements of the status quo, such as historic political party alignments, traditional institutions, attitudes and values, or long-existent economic patterns. There is always something old in anything new.

The Stages of Historical Consciousness

Even at this stage it should be clear that thinking historically is not as easy as it might at first appear. Below we list the four stages one passes through on the road to a more sophisticated appreciation of history and mastery of historical thinking. You are probably farther along that road than you think. At what stage are you?

Stage I: History as Fact

> To me (says the typical Stage I student) history is a bunch of facts—dates, names, events—
> that I have to memorize for the test. The books and lectures are full of facts, but I really
> don't see how they all fit together. I take history because I have to, and it bores me. Once I
> get my requirements out of the way, I plan to avoid history like the plague.

Too many people in our society never get beyond this view of history. It is not always their fault: When teachers present history as the rote memorization of facts and dates, it should come as no surprise that many of their students turn their back on the subject at the earliest opportunity. Such people lack any sense of the causal relationships that give meaning to the study of the past, and they certainly don't have the faintest understanding of the role interpretation plays in history writing.

Stage II: History as Causal Sequence

> I now see (says the student at Stage II) that history is more than facts. History provides a
> story of sequential developments over time, you know: Event A leads to event B, which
> leads to event C, and so forth. The stories are often interesting (my teacher tells some great
> anecdotes!) and it is satisfying to know why things happened as they did. More important,
> I am now beginning to see where I fit into the picture. I understand my own origins a bit
> better. The only thing that bothers me is that my textbook and my instructor sometimes
> contradict each other. It's a shame that historians can't get their act together and come to
> some sort of agreement on the true causes of events. Maybe in time they will.

Generally, a large number of people reach this stage. Stage II "consciousness" is still quite basic, but it is far beyond the very simplistic outlook of Stage I. People at Stage II can be fascinated by history and can understand cause-and-effect relationships.

But they still do not realize the complexity of such relationships and cannot accept the possibility of alternative interpretations. When they come across contradictions, they assume that one version is, of necessity, false and the other true. Furthermore, the notion that both versions could be false yet could contain a part of the truth never occurs to them. Put another way, what they seek from a history book is *the* truth, not *a* truth. Such people also have difficulty in perceiving the difference between fact and opinion.

Stage III: History as Complexity

I'm confused, says the Stage III student. History is a subject in which there is so much to learn, I no longer know where to begin. There are too many variations in the accounts you read, even accounts of the same time and place! Some books (or lecturers) emphasize politics and war, others emphasize social life, or economics, or ideas, or art, or science and technology. Studying history is like looking in a kaleidoscope in which the picture changes with each turn of the cylinder. History certainly isn't like math or chemistry, where you can get exact and certain answers. In history there seem to be so many ways of looking at the same event or period that I often don't know what I should be studying anymore.

People at this stage are (at last!) conscious of the relativistic character of history. The paradox of Stage III is that people who reach it often feel themselves to be more confused and ignorant than they did at Stages II and I. It is at Stage III that students realize how complex human affairs really are and how much there is to be learned about even tiny segments of the past. They also begin to realize how little they know compared to the immensity of what there is to know. But this feeling of helplessness is really a positive sign. The recognition of ignorance is the first step to real understanding and wisdom.

At this level people begin to think like historians. They finally realize that, due to the enormity and complexity of the historical record, accounts of even the smallest segment of the past are very selective and limited in what they cover. They understand, further, that individual historians are the ones who ultimately decide what to include and exclude in any history of any subject. Historians tell different stories depending on their interests and points of view. This awareness is an important insight. Even at Stage III, however, people still lack a full appreciation of the inherently interpretive nature of history.

Stage IV: History as Interpretation

Last year, remarks the increasingly confident student at Stage IV, a professor said that history is as much a product of the historian who writes it as of the actual people who lived it. At the time I didn't understand the comment at all; now I do. Just as individual historians will choose their topics differently, and disagree on what evidence should be included or excluded, historians, of necessity, interpret their materials differently. Not only that, but I now realize that studying the various interpretations of an event, and how historians support and develop their interpretations, is much more interesting than just trying to memorize facts.

Students at this stage will derive the most intellectual satisfaction from the study of history. They have come to terms with the interpretive nature of written history.

They understand that the evidence for any historical event is contradictory, complex, and incomplete. At the same time, paradoxically, they know that there is far more evidence available (for most events) than any historian can handle comfortably. Moreover, historians will approach the evidence with different questions, different personalities, different value systems, and different abilities. The result: history as interpretation. These realizations are uncomfortable for individuals who crave moral certainty and loath ambiguity. However, the sooner they realize that history cannot provide absolute truth, the sooner they will be able to extract the maximum intellectual benefit from its study.

> **WRITING CAPSULE 2**
>
> ## The Literature Review
>
> Since the study of history is as much the study of interpretations as the study of "facts," a good history paper should include a brief overview of what others have said about the problem you are researching. Some call this a "literature review," in that you are summarizing some of the existing books and articles on your topic. Historians often refer to such a review as the "historiography" of the subject.

EXERCISES

SET A   *Exercise 1*

In this chapter we discussed the theme of "historical thinking," which includes (1) sensitivity to multiple causation, (2) sensitivity to context, or how other times and places differ from our own, and (3) awareness of the interplay of continuity and change in human affairs.

Each of the passages below in some way reflects one or more of the elements of historical thinking. Although most written history includes all of these elements in varying degrees, in each of the passages below, your task is to decide which of the elements of historical thinking is **most visible**. You may use a category more than once, but all the categories are represented. Give the reasons for your selection in each case.

Use the letters below to indicate whether the historian in each case:

A. Describes **numerous changes** occurring in rapid order in a given time period or explains the **nature of a significant change**.

B. Emphasizes **continuity**: showing how specific conditions/elements/ideas from an earlier time carried forward from a relatively distant past—distant, that is, from the period under discussion.

C. Cites **multiple causes and factors** as an explanation of an event or situation.

D. Describes a historical or cultural setting (**context**) vastly different than our own.

1. Once the C.I.O. [i.e., the unions] pierced the fortifications of G.M. [General Motors] and U.S. Steel, it was able to overrun much of the rest of industry. By the end of 1937, the U.A.W. [United Auto Workers] had brought every car manufacturer save Ford into line. The pace of organization moved so swiftly that workers outdistanced union leaders. "Many of us," reflected a Dodge unionist, "had the feeling we were like the kid that gets a little fire started in the hayfield." In a year, the U.A.W.'s membership jumped from 30,000 to 400,000. By early May, 1937, S.W.O.C. [Steel Workers' Organizing Committee], formed less than a year before, claimed 325,000 members; by the end of the month, it had signed up all the subsidiaries of U. S. Steel, and such important independents as Jones and Laughlin, Wheeling Steel, and Caterpillar Tractor. As steel and auto went, so went much of the nation. After an eight-week strike in March and April, 1937, Firestone Tire & Rubber capitulated to the United Rubber Workers. By the end of 1937, General Electric, RCA-Victor and Philco had recognized the United Electrical and Radio Workers. The Textile Workers Organizing Committee, run by Sidney Hillman, brought into line industry titans like American Woolen in Lawrence; by early October, it boasted 450,000 members.

Category: _____

Basis: _____

_____

2. The causes of the postwar boom [in the U.S. after World War II] were both numerous and complex. Because of wartime rationing, an enormous pent-up demand existed in 1945 for housing and for all sorts of consumer goods. American consumers, both civilian and military, had accumulated huge savings; and even poorer Americans eagerly awaited the goods promised by American manufacturers at the conclusion of the war. The American economy was also boosted by several long-term factors. The "baby boom" stimulated expansion in consumption and demand, not only for goods, but also for a variety of services. Overall, the American economy experienced great increases in productivity . . . both in agriculture and industry. Between 1947 and 1964, for example, productivity in the entire American economy grew by 70 percent. Finally, the new industries of the 1920s—electrical appliances, chemicals . . . and automobiles—grew tremendously, largely because of the ready supply and cheap price of oil and other forms of energy.

Category: _____

Basis: _____

_____

3. The next step in complex marriage [in the Oneida settlement, a Utopian community of the nineteenth century] was a program of eugenics that was initiated

as "stirpiculture" [planned breeding] in 1869. Its goal was scientific procreation to create a genetic stock predisposed to the religious, intellectual, and physical requirements of spiritual perfection. A resolution was signed by all women of childbearing age to the effect that they did not belong to themselves in any respect, that they belonged first to God and second to John Humphrey Noyes [the founder of the community] as God's true representative. The declaration further stated that they had no rights or personal feelings in regard to childbearing that would in the least embarrass or oppose him in his choice of scientific combination. They agreed to put aside all envy, childishness, and self-seeking, and to rejoice with those who are the chosen candidates. They would, if necessary, become martyrs to science and cheerfully resign all desire to become mothers if for any reason Noyes deemed them unfit for propagation. Above all, they offered themselves as "living sacrifices" to God and true communism. Thirty-eight young men of the community signed a similar statement.

Category: _____

Basis:_____

_____

4. [From a history of the environmental movement.] First, America's economic modernization played a formative role in conservationism and environmentalism. Commercial and industrial growth created scarcities of resources and environmental degradation both in the countryside and the city. . . . The growth of a consumerist, leisure-based society and the vicissitudes of a capitalist economy in the 1920s and 1930s led to further changes in the movement, as its activists tried to adapt to the widespread use of the automobile and the resulting recreational abuse of the environment by sightseers, campers, and sportsmen. The Great Depression supplied the justification for a massive federal commitment to conservation programs as a spur to job creation and a stimulus to economic expansion in poor communities. Further economic changes altered the nature of conservationism to evolve into an environmental movement after World War II. Post-war affluence and suburbanization created a new society that focused less on its subsistence and more on its amenities, such as an aesthetically pleasing and healthy environment.

Category: _____

Basis:_____

_____

5. When the Eagle Forum's Kathleen Teague claimed [in 1980] that American women have "the right to be . . . ladies" she was . . . squarely in the middle of an antique legal tradition that substituted married women's obligations to their husbands for obliga-

tions to the state. This tradition had largely eroded when she spoke, but her ability to articulate it meant it was not yet dead. From the era of the American Revolution until deep into the present, the substitution of married women's obligations to their husband and families for their obligations to the state has been a central element in the way Americans have thought about the relation of all women, including unmarried women, to state power. One by one, most of these substitutions have come to seem inappropriate and have been abandoned, but in each case only after a long and complicated struggle.

Category: _____

Basis:_____

_____

Sources
1. William E. Leuchtenburg, *Franklin D. Roosevelt and the New Deal* (New York: Harper & Row, 1963), 240.
2. William A. Link, Arthur S. Link, *The Twentieth Century: A Brief American History in Two Volumes*, Vol. 2 (Arlington Heights, IL.: Harlan Davidson, Inc., 1992), 242.
3. Ira L. Mandelker, *Religion, Society, and Utopia in Nineteenth-Century America* (Amherst: The University of Massachusetts Press, 1984), 119.
4. Thomas R. Wellock, *Preserving the Nation: The Conservation and Environmental Movements, 1870–2000* (Wheeling, IL: Harlan Davidson, Inc., 2007), 7.
5. Linda K. Kerber, *No Constitutional Right to Be Ladies* (New York: Hill and Wang, 1998), 11.

SET A   *Exercise 2 — Writing about History*

Read the documents in Appendix A (pages 257–264) regarding the beginnings of American fur trade on the upper Missouri River. This trade had great potential economic value, since animal furs and hides were regarded as the major resource of the developing West. The events described in the documents took place within what was legally American territory (part of the Louisiana Purchase of 1803). One must remember, however, that for more than a hundred years British fur traders had operated successfully throughout the forest and mountain areas of North America, no matter who owned them.

Using only the information given in the documents, your task in this exercise is to write a paragraph that begins with a generalization about some facet of the Ashley expedition, followed by specific sub-points that give support to your general statement. There are many possible themes you might choose to develop, such as the role of the British in the failure of the Ashley expedition, leadership deficiencies of General Ashley, blunders by the federal government, justification for Arikara Indian attacks, or the attitudes and outlooks of the men on the expedition. Naturally, there are other possibilities.

Write a single fully developed paragraph, one that provides support for your particular analysis of the documents. Remember, the documents in Appendix A (along with the preliminary remarks) are all you have to work with. Give your paragraph (or paper) a good title that summarizes the theme you have chosen to develop.[8]

Before you begin you may wish to consult Writing Capsule 1 (p. 9) and Writing Capsule 3, below.

Instructors:

Alternative 1: Instead of a paragraph, assign a brief paper, about two pages (3–4 paragraphs) in length.

Alternative 2: Use the Appendix A documents to assign the slightly longer paper called for in Chapter 12: Writing the History Paper (Set A, Exercise 5). This is our recommendation. This assignment forces students to write as historians, making claims supported with primary sources.

WRITING CAPSULE 3

Coherent Paragraphs: Transitions[9]

As noted in Writing Capsule 1, readers expect to find the main point of a paragraph in the topic sentence. The rest of the paragraph should expand on the topic sentence, either directly or indirectly. That is, if a sentence does not support the topic sentence directly, it should support an earlier sentence that is linked directly to the topic sentence.

To help a reader follow your train of thought you have to take care to indicate clearly the connections that link the ideas (sentences) together. A common device is to list points in some sort of logical or temporal order: First . . . , second . . . , finally.

Other useful transitional phrases can be found in the following list:

Additions: *and, also, furthermore, moreover, in addition, too, second, third*

Providing examples: *for example, for instance*

Contrasts: *but, however, on the other hand, although, nevertheless, on the contrary*

Comparisons: *similarly, likewise, also*

Temporal shifts: *while, when, meanwhile, after, before, during, finally, then*

Cause and effect: *thus, therefore, consequently, as a result*

To summarize: *in conclusion, finally, in short, in summary, therefore*

Finally, just as you need smooth transitions between sentences, you must provide clear transitions between paragraphs. For more on this subjects see Chapter 12: Writing: The History Paper, page 205.

---

[8] The concept for this exercise was drawn from Harold D. Woodman, "Do Facts Speak for Themselves?" *Perspectives*, American Historical Association, 25 (April, 1987), 18–20.
[9] For much of the material in this capsule we are indebted to Diana Hacker, *A Writer's Reference*, 5th ed. (Boston: Bedford/St. Martin's, 2003), 31–35.

SET B   *Exercise 1*

In this chapter we discussed the theme of "historical thinking," which includes (1) sensitivity to multiple causation, (2) sensitivity to context, or how other times and places differ from our own, and (3) awareness of the interplay of continuity and change in human affairs.

Each of the passages below in some way reflects one or more of the elements of historical thinking. Although most written history includes all of these elements in varying degrees, in each of the passages below, your task is to decide which of the elements of historical thinking is **most visible**. You may use a category more than once, but all the categories are represented. Give the reasons for your selection in each case.

Use the letters below to indicate whether the historian in each case:

A. Describes **numerous changes** occurring in rapid order in a given time period or explains the **nature of a significant change**.

B. Emphasizes **continuity**: showing how specific conditions/elements/ideas from an earlier time carried forward from a relatively distant past—distant, that is, from the period under discussion.

C. Cites **multiple causes and factors** as an explanation of an event or situation.

D. Describes a historical or cultural setting (**context**) vastly different from our own.

1. [T]he looming figure of [Martin] Luther makes the personal factor important in the causation of the Reformation. . . .

The circumstances were ready for the man, and his religious zeal furnished a focal point for the hitherto diffused causes for the Reformation. One may legitimately question if one single force, albeit as powerful as this one, could in itself have altered the course of history. From our perspective, at least, a number of social forces seem to converge upon the developing events and carry them forward.

We have seen gunpowder and the better ocean-going vessels make possible the expansion of the European into other parts of the world. The printing press, another technological advance, served as a tool of incalculable importance in the Reformation. Someone might argue very plausibly that no Reformation could have occurred had it not been for the invention of the printing press. Without this method of spreading ideas, the Lutheran doctrines could not have been disseminated so rapidly. . . .

Social forces emerging from economic motives, powerful as they were, must have exercised an important influence on these events. The kind of merchant that we encountered in Florence or in sixteenth-century England, and who was also active in Germany, would deplore the constant flow of money to Rome. . . . Especially would the growing middle class deplore the drag on productivity caused by the clerical possession of land, the numerous church festivals, and the presumed idleness of the monks. . . .

We know that the nobles were always eager to expand their holdings. They had long eyed the lands of the Church, and the Reformation, with its expropriation of clerical wealth, offered the awaited opportunity.

Category: _____

Basis:_____

_____

2. The first order of business for the new administration [in 1933] was to unclog the channels of finance. On his second day in office, [President Franklin] Roosevelt called for a special session of Congress, and he then declared a four-day banking holiday. It took Congress only seven hours to pass the Emergency Banking Relief Act, which permitted sound banks to reopen under approval from the Treasury, and provided managers for those still in trouble. On March 12, 1933, in the first of his radio "fireside chats," the president told his audience that it was safer to "keep your money in a reopened bank than under the mattress.". . . In rapid order Roosevelt next slashed military pensions and government payrolls and then urged Congress to pass the Twenty-first Amendment, which the states ratified on December 5, ending prohibition.

Category: _____

Basis:_____

_____

3. [In the mid-1920s Alfred P. Sloan, president of General Motors, made the decision to institute an annual model change in all of the company's automobile divisions. It was a daring move considering that the best-selling car in the country, the Ford Model T, had not been changed since 1910.]

The annual model was an answer not only to the growing American demand for newness. While it institutionalized novelty, it responded to other distinctively American needs. In a democracy of cash, how were people to prove that they really were climbing the social ladder? The annual model, as Sloan elaborated it, provided a visible and easily understood symbol of personal progress, and so produced what we could call a "ladder of consumption." When the Model T became cheap and reliable and almost universal, cheapness and reliability were no longer enough. Universality and uniformity actually became drawbacks. As the Model T helped more and more Americans to move around the country, it became less useful than ever in helping Americans show that they were moving up in the world. While Sloan, in order to keep the automobile industry and General Motors flourishing, elaborated the idea of the annual model, he incidentally gave the automobile a new and wider symbolic role in American life.

Category: _____

Basis:_____

_____

4. One sound rose ceaselessly above the noises of busy life and lifted all things unto a sphere of order and serenity: the sound of bells. The bells were in daily life like good spirits, which by their familiar voices, now called upon the citizens to mourn and now to rejoice, now warned them of danger, now exhorted them to piety. They were known by their names: big Jacqueline, or the bell Roland. Every one knew the difference in meaning of the various ways of ringing. However continuous the ringing of the bells, people would seem not to have become blunted to the effect of their sound. Throughout the famous judicial duel between two citizens of Valenciennes, in l455, the big bell, "which is hideous to hear," says Chastellain, never stopping ringing. What intoxication the pealing of the bells of all the churches, and of all the monasteries of Paris, must have produced, sounding from morning till evening, and even during the night, when a peace was concluded or a pope elected.

Category: _____

Basis:_____

_____

5. Yet New England witchcraft had its roots in the villages and towns of England. It was so much a part of the culture the settlers transported from the old world to the new that the continuities rather than the differences stand out. The colonists shared with their counterparts in England many assumptions about what kinds of people witches were, what kinds of practices they engaged in, and where and how they attained their supernatural power. They also knew how to detect witches and how to rid their communities of the threat witches posed. Indeed, belief in the existence and danger of witches was so widespread, at all levels of society, that disbelief was itself suspect.

Category: _____

Basis:_____

_____

Sources

1. Carl G. Gustavson, *A Preface to History* (New York: McGraw-Hill, 1955), 58–60.
2. George Brown Tindall and David E. Shi, *America: A Narrative History*, Brief 2nd ed. (New York: W. W. Norton & Company, 1989), 708–709.
3. Daniel J. Boorstin, *The Americans: The Democratic Experience* (New York: Vintage Books, 1974), 552–53.
4. J. Huizinga, *The Waning of the Middle Ages* (Garden City, NY: Doubleday Anchor Books, 1954), 10–11.
5. Carol F. Karlsen, *The Devil in the Shape of a Woman: Witchcraft in Colonial New England* (New York: W. W. Norton & Company, 1998), 2–3.

SET B   *Exercise 2 — Writing About History*

See Set A, Exercise 2

CHAPTER 4

HISTORICAL THINKING: MULTIPLE CAUSALITY IN HISTORY

"It is better to know some of the questions than all of the answers."
—JAMES THURBER

"Nothing is inevitable in history until five minutes before it happens."
—JOEL HURSTFIELD[1]

One of the leaders of the Russian Revolution of 1917, Leon Trotsky, said that war is the locomotive of history, dramatically moving society in new directions. It was a perceptive remark, especially since the war that spawned the Russian Revolution, World War I (1914–18), was destined to put a permanent stamp on the remainder of the twentieth century. The Great War—as contemporaries knew it—was a destroyer of empires and led, among other things, to World War II (1939–45), which in turn led to the Cold War (ca. 1946–89). "By entering into military conflict in 1914," laments one historian, "the European states unleashed the mayhem from which were born not one but two revolutionary movements—one of which [Nazism] was crushed in 1945, the other [Soviet Communism, one of Trotsky's legacies] left to crumble in the dramatic events of 1989–91."[2]

How can we explain the decades-long shadow that World War I cast over the twentieth century? There were many contributing factors, but one of them certainly was a grave mistake made in the immediate aftermath of the war. The victors of World War I decided to blame the entire conflict and its attendant destruction on Germany, the defeated enemy. The causes of the war were tangled and complex, and many nations participated in the conflict, yet the victors chose to identify and punish a single culprit. Not only was the decision intellectually indefensible, but it was to have unimagined, truly horrific, consequences.

World War I, which began in 1914, began to wind down in the spring and summer of 1918 after Germany's last desperate drive failed. The "Allies" (essentially France, Britain, and the United States) seized the initiative, and by mid-August the Germans began to seek peace. With their backs against the wall, they accepted the generous terms offered them by U.S. President Woodrow Wilson, and an armistice ended the fighting on November 11. What the Germans were ultimately forced to accept, however, was the Treaty of Versailles (1919), the most notable of the settlements drawn up during the Paris Peace Conference of 1919. The Treaty of Versailles bore little relationship to the peace terms promised by President Wilson. It was a harsh,

---

[1] Quoted in M. J. Tucker, "Joel Hurstfield: Historian for All Seasons," in *Recent Historians of Great Britain,* ed. Walter Arnstein (Ames : Iowa State Univ. Press, 1990), 51.

[2] Norman Davies, *Europe: A History* (Oxford: Oxford University Press, 1996), 900.

punishing document that took away much German territory, sharply reduced its industrial capacity, virtually destroyed the German military, and required Germany to pay huge war reparations. Worse, by the terms of the infamous Clause 231, the treaty required Germany to accept entire responsibility for having caused the war.

This "War Guilt" provision caused a firestorm in Germany. "May God palsy the German hand that signs the Versailles Treaty," cried one patriot. But under duress the document was signed, and the clause became an enduring symbol to Germans of all that was wrong with the treaty. It was an emotional sore spot that never failed to arouse resentment, which a clever politician named Adolf Hitler effectively exploited in his rise to power in the 1920s and 1930s.

Without having to read a page of history the German people instinctively knew that wars don't happen in a one-factor vacuum. The world is more complicated than that. And historians of the origins of World War I have agreed with this instinctive wisdom. Even the most anti-German of historians would acknowledge that no single cause—the Treaty of Versailles notwithstanding—could ever be a satisfactory explanation of even seemingly simple events. And World War I was hardly simple. Historians have used countless gallons of ink debating the origins of World War I. And, whatever their disagreements, they agree on one thing: There was no single cause,

President Woodrow Wilson brings the United States into World War I in April 1917. (Cartoon by Clifford Kennedy Berryman, 1869–1949.) *U.S. National Archives, ARC Identifier 306092.*

but many, including intense nationalism, an interlocking alliance system, imperial rivalries, internal political pressures in several countries, a sensation-seeking press in all countries, a weapons buildup on all sides, and more—much more. In other words, the key to understanding the onset of World War I is multiple causality.

The Importance of Questions

Viewing history through the lens of multiple causality is a basic ingredient of thinking historically. To explain how and why some given event happened as it did, the historian must make a thorough inquiry into all relevant conditions and circumstances. If taken literally this is clearly an impossible task, since the circumstances and conditions that determine the direction of human affairs are almost numberless. In the real world, however, the task can be simplified, if not made simple.

The skill is called "analysis," which means nothing more than breaking the whole into its parts to find out how it works. Applied to a historical event, this means you begin by looking at separate "pieces" of the event in isolation as a step toward understanding the event in its totality. How do you do this? *You ask questions*—appropriate questions—that will lead you through an event step by step. James Thurber remarked that knowing questions is more important than knowing answers. He was right. In many endeavors and walks of life the ability to ask the right question at the right time often separates success from failure, the great scholar (or journalist, manager, or physician) from the not so great.

Teachers want students to know the events of the past, of course, but more than that they want them to develop the habit of asking—in a systematic way—certain broad questions in order to understand those events. In the long run this mental habit of seeing events with wider vision is one of the crucial intellectual skills to be gained through the study of history.

What sorts of things does a historian seek to know in order to understand the hows and whys of a historical event? A list of specific questions that historians might ask would be endless, but certain broad categories of questions are more or less standard:

- How did *ideas,* both emergent and traditional, affect the situation?
- Which important *individuals* and *groups* influenced events?
- Were *class* or *gender relationships* important?
- What role was played by *economic* and *technological* factors?
- Did *geographical location, terrain,* or *environmental conditions* play a role?
- How influential were *long-standing legal, customary,* and *diplomatic practices* or situations?
- Were there any *contingent factors*?

Before we examine these questions, a couple of important qualifications are in order.

First, these questions are "starter" ones. They are designed to help ensure that you "touch all the bases," that you follow a systematic search pattern. You will find some of the questions less relevant than others when you apply them to a particular historical situation. Others will lead to promising conjectures that must be checked against the evidence—a process that leads to more pointed and precisely phrased questions. In any event, the lists of questions below are meant to be suggestive, not definitive. Also, note well, *there is considerable overlap between the categories discussed below*—e.g., an important individual might have acted according to a distinctive set of ideas or economic interests.

Second, while it is true that historians must ask the standard questions while studying a given historical event, it is also true that they usually, as a matter of personal inclination, wind up emphasizing only one or two of the standard questions when presenting the story. The writers of survey textbooks sometimes try to cover all the bases, usually to the numbing frustration of their readers. Most historians choose just one or two main themes, which results in the many varieties of history (economic, political, intellectual, etc.) that exist.

Ideas in History

The adage that "men do not possess ideas, rather they are possessed by them" has considerable truth, especially if "ideas" are taken to include ideals, attitudes, and values. Often ideas are below the surface, not mentioned in a direct way, but present nevertheless as assumptions. In his public addresses, for example, President John F. Kennedy never specifically cited Keynesian economic principles, but he used them to revitalize the American economy in 1962.

At least as often ideas are "out front" in the movement of events. When British power in North America was at its height, in the seventeenth and eighteenth centuries, Britain's statesmen publicly espoused and followed the principles of mercantilism. The American radicals in 1776 just as candidly borrowed the main ideas of Englishman John Locke in their *Declaration of Independence.* Other examples include the impact of *Uncle Tom's Cabin* (written by Harriet Beecher Stowe), which changed Northerners' perceptions of slavery in the pre–Civil War period; Alfred T. Mahan's ideas on the role of sea power in history, which prompted an enormous naval buildup in late-nineteenth-century Germany; the Marxist ideas that formed the core ideology of the Russian revolutionaries of 1917; and the ardent feminism that emerged from the publication of Betty Friedan's *The Feminine Mystique* in 1963. In any case the historian must remember to look for both emergent ideas of compelling power and traditional ideas with an enduring hold on people's loyalties.

In dealing with the role of ideas, whether political, economic, religious, scientific, or social, there are various questions one might ask in assessing their impact:

- Had any particular idea(s) become newly fashionable?
- Which traditional ideas remained influential; which had begun to be questioned?
- Did any individual's (or group's) ideology, religious beliefs, or value system play an important role?
- Was there a distinctive public mood that appears to have aided any groups or individuals?
- Did the "intellectuals" have a marked influence at any particular point?

Again, these questions are merely suggestive of the angles of inquiry one might pursue. Also, it should be obvious that few of them permit spontaneous answers. Rather, they point in the direction of further reading and research.

Finally, in recent decades a significant development in historical studies revolves around the concept of "mentalities." Traditional history has always given due attention to ideas, whether considered as "principles" (e.g. "separation of church and state," or "one person, one vote") or "ideologies" (Puritanism, communism, Social Darwinism, isolationism, etc.). But some modern scholars widen the range of inquiry to include the outlooks and attitudes of society as a whole or in part—e.g., typical life ambitions, value systems, common anxieties, unspoken assumptions, and popular attitudes. Such inquiries go beyond the details of political or economic events to explore the various ways the common people of a given era perceived, experienced, and reacted to the world. Thus, the history of mentalities is a type of social history that considers occupational outlooks, family associations, religious tendencies, but also popular culture preferences.

Economic and Technological Factors

There is a popular axiom that to understand puzzling events one simply needs to "follow the money." Good advice indeed, especially for historians. "Economics" refers to the processes by which a society and its members make a living. That immediately involves us in such matters as market demand, trade patterns, accessibility to raw materials, the interests of economic classes and subgroups, productivity, and employment levels. While this is not the place for a mini-course in economics, the following sorts of questions can be quite helpful in sorting out the relevant factors of a historical situation.

- Were serious clashes occurring among different economic classes/groups within the population?
- Did entrenched economic interests feel endangered by new government policies? By competitive pressures?
- Did any economic group have especially strong political muscle, giving it an advantage over other interests?
- Were the markets for a nation's or region's major products and services improving or declining?
- Were existing trade patterns within and without the nation or region being disrupted by new developments?
- Was the nation or region in a discernible stage of an economic cycle (depression, recovery, boom, recession)?

Now, these are large-scale questions that, while useful in framing the overall picture, are not sufficiently focused to define a more localized situation. One must ask "small-scale" questions as well, perhaps something like:

- What were the economic stakes involved in a particular strike for both workers and employers?
- To what extent did an office-seeker's financial resources affect the outcome of an election?
- Were any key figures in any way motivated by greed, perhaps leading them to cut corners on a building project or manipulate the contract-awarding process?

We will have more to say later in this chapter about such small-scale inquiries. You'll note that some of the above questions, particularly several of the large-scale ones, do require a certain amount of economic literacy, though not at a level much beyond that obtained by reading about current events.

Related to economic factors are technological developments that influence a society's production processes and its lifestyle. Such developments can bring sharp changes in a society's direction, as happened in America in 1793. Before that date slavery was commonly regarded in the South as a crumbling system, for Southerners lacked a profitable cash crop to support its expenses. Then, while visiting at a South Carolina plantation, young Eli Whitney put together a simple but ingenious device called a "cotton gin." It made what was then called "green-seed cotton" a viable crop—this at exactly the time when English mills were voraciously consuming every fiber of cotton that could be produced. Thus, for the South, cotton became, in the words of *New York Times* writer Anne O'Hare McCormick, "map-maker, trouble-maker, history-maker."[3]

Rarely are technological developments in the foreground of historical situations. Rather, they become integrated with a society's economy, creating new products that displace others, enhancing one region's economic potential at the expense of another's, and shifting balances in international trade. So while technology is in a sense submerged, it is an area that calls for occasional scrutiny because of its impact on the economy and popular culture.

Organized Groups (and Some That Aren't)

There are few historical situations that can be understood without careful consideration of the role that group interests played in shaping the course of events. We use "interests" here in a very broad sense. Examples include organized political parties, factions within parties, interest groups of all kinds, lobbying organizations, non-profit public interest groups, government bureaucracies, legislative bodies, commissions, or simply "the gang in the back room."

The variety of organizations and groups listed above suggests a daunting complexity to human affairs. Fortunately, in most historical situations only a few such groups play a significant role at any given time. The key is for us to keep in mind David Potter's dictum that historians deal with human beings less as individuals than as groups—religious groups, cultural groups, ideological groups, interest groups, occupational groups, or social groups.[4] This means that the historian must remain acutely conscious of groups, and in research and reading see them as the focal points both of change and resistance to change. Put another way, human affairs should be viewed as an arena in which groups with differing interests band together or oppose one another to achieve their goals.

---

[3] Quoted in J. G. Randall, *The Civil War and Reconstruction* (Boston: D.C. Heath and Co., 1937), 8.
[4] David M. Potter, "The Historian's Use of Nationalism and Vice Versa," *American Historical Review*, 68 (July 1962): 924.

Some questions worth considering when addressing any historical situation are:

- What organized groups played an important role in the situation you are investigating?
- How well organized and how disciplined were each of the various groups involved in the situation? How committed was each group to the issues involved in this situation?
- Where was a given group in the "pecking order" of political, economic, and social prestige?
- How much political clout did each group have? How much access to the power centers? What methods did they utilize to achieve their ends?

When considering the influence of organized groups it is important to remember that most groups achieve their aims through government action. In a democracy, at least, this involves political activity to influence public opinion and the legislative process. The story of a society can scarcely be told without recurrent reference to the ongoing competition for control of the levers of power. This is not to disparage the importance of social history, but only to reiterate that power struggles in the political arena are, and will remain, essential ingredients of any people's history.

Class and Gender

Finally, remember that *group* is an ambiguous term. We have been commenting on the role of "organized groups," but there are myriad other "groupings" one must consider. It has long been a staple of American politics, for example, that women vote differently than men and African Americans vote differently than whites, Hispanics, or Asians. Workers have different interests than employers. Recent immigrants see things differently than do long-term residents. Now, individuals from all of these "groups" may belong to formal organizations of various sorts, but it would be a mistake to focus our attention solely on such "organized groups" without also examining the broader impact of these class, gender, racial, and ethnic differences.

Individuals in History

This is not the place to engage in the debate over whether "the individual makes the times" or "the times make the individual"—the "superperson or any person" argument. It will suffice to say that since human beings do act, their personalities, characters, and motives inevitably influence events. In England, for example, King Henry VIII's personal quest for a divorce from his wife Katherine of Aragon in the 1530s was perhaps *the* critical factor in assuring the triumph of the Protestant Reformation in that country. Woodrow Wilson (U.S. president, 1913–21) was a man of such lofty moral principles that he found it impossible to compromise with more mundane souls over the issue of his "morally right" League of Nations. Did his behavior thus help set the stage for World War II? The courage and eloquence of Rev. Martin Luther King, Jr., profoundly shaped the American civil rights movement of the 1950s and 1960s. Even these few examples sufficiently show that individuals—with their personal quirks, principles, virtues, and vices—do affect the course of events.

Some questions you might want to ask about key individuals are:

- What qualities of leadership did the individual conspicuously display or lack?
- What were the person's skills and abilities, defects and weaknesses?
- What was the person's ideology or worldview?
- What aspects of the individual's personality or worldview influenced the situation?
- What was the individual's social and economic background, and how did it influence his/her actions?

Long-standing Legal, Customary, and Diplomatic Conditions

In a sense this category overlaps each of those preceding it, but it deserves to be treated independently. To understand any historical event we must not only look at the influence of groups, ideas, and individuals, but we must also consider the basic "rules of the game" that serve as a permanent backdrop to all human dramas. More concretely, the historian must understand the established ways of the society in question, including common beliefs and attitudes, fixed elements of the social structure, long-existing economic arrangements, and relatively permanent institutions and governmental patterns. Without knowledge of such basic continuities, any concept of change is meaningless. (See Chapter 3.)

This is an admittedly foggy category, but it refers to all those habitual and relatively consistent patterns of behavior that most of us take for granted in our day-to-day lives. These patterned responses, sometimes based on formal law and sometimes on custom or social convention, do affect the course of events and must be taken into account by the historian. The laws, institutions, traditions, diplomatic ties, and social customs of a people live beyond the events of the moment or even the lives of individuals. Naturally these things change, but, periods of revolution excepted, not quickly. Most historical situations are, to a greater or lesser degree, influenced by the weight of legal and behavioral tradition. As William Faulkner said in *Absalom, Absalom!* "The past is never dead, it's not even past." Two examples might make this clearer.

The historian who is trying to write the history of a given presidential election, say John McCain vs. Barack Obama in 2008, will certainly ask several of the questions we have discussed: What was the role played by key individuals and groups and how did economic and ideological factors influence the outcome? To answer those questions our imaginary historian will also have to know, at minimum, something about the laws that govern the nominating process (such as the workings of the Electoral College), the key issues of the election, and the traditional voting behavior of various ethnic, religious, regional, and professional groups. The sensitive historian will also have to know something about the intangible and unwritten "rules" that set limits as to how candidates can and cannot behave. For example, there is no law that says a male candidate must wear a suit and tie while campaigning, but almost all of them do—at least most of the time. (When was the last time you saw a presidential candidate giving a major speech wearing Levi's and a sweater?)

Sometimes habitual behavior patterns become so entrenched that they frustrate the best attempts of individuals and groups to initiate change. Such behavioral inertia is a characteristic of many large bureaucracies. For instance, beginning in the early 1920s Soviet leaders had serious problems in directing the large-scale collectivization of Russian industry and agriculture. Soviet leader V. I. Lenin complained five years after the Revolution that though he had in place a "vast army of governmental employees," he lacked any real control over them, and that "down below . . . the bureaucrats function in such a way as to counteract our measures."[5] Institutions in the United States can also be maddeningly inflexible. An environmental lawyer, Victor Yannacone, once complained about "self-perpetuating, self-sufficient, self-serving bureaus [which] are power sources unto themselves, effectively insulated from the people and responsible to no one but themselves."[6]

Contingency in History

Engaging in historical inquiry is like peeling an onion. It must be done from the outside, with each layer separately removed, each of the "starter" questions separately asked. As we get closer to the onion's center we sometimes get to layers we can't at first name—in history we can call these "special" or "chance" factors. Since these factors are so close to the heart of the onion (the historical occurrence), they must be studied carefully, even though, strictly speaking, they may not be classifiable under one of the major headings given in this chapter.

One of the difficulties in explaining historical events is that each of them is more or less unique. This is so in no small part because of unforeseen events and accidents (the meaning of "contingency") that decisively affect the situation. As a recent article on history teaching put it, "The core insight of contingency is that the world is a magnificently interconnected place. Change a single prior condition, and any historical outcome could have turned out differently."[7] As examples, consider the following:

- The assassination of the Austro-Hungarian crown prince at Sarajevo in 1914 provoked his government into a harsh line against Serbia, thus setting into motion a chain of events that soon brought the onset of World War I five weeks later.
- The news that Democratic candidate Grover Cleveland had fathered an illegitimate child changed the tone of the presidential election of 1884.
- On D-Day, June 6, 1944, when Allied forces assaulted the Normandy beaches, Germany's most skillful field commander, General Erwin Rommel, was back in Germany visiting his family. His absence from the scene of operations almost surely contributed to the Allied success in establishing a beachhead on that vital day.

[5] Merle Fainsod, "The Pervasiveness of Soviet Controls," in Michael Dalby and Michael Werthman, *Bureaucracy in Historical Perspective* (Glenview, IL.: Scott Foresman, and Co., 1971), 121.
[6] Quoted in Gerald N. Rosenberg, *The Hollow Hope: Can Courts Bring About Social Change?* 2nd ed. (Chicago: University of Chicago Press, 2008), 23.
[7] Thomas Andrews and Flannery Burke, "What Does It Mean to Think Historically?" *Perspectives* (January 2007), 34.

- The Iranian hostage crisis of the 1970s, along with the intense media coverage of futile U.S. attempts to recover the hostages, contributed in a major way to Jimmy Carter's defeat in the presidential election of 1980.

Other particular and unpredictable events can change the course of history: the delivery of an effective speech; a sudden illness; a badly handled press conference; the Boston Tea Party; the sinking of the battleship *Maine* in 1898; the breaking of the German code during World War II. Such events can change a historical situation and push the larger forces into the background, though not eliminate them entirely. Chance events are like "wild cards" in a poker hand, decisively changing its value and thus affecting the outcome of the game.

Conclusion

Use of the categories discussed in this chapter will help assure you that you have asked the important questions. Still, we hasten to add that there are situations in which other categories enter into the picture, and you must be ready to identify them and pursue them if necessary. For example, in many historical situations demographic (population), environmental, or geographic factors play a central role. It is impossible to understand English foreign policy, for example, unless one takes into account the fact that England is an island. The greatest catastrophe in European history, the Black Death epidemic of the fourteenth century, is inexplicable without close study of the environmental conditions at the time as well as our relatively recent knowledge about how infectious diseases operate in human populations.

Finally, a word of caution: In Chapter 2 we discussed historians' "frames of reference." Each of us perceives and measures the world according to a set of values and interests that is distinctively our own. This is natural, but we run the risk that our own frame of reference may become so narrow as to constrict severely our understanding of the historical situation under consideration. Bringing to our historical investigation the categories of questions described in this chapter should assure a more-balanced perspective.

As you complete the exercises below, remember that whatever question historians ask concerning an event or situation, they are looking for two things: (1) factors that upset the status quo and (2) elements in the status quo that were strongly resistant to change and that made whatever change that occurred less far-reaching than it otherwise might have been.

EXERCISES

SET A   *Exercise 1 — Questions*

The following exercise is intended to deepen your awareness of the variety of factors that can enter into a historical situation. The excerpt below ranges across many of the categories we have discussed, showing that the historian who wrote it asked many of the questions we have emphasized in this chapter. Your task is not to try to identify "causes," but only to note the factors that somehow helped shape the situation, at least in this historian's view. Read the passage and then respond to the questions that follow. (As you read be alert for evidence of the influence of ideas and attitudes, economic and technological factors, group initiatives, important individuals, entrenched behavior patterns, contingencies and the like.)

This excerpt is from, *Give Me Liberty! An American History,* Volume 2 by Eric Foner, 878–79. Copyright © 2005 by Eric Foner. It discusses the "new environmentalism," which Foner sees as one of a variety of new American social and political movements during the 1960s. Used by permission of W. W. Norton and Company, Inc.

THE NEW ENVIRONMENTALISM

❊1 Liberation movements among racial minorities, women, and gays challenged long-standing social inequalities. Another movement, environmentalism, called into question different pillars of American life—the equation of progress with endless increases in consumption and the faith that science, technology, and economic growth would advance the social welfare. Concern for preserving the natural environment dated back to the creation of national parks and other conservation efforts during the Progressive era. But in keeping with the spirit of the Sixties, the new environmentalism was more activist and youth-oriented, and it spoke the language of empowering citizens to participate in decisions that affected their lives. Its emergence reflected the very affluence celebrated by proponents of the American Way. As the "quality of life"—including physical fitness, health, and opportunities to enjoy leisure activities—occupied a greater role in the lives of middle-class Americans, the environmental consequences of economic growth received increased attention. When the 1960s began, complaints were already being heard about the bulldozing of forests for suburban development and the contamination produced by laundry detergents and chemical lawn fertilizers seeping into drinking supplies.

❊2 The publication in 1962 of *Silent Spring* by the marine biologist Rachel Carson brought home to millions of readers the effects of DDT, an insecticide widely used by home owners and farmers against mosquitoes, gypsy moths, and other insects. In chilling detail, Carson related how DDT killed birds and animals and caused sickness among humans. Chemical and pesticide companies launched a campaign to discredit her—some critics called the book part of a communist plot. But Carson launched the modern environmental movement. The Sierra Club, founded in the 1890s to preserve forests, saw its membership more than triple, and other groups sprang into existence to alert the country to the dangers of water contamination, air pollution, lead in paint, and the extinction of animal species. Nearly every state quickly banned the use of DDT. In 1969, television brought home to a national audience the death of birds and fish and the despoiling of beaches caused by a major oil spill off the coast of California, exposing the environmental dangers of oil transportation and ocean drilling for oil.

❊3 Despite vigorous opposition from business groups that considered its proposals a violation of property rights, environmentalism attracted the broadest bipartisan support of any of the new social movements. Under Republican president Richard Nixon, Congress during the late 1960s and early 1970s passed a series of measures to protect the environment, including the Clean Air and Clean Water Acts and the Endangered Species Act. On April 22, 1970, the first Earth Day, some 20 million people, most of them under the age of thirty, participated in rallies, concerts, and teach-ins.

¶4 Closely related to environmentalism was the consumer movement, spearheaded by the lawyer Ralph Nader. His book *Unsafe at Any Speed* (1965) exposed how auto manufacturers produced highly dangerous vehicles. General Motors, whose Chevrolet Corvair Nader singled out for its tendency to roll over in certain driving situations, hired private investigators to discredit him. When their campaign was exposed, General Motors paid Nader a handsome settlement, which he used to fund investigations of other dangerous products and of misleading advertising.

¶5 Nader's campaigns laid the groundwork for the numerous new consumer protection laws and regulations of the 1970s. Unlike 1960s movements that emphasized personal liberation, environmentalism and the consumer movement called for limiting some kinds of freedom—especially the right to use private property in any way the owner desired—in the name of a greater common good.

Questions:

Indicate in the spaces provided in what way any of the following were involved in the situation. In each instance note the appropriate paragraph number(s). Include **all** relevant possibilities under each category. If you feel a given factor was not present, write "none." Of course, a given factor legitimately may be placed in more than one category. Be prepared to defend your answers.

1. Ideas/Attitudes/Public Opinion:

_____

_____

_____

_____

2. Economic and Technological Factors:

_____

_____

_____

_____

3. Groups (Organized and Otherwise):

_____

_____

_____

_____

4. Individuals (and their specific contribution):

_____

_____

_____

_____

5. "Rules of the Game" (i.e. long-standing legal, customary, diplomatic practices and situations):

_____

_____

_____

_____

6. Contingencies (unforeseen/accidental developments):

_____

_____

_____

_____

SET A   *Exercise 2 — The Historian's Frame of Reference*

In the final segment of this chapter (and in Chapter 2) we discussed how a frame of reference can shape a historian's explanation of an event. Remember, a frame of reference influences the questions historians ask as well as the elements of a historical situation they choose to emphasize in their writings. This is true even in supposedly "objective" and "value free" textbooks.

Each of the textbook passages below tries to explain the governmental corruption during the administration of the Republican president Ulysses S. Grant (1869–77). And each explanation emphasizes the importance of one (possibly two) of the following variables at the expense of the others: ideas, economic or business interests, Grant's individual personality traits, or the "rules of the game" (in this case primarily political "rules"). Read each passage, then in the spaces provided classify the author's frame of reference according to whether the passage emphasizes (1) ideological factors (formal ideologies or popular attitudes or values), (2) economic/business interests, (3) elements of the political system (rules of the game), or (4) individual traits as **most** responsible for the corruption under Grant.

*More than one orientation might be present, but you should attempt to single out the **dominant** orientation. Underline the sections of the passages that support your conclusions. Be prepared to defend your answers in discussion.*

1. The Liberal Republican challenge [by those who left the party in 1872] reflected growing dissatisfaction with Grant's administration. Strong-willed but politically naïve, Grant made a series of poor appointments. His secretary of war, his private secretary, and officials in the Treasury and Navy departments were all involved in bribery or tax-cheating scandals. Instead of exposing the corruption, Grant defended some of the culprits. As the clamor against dishonesty in government grew, Grant's popularity and his party's prestige declined.

Orientation: _____

Basis:_____

2. One of the many ironies in the Reconstruction story is that some of the radical Republicans took the first steps toward destroying the political alliances on which the Republican political position in the South depended. During the first Grant administration a new set of leaders won a dominant position in the presidential circle. These were men who were most responsive to the economic pressures created by the cyclonic growth of American capitalism after the Civil War. They helped to make Congress, the state legislatures, and state political machines the willing collaborators of railroad, oil, textile, and steel interests that wanted government favors. The older crusading radicals found this new Republican leadership appalling, particularly as evidence of corruption began to come to light. "Like all parties that have an undisturbed power for a long time," wrote Senator James Grimes of Iowa, "(the Republican

Party) has become corrupt, and I believe it is today the most corrupt and debauched political party that has ever existed."

Orientation: _____

Basis:_____

3. There can be no doubt that in statecraft Grant was inexperienced and naïve, and that posterity would think better of him if he had not ventured out beyond his depth into the whirlpool of public affairs. But if one is to apportion blame, one cannot avoid pointing an accusing finger at the American people. They displayed a lack of political maturity that matched Grant's when they drafted yet another war hero for this exalted office. He was twice nominated unanimously by the Republican national convention and both times won the ensuing election by a substantial margin. . . . If he was a disaster as President, the voters evidently did not think so. . . .

Moral standards had broken down, primarily as a result of the Civil War, and corruption was rampant. The "eight long years of scandal" probably would have existed with or without Grant, though perhaps in a less acute form.

Orientation: _____

Basis:_____

President Ulysses S. Grant. Photograph by Mathew Brady, taken between 1869 and 1877. *Library of Congress, Prints & Photographs Division, (LC-USZ62-21986).*

4. But even the most determined presidential effort could not have immediately tamed the spoils system. The sheer numbers, combined with the cost of maintaining party machinery, led to the development of a system which obliged party workers to pay fees for appointments, or incumbent officeholders were taxed an annual assessment on their salaries. Officeholders, well aware that their tenure was impermanent, unsurprisingly took it for granted that they were to milk the post for all it was worth. The result was inescapably a pervasive corruption. Efforts to control the system, as more than one president swiftly discovered, ran afoul of the congressional presumption that spoils were its peculiar prerogative—a presumption which if defied was promptly sustained by congressional refusals to support executive proposals.

Orientation: _____

Basis:_____

5. [During the Grant administration] some of the nation's most prominent politicians routinely accepted railroad largesse. Republican senator William M. Stewart of Nevada, a member of the Committee on the Pacific Railroad, received a gift of 50,000 acres of land from the Central Pacific for his services. Republican senator Lyman Trumbull of Illinois took an annual retainer from the Illinois Central. The worst scandal of the Grant administration grew out of corruption involving railroad promotion. As a way of diverting funds for the building of the Union Pacific Railroad, an inner circle of Union Pacific stockholders created the dummy Crédit Mobilier construction company. In return for political favors, a group of prominent Republicans received stock in the company. When the scandal broke in 1872, it ruined Vice-President Schuyler Colfax politically and led to the censure of two congressmen.

Orientation: _____

Basis:_____

Sources
    1. Mary Beth Norton, et al., *A People and a Nation: A History of the United States* (Boston: Houghton Mifflin Co., 1994), 490.
    2. Edwin C. Rozwenc, *The Making of American Society*, Vol. II (Boston: Allyn and Bacon, 1973), 596.
    3. Thomas A Bailey, *Probing America's Past*, Vol. II (Lexington, MA.: D. C. Heath and Co., 1973), 434–35.
    4. J. P. Shenton and Alan M. Meckler, *U.S. History Since 1865* (Homewood, IL.: Learning Systems Co., 1975), 16.
    5. John Mack Faragher, et al., *Out of Many: A History of the American People*, Vol. II (Englewood Cliffs, NJ: Prentice Hall, 1994), 537–38.

SET B *Exercise 1 — Questions*

See Set A, Exercise 1. (Instructors: An alternative would be to ask students, using the categories in Set A, to suggest possible factors involved in a recent event with which they are all familiar—an election, international crisis, business merger or collapse, local scandal, etc.)

SET B *Exercise 2 — The Historian's Frame of Reference*

In the final segment of this chapter, and in Chapter 2, we discussed how a frame of reference can shape a historian's explanation of an event. Remember, a frame of reference influences the questions historians ask as well as the elements of a historical situation they choose to emphasize in their writings. This is true even in supposedly "objective" and "value-free" textbooks.

Each of the textbook passages below tries to explain why the Versailles Treaty (1919), which ended World War I and provided for the establishment of a League of Nations (in addition to blaming the Germans for the war), failed ratification in the United States Senate. Each explanation emphasizes the importance of one of the following factors: the influence of ideology, political partisanship, or President Woodrow Wilson's personality traits. (Wilson had personally negotiated the treaty.) Read each passage, then, in the spaces provided, classify the author's frame of reference according to whether the passage emphasizes (1) ideological factors (formal ideologies or popular attitudes or values), (2) political conflict, or (3) individual personality traits as **most** responsible for the Senate's rejection of the Versailles Treaty.

*More than one orientation might be present, but you should attempt to single out the **dominant** orientation. Underline the sections of the passages that support your conclusions. Be prepared to defend your answers in discussion.*

1. Polls showed that most Americans favored the League [of Nations] in some form. All Wilson had to do was compromise with the Senate and the treaty would pass. Instead, he returned to Washington in July itching for a fight, and he grew more stubborn and frustrated as the summer wore on. Dismissing his opponents as "blind and little provincial people," Wilson declared that the "Senate must take its medicine." His use of a medical metaphor was telling, for Wilson's health had deteriorated under the strain of the war. In fact, in Paris [where the treaty had been written] he had suffered a severe attack of indigestion that was probably a mild stroke. . . .

Wilson was clearly to blame for the Senate's failure to reach a compromise.

Orientation: _____

Basis:_____

2. His [Wilson's] most extreme enemies in the Senate were a group of about eighteen "irreconcilables," opposed to a treaty in any form. Some were isolationist progressives, such as Republicans Robert M. LaFollette of Wisconsin and William Borah of Idaho,

who opposed the league as steadfastly as they opposed American entry into the war. Others were racist xenophobes like Democrat James Reed of Missouri. . . .

The less dogmatic but more influential opponents were led by Republican Henry Cabot Lodge of Massachusetts, powerful majority leader of the Senate. They had strong reservations about the League of Nations, especially the provisions for collective security in the event of a member being attacked. Lodge argued that this provision impinged on congressional authority to declare war and placed unacceptable restraints on the nation's ability to pursue an independent foreign policy. Lodge proposed a series of amendments that would have weakened the league. But Wilson refused to compromise, motivated in part by the long-standing hatred he and Lodge felt toward each other.

Orientation: _____

Basis:_____

3. At the core of the debate lay a basic issue in American foreign policy: whether the United States would endorse collective security or continue to travel the path of unilateralism articulated in George Washington's Farewell Address and in the Monroe Doctrine. In a world dominated by imperialist states unwilling to subordinate their selfish acquisitive ambitions to an international organization, Americans preferred their traditional nonalignment and freedom of choice over binding commitments to collective action. That is why so many of Wilson's critics targeted Article 10 [which seemingly would allow the League of Nations to use American troops independently of Congressional approval] and why the president was so adamant against its revision.

Orientation: _____

Basis:_____

4. The leading opponent of the League of Nations in the Senate was Henry Cabot Lodge, a prominent Republican who was a lifelong friend of Theodore Roosevelt's. It has often been said that Lodge defeated the treaty. That is assuming a great deal. Mr. Lodge was not a big enough man to defeat anything that had a popular following. . . .

No; the League Covenant was defeated by the American people. Wilson realized that public opinion was opposed to his cherished measure. He thought the people were not informed clearly as to its purport, and he went on a long speaking tour for the purpose of instructing them.

He was already a sick man, and the cold reception that he encountered broke his heart. At Pueblo, Colorado, on September 26, 1919, he had a paralytic stroke from which he never recovered.

On March 19, 1920, the treaty was voted down in the Senate [for the final time].

Orientation: _____

Basis:_____

5. In the final analysis the treaty was slain in the house of its friends rather than in the house of its enemies. In the final analysis it was not the two-thirds rule, or the "irreconcilables," or Lodge, or the "strong" and "mild reservationists," but Wilson and his docile following who delivered the fatal stab. If the President had been permitted to vote he would have sided with Borah, Brandegee, Johnson, and the other "bitter-enders"—though for entirely different reasons.

Wilson had said that the reservation to Article X was a knife thrust at the heart of the Covenant. Ironically, he parried this knife thrust, and stuck his own dagger, not into the heart of the Covenant, but into the entire treaty.

This was the supreme act of infanticide. With his own sickly hands Wilson slew his own brain child—or the one to which he had contributed so much.

Orientation: _____

Basis:_____

Sources
1. James K. Martin, Randy Roberts, Steven Mintz, Linda O. McMurry, James H. Jones, *America and Its People* (Glenview, IL.: Scott, Foresman and Company, 1989), 736–37.
2. John Mack Faragher, et al., *Out of Many*, vol. II (Englewood Cliffs, NJ: Prentice Hall, 1994) 714.
3. Mary Beth Norton, David M. Katzman, Paul D. Escott, Howard P. Chudacoff, Thomas G. Paterson, William M. Tuttle, Jr., *A People and a Nation*, Vol. II (Boston: Houghton Mifflin Company, 1994), 714.
4. W. E. Woodward, *A New American History* (New York: Literary Guild, 1937), 798–99.
5. Thomas A. Bailey, "The Supreme Infanticide," in Sidney Fine and Gerald Brown, *The American Past*, Vol. II (London: The Macmillan Company, 1970), 368.

CHAPTER 5   HISTORICAL THINKING: CONTEXT

"Men resemble their times more than they do their fathers."

—ARAB PROVERB

"The past is a foreign country; they do things differently there."

—L. P. HARTLEY

Historians are firm believers in the cliché that truth is stranger than fiction. What could be stranger, for instance, than the episode recounted by Robert Darnton in his intriguing essay, "Workers Revolt: The Great Cat Massacre of the Rue Saint-Séverin."[1] The essay deals with a rather grisly episode in the Paris of the late 1730s—the attempt one day of a number of printer's apprentices to kill every cat they could get their hands on. After killing the favorite cat of their master's (employer's) wife, the workers "drove the other cats across the rooftops, bludgeoning every one within reach and trapping those who tried to escape in strategically placed sacks. They dumped sackloads of half-dead cats in the courtyard. Then the entire workshop gathered round and staged a mock trial. . . . After pronouncing the animals guilty and administering last rites, they strung them up on an improvised gallows."

Does this episode strike you as barbaric? Most people today would think so. But there is something decidedly peculiar about the whole thing: The workers who participated in the slaughter thought it was all a hilarious joke. The apprentices, says Darnton, were overcome with laughter and joy as they gathered and dispatched the local cats, and, in the days that followed, they riotously reenacted the comic events of the massacre over and over again. The fact that we have trouble appreciating the humor of the slaughter of animals often considered cuddly pets is an indication that we don't know enough about the era and culture we are studying. As Darnton notes: "Our own inability to get the joke, is an indication of the distance that separates us from the workers of preindustrial Europe."[2]

Darnton has presented an interesting puzzle. Why did those eighteenth-century workers think killing and torturing cats was so hilariously funny? We can find the answer, as Darnton shows, by examining the historical context in which the event took place. To get the "joke" of the cat massacre we have to enter the thought-world of eighteenth-century popular culture. On one level the frolicsome massacre of cats, as it turns out, represented the venting of worker hostility against an overbearing and unpopular employer. For a number of nights the workers had yowled like cats

---

[1] See Robert Darnton, *The Great Cat Massacre and Other Episodes in French Cultural History* (New York: Basic Books, 1984).
[2] Darnton, *Cat Massacre*, 76–78.

in order to irritate the master who had been mistreating them. In desperation the master ordered the apprentices to get rid of the offensive "cats." The workers did so with great glee, and in the process killed the house pet of their employer's wife. The master and his wife were outraged but helpless, in that they themselves had given the order to eliminate the cats.

This helps a little, but it is not enough. The core of Darnton's analysis is his discussion of popular amusements in eighteenth-century Europe and the role cats played in the popular mind. First, the torture of animals of all kinds, but especially cats, was a popular form of entertainment in that era. More important, cats had long been popularly associated with witchcraft, sexuality, and fertility. By first imitating cat cries and then executing the mistress's cat, the apprentices, according to Darnton, were both accusing their master's wife of witchcraft and "assaulting" her in a sexually symbolic way, thus ridiculing the master as having been cuckolded (our phrase would be "cheated on"). To workers who had grown up in a culture that tortured animals for amusement, who had long suffered insults and mistreatment from an unpopular master, the "great cat massacre" was both funny and deeply satisfying.

This bare outline hardly does justice to the sophistication and intricacy of Professor Darnton's analysis, but the essential point should be clear: To "understand" even this relatively minor incident in the history of pre-modern France, the historian must uncover the rich texture of beliefs, customs, and values within which the event took place. The historian must, in short, pay very close attention to context.

Context and Historical Understanding

The importance of context in history is based on the simple premise that the past is different than the present, and to interpret the past using the values and beliefs of the present will distort and misrepresent that past.[3] A distinguishing mark of the good historian is the ability to avoid judging past ages by the standards of the present, and to see former societies (to the greatest extent possible) as those societies saw themselves.

It is extremely difficult, even for the most fair-minded of observers, to understand and evaluate the habits, thoughts, and values of people who lived long ago and far away. An analogy would be the difficulty faced by anyone today venturing into a foreign culture. Even in the early twenty-first century, travelers abroad encounter a bewildering array of customs, practices, laws, and values that may seem to them "strange" and even "illogical." For instance, the reverence toward cows that one finds in India can bewilder a visitor for whom beef is simply a meal. A siesta during the searingly hot hours of midday is simple common sense to residents of many tropical countries, but to some Americans such behavior smacks of laziness. Western visitors to the Middle East or parts of Asia may unwittingly insult the locals by crossing their legs and pointing the sole of their shoe at someone. And so it goes. The successful traveler is the individual who is open-minded enough to try to understand these cultural differences and adapt to them.

---

[3] The realization that the past is radically different than the present is a surprisingly modern notion. Throughout much of history, people thought of past events as though they were part of present reality. Note the countless Italian Renaissance paintings of Biblical scenes in which the figures are dressed in the height of fifteenth-century Florentine style!

The same is true of the historian embarking on an intellectual journey into the past. In the words of British novelist L. P. Hartley, "The past is a foreign country; they do things differently there."[4] Just as the conscientious traveler today must learn the local customs, values, laws, and language to feel at ease in a foreign country, historians must become fully acquainted with the institutions, cultural habits, and beliefs of the society they are studying. Only then can they appreciate the significance and complexity of historical events. As Robert Darnton put it, "other people are other. They do not think the way we do. And if we want to understand their way of thinking, we should set out with the idea of capturing otherness."[5]

To think historically, then, you must constantly remind yourself that the past is different from the present and that historical events must not be evaluated in isolation from the total cultural and intellectual environment of the time in which they took place. To do so is to risk massive oversimplification or, worse, to misunderstand the events completely. You need to know as much as possible about the historical period you are studying in order to interpret the past in a fair-minded manner. The investigator's knowledge, as Jacques Barzun and Henry Graff see it, "must include an understanding of how men in other eras lived and behaved, what they believed, and how they managed their institutions."[6] To the best of your ability you should attempt to see the world through the eyes of those you are trying to study. You need not abandon your own values in favor of those of a different place or time. (No need, for instance, to see a massacre of helpless cats as a grand joke.) But you should be able to distance yourself from your own values sufficiently to be able to *understand* why the printer's apprentices thought killing the local cats was so funny. The exercise of such *imaginative sympathy* is a prerequisite of sound historical thinking.

All of this is easier said than done. Very often the tendency to judge the past according to one's own values and standards seems a deeply ingrained human habit. It is often impossible for the historian to see events exactly as contemporaries saw them for the simple reason that the historian knows "how things came out," whereas the participants did not. Historians narrate and interpret the past with the enormous advantage of hindsight, and it is much easier to be an armchair quarterback than to play the game itself. Hindsight makes it very tempting for the historian to make grand generalizations about the incompetence, naiveté, and shortsightedness of those in the past who could not, as we do, know their future. Allan Nevins, in *The Gateway to History*, points out the fallacy involved with this sort of history. Historical hindsight, he warns, makes past problems seem much more simple (and more easily solvable) than they actually were, and "the leaders that dealt with them . . . smaller men."[7] Hindsight, in short, makes it very difficult for even the best-intentioned investigators to approach the trials and triumphs of past ages with true imaginative sympathy.

The difficulty of judging the past by its standards rather than your own increases when you are trying to understand behaviors repugnant to contemporary moral codes (e.g., "the great cat massacre"). It is difficult to get beyond moral outrage, yet true understanding demands that you do so. The same problem besets historians

---

[4] Quoted in David Lowenthal, *The Past is a Foreign Country* (Cambridge: University Press, 1985), xvi.

[5] Darnton, *Cat Massacre*, 4.

[6] Jacques Barzun and Henry Graff, *The Modern Researcher*, rev. ed. (New York: Harcourt, Brace, and World, 1970), 116.

[7] Allan Nevins, *The Gateway to History* (Chicago: Quadrangle Books, 1963), 257.

King James I of England, ruled 1603–25. (From Charles Johnston and Carita Spencer, *Ireland's Story: A Short Story of Ireland* [Boston, New York and Chicago: Houghton Mifflin and Co., 1905]. *[From the private collection of Mr. Gerry Lee] Courtesy of the CUNY Institute for Irish-American Studies.*

who write biographies of villains, scoundrels, or the merely unsavory. David Harris Willson confronted this problem when working on a biography of King James I of England (ruled 1603–25). This biography, still one of the best treatments of this rather flawed and obnoxious king, is a model of impartiality. Willson succeeded in writing a fair and sympathetic treatment of James, in spite of the fact that he never really liked the English king, no matter how hard he tried to do so.[8]

Context and Moral Judgments in History

Above we referred to King James I of England as a "rather obnoxious king." In its most basic sense "obnoxious" means "very unpleasant" or "objectionable." What right do we have to be so moralistic and judgmental? Does not such a label violate the central lesson of this chapter—i.e., thou shalt not judge the past by the standards of the present? Is this not a violation of a basic tenet of historical thinking? Perhaps.

But if, after carefully reading and evaluating the relevant original sources of James's reign, we conclude that many of James's seventeenth-century contemporaries thought him "obnoxious" (even if they used different words to express it), then we are justified in "calling 'em as we see 'em." That is, the evidence would have justified the use of the term. On the other hand, if we deem James "obnoxious" because *we* find his behavior morally objectionable, that is a different situation altogether. In the latter case we could be accused of interpreting events "out of context." But even in this case the verdict of practicing historians would not be unanimous. There is marked disagreement among professional historians as to the legitimacy of passing moral judgments on past events and individuals.

---

[8] D. H. Willson, *King James VI and I* (New York: Oxford Univ. Press, 1967).

Any discussion of the importance of thinking contextually about the past ventures into troubled waters when the issue of moral values surfaces. Many practices that today we consider morally reprehensible have been viewed quite differently in the past. Slavery and serfdom, for example, although almost universally (and rightly) condemned today, were once considered part of the natural order of things. Slavery was a prominent feature of ancient Greek and Roman life; in the European Middle Ages (and much later in Russia and Eastern Europe) serfs lived lives not far removed from those of slaves; and, as everyone knows, slavery was an integral part of the culture of the American South for over two hundred years. In cases such as this, what position should the conscientious historian take? Should these past cultures be condemned as "immoral" because they countenanced slavery? Should the historian become a moral "relativist" and judge those societies in terms of his or her own standards of right and wrong? Or should the historian avoid making moral judgments altogether?

Herbert Butterfield, a British historian, believed that moral judgments should be irrelevant to historical understanding. If readers did not recognize the immorality or morality of past deeds, he argued, the historian's moralistic pronouncements would certainly not change their mind. Further, moral judgments would do nothing to help researcher or reader understand the past in any meaningful way. Says Butterfield: "Moral judgments on human beings are by their nature irrelevant to the enquiry and alien to the intellectual realm of scientific history. . . . These moral judgments must be recognised to be an actual hindrance to enquiry and reconstruction. . . ."[9]

Butterfield and those like him are sometimes called "amoralists." That is, they believe that moral judgments do not serve any useful purpose in a historical narrative. Ranked opposite are those who believe historians have a duty to inject moral pronouncements into their work. Their case also has merit. This group believes that certain moral and ethical norms are universal and transcend time and space. It is appropriate, then, to point the finger at evil and condemn it wherever one finds it. As Lord Acton, the planner of *The Cambridge Modern History,* said in 1895, "I exhort you never to debase the moral currency or to lower the standard of rectitude, but to try [judge] others by the final maxim that governs your own lives, and to suffer no man and no cause to escape the undying penalty which history has the power to inflict on wrong."[10] Acton's contemporary, Goldwin Smith, agreed, saying "Justice has been justice, mercy has been mercy, honour has been honour, good faith has been good faith, truthfulness has been truthfulness from the beginning."[11] We sacrifice too much, in other words, if we rank "understanding" above defending solid moral values.

There are others who occupy a middle ground. This group believes it is legitimate and important for historians to provide moral critiques of the past, but they also believe (along with Butterfield) that the historian should not play the role of the judge, condemning the guilty and absolving the innocent. This position is held by American historian John Higham, who believes that what he calls "moral history" can be an important spur to historical understanding. Moral history can help us appreciate the nature and importance of moral imperatives in different times and places. It can help us understand how certain values—honor, courage, and other

---

[9] Quoted in Hans Meyerhoff, ed., *The Philosophy of History in Our Time* (New York: Doubleday, 1959, 230.
[10] Quoted in Frtiz Stern, ed., *The Varieties of History* (Cleveland: Meridan Books, 1956), 247.
[11] Meyerhoff, *Philosophy of History,* 225.

concepts of "character"—changed over time. It can also help us "ponder the moral responsibility of the agents of decision [leaders]," by helping us understand the real alternatives available to leaders at key moments in history. In Higham's words, "The historian is not called to establish a hierarchy of values, but rather to explore a spectrum of human potentialities and achievements."[12] Higham's position, then, is somewhat "relativistic." The historian can and should venture into the realm of moral judgments, but those judgments must take into account the broad context of the time and place being studied.

And the debate goes on. Wherever your sympathies lie on this issue, it is necessary to keep in mind that there is a problem here for which there is no easy solution. It is the historian's job to understand and interpret the past, and this is most difficult if basic moral values are in conflict. Perhaps the best advice is this: Be aware of the dilemma, so that in your own studies and research you can act out of conscious choice rather than ignorance.

Context and Success in Business

We have been considering the importance of context in historical inquiry. It should be clear that the principles we have outlined are not important only for the "ivory tower" world of the university classroom. Contextual awareness is equally vital in a wide variety of professional activities. Journalists who ignore the lessons of context do so at their own risk. It is difficult to report and assess the significance of world events if those events are studied independently of cultural and historical context. Likewise government officials would be well advised to consider the "big picture" whenever considering specific policies and proposals. Doctors know it is not enough merely to ask their patients for a list of their symptoms. It is often vital to know as much as possible about the totality (i.e., context) of a person's life in order to prescribe the best treatment.

Finally, a failure to appreciate the importance of context can cost money, as numerous corporations have discovered. Businesses have made embarrassing and costly errors simply because they were unaware of critical cultural differences in foreign markets. Gary Stoller wrote recently in *USA Today*: "Every day deals are jeopardized or lost when foreign associates are offended by Americans unaware of other countries' customs, culture or manners . . . ." For instance:

1. In many cultures the left hand is deemed unclean and should not be used, especially for eating. In India a left-handed American cut a ribbon at a bank opening with his left hand. The left hand is considered "inauspicious" in India, and the ribbon-cutting had to be repeated with the right hand.

2. In Egypt crossing ones legs when sitting is an insult and the thumbs up sign is an obscene gesture. In Greece hailing a cab with your palm faced outward is considered offensive.

(continued)

---

[12] John Higham, *Writing American History* (Bloomington: Indiana University Press, 1970), 150–56.

And, advertising and marketing gaffs are legion:

3. One firm tried advertising refrigerators in the Islamic Middle East by using pictures of the refrigerator full of appetizing food, including a very prominent ham. Muslims do not eat pork.

4. Advertising disasters have also resulted from ignorance of the significance of certain colors in various countries. In Japan white is the color of death. In Africa green is the color of disease.

As the above examples testify, it is not only the historian who has to cultivate some of the key attributes of historical mindedness. Abandon the concept of context only at your own peril.

(Items 1 and 2 are taken from Gary Stoller, "Doing Business Abroad? Simple Faux Pas Can Sink You," *USA Today*, Aug. 24, 2007, B 1–2; items 3 and 4 from "Business Blunders: Some Funny, but, All Costly," *St Louis Post-Dispatch*, November 13, 1980.)

EXERCISES

SET A *Exercise 1 — Cromwell in Ireland*

The following excerpts are intended to help you appreciate the importance of trying to understand past events within the proper historical context. The passages (drawn from secondary sources) are all concerned with a notorious episode in the life of Oliver Cromwell (1599–1658), the English revolutionary leader who led the anti-royalist Parliamentary forces during the English Civil War (1642–49). By 1649 Parliament had won the civil war, had executed the king, Charles I, and Cromwell had become the effective ruler of England. In the same year Cromwell led an army to Ireland to snuff out an anti-English rebellion that had been raging since 1641. It is Cromwell's behavior in Ireland that is the primary concern of the passages that follow. When in Ireland, Cromwell's soldiers massacred the inhabitants of two towns, Wexford and Drogheda.

Keep in mind that in the 1640s the great upheaval in Western Christianity, the Protestant Reformation, was not that far in the past, and violent hatred between Catholics and Protestants continued to fuel many international disputes. England, of course, was a Protestant country at this time, but Ireland remained steadfastly Catholic. To complicate matters, the Protestants in Britain were split between the state-sanctioned Anglican Church and the Puritans who wanted even more radical religious reforms. The one thing both Protestant groups could agree on was their distrust of and distaste for the rebellious Catholics in Ireland.

The following passages attempt to examine the event by putting it in a broader historical context. The aim is not to justify a military atrocity, but to help you *understand* the event in all its dimensions. After reading the initial passage, read the subsequent passages carefully in order to ascertain what *new pieces of information* each presents. Note how a wider appreciation of the situation in 1649, the mind-set of Cromwell, the worldview of the seventeenth century, and the relevant historical background all help us to understand better the complex dynamics of a seemingly straightforward occurrence. Then answer the questions that follow.

The Event:

Cromwell stayed in Ireland for a little over nine months—from August 1649 to May 1650. His siege of Drogheda lasted ten days (September 2–11), and its successful conclusion was followed by four days of general massacre directed by Cromwell himself, during which period some four thousand people were murdered. When, on October 1, Wexford too was stormed, the same vengeance was exacted, and two thousand people more—men, women, and children, priests, nuns, and laymen—were put to death. . . . Having given this grim warning, Cromwell refrained from further atrocities in Ireland. . . . Nevertheless, on account of Drogheda and Wexford, Cromwell left behind him in Ireland a name for cruelty such as the passage of three hundred years has scarcely erased from memory.

Supplementary Information:

A. What then is the explanation of Cromwell's cruel and compulsive behavior in Ireland? From childhood he had been raised in an atmosphere of paranoiac hatred for Catholicism. When he was only six, a group of desperate English Catholics had tried to blow kings, Lords, and Commons sky-high; after the Gunpowder Plot of 1605, a fear and loathing of Catholicism that was to last for many years swept England and formed the background of Cromwell's childhood education. . . . Finally, in Cromwell's adult years came the reports of the unspeakable atrocities committed by Irish Catholics in 1641—reports that, as we have seen, were grossly overstated but that seemed to establish irrefutably the unchanging nature of the evil that was Catholicism.

B. The rules of war of the time, with regard to sieges, were clear. If a commander refused to accede to a summons to surrender, and the town was subsequently won by storm, then he put at risk the lives not only of all his men, but of all those who could be held to be combatants. The significant moment was when the walls were breached by the opposing side: thereafter quarter [i.e., mercy] could not be demanded. . . . Nor was the civilian population of the town necessarily protected from the rash consequences of the commander's refusal to surrender. . . . Grotius in *De Jure Belli ac Pacis*, a work first printed in 1625, that attempted to prescribe some limits to the vengefulness of war as a result of the appalling slaughters of the Thirty Years' War [1618–48], still postulated that it was lawful to kill prisoners of war, and furthermore, that "the slaughter of women and children is allowed to have impunity, as comprehended in the right of war and 137th Psalm."

C. Cromwell's Irish policy was not personal but national. When he crossed to Ireland in 1649 the Irish revolt against English rule . . . had dragged on for eight years. So long as it continued, Ireland offered a backdoor to foreign intervention against the regicide republic [Cromwell's Parliamentary party had beheaded King Charles I in January 1649], now isolated in monarchical Europe. . . . The government of the English republic decided that Ireland must be subdued quickly. Hence the massacres of Drogheda and Wexford, for which Cromwell is remembered in Ireland to this day.

D. In England [Cromwell] was prepared in fact to tolerate Catholics as well as Episcopalians [Protestants to be sure, but not "progressive" enough for Cromwell and his Puritan allies]: Roman Catholic historians agree that their coreligionists were better off during the Protectorate [the period of Cromwell's rule] than they had ever been under James or Charles I. But in Ireland it was different. . . . Again we must refer, by way of explanation though not justification, to the political associations of Irish Catholicism. . . . It was a political religion in a sense in which Catholicism in England had ceased to be political.

E. It is necessary to set this story in perspective because it has so often been used to picture Cromwell as a monster of cruelty, differing from other generals and statesmen in English history, and secondly because it is frequently assigned as a main reason for the poisoning of Anglo-Irish relations in modern times. In fact, Cromwell's Irish policy—wrongheaded as it may have been—was identical with that of Queen Elizabeth I, King James I, Strafford, and Pym. All of them sponsored the colonization of Ireland by Protestant settlers. To the Puritans [the more radical English Protestants] Ireland was a nearer alternative to Massachusetts or Virginia and the natives as capable of absorption or extrusion as the Indians.

Sources
"The Event" and passage A. Giovanni Costigan, *A History of Modern Ireland* (New York: Pegasus, 1970), 76–77, 79.
B. Antonia Fraser, *Cromwell* (New York: Knopf, 1973), 335–36.
C. Christopher Hill, "Political Animal," *New York Review of Books*, June 9, 1977, 40.
D. Christopher Hill, *God's Englishman* (New York: Harper & Row, 1972), 121–22.
E. Maurice Ashley, *The Greatness of Oliver Cromwell* (New York: Collier Books, 1966), 233–34.

Questions

1. For each passage (A through E) note the specific *additional* pieces of information that enable you to put the massacres of Wexford and Drogheda into a broader historical context:

Passage A: _____

Passage B: _____

Passage C: _____

Passage D: _____

Passage E: _____

2. The quoted passages help put Cromwell's expedition into historical perspective by supplying: (1) information on Cromwell the individual (personal values and beliefs); (2) commentary on the *immediate* political situation (i.e., 1649); (3) insights into the broad cultural, religious, and moral values of seventeenth-century society (the

"worldview"); and (4) relevant historical background information (developments in England and Ireland *before* 1649) that had an impact on events.

Indicate by letter (A–E) the specific passage or passages above that contain important information related to each of the general categories just listed. Multiple answers are possible, and you may use each letter more than once.

a. Cromwell the individual: _____

b. *Immediate* political situation (ca. 1649): _____

c. Societal values/worldview: _____

d. Historical background (*pre*-1649 in England): _____

Discussion Topics:

1. Generally, the quoted passages allow you to make a more balanced appraisal of Cromwell's Irish campaign because they suggest what a modern-day court of law would call "mitigating circumstances." The purpose is not to condemn or exonerate Cromwell's behavior, but to allow you to view Cromwell's actions as his fellow countrymen in the seventeenth century might have viewed them. In what ways do you think the seventeenth-century assessment would differ from a twenty-first-century judgment? Why?

2. Which passage or passages added most to your understanding of the events in question? Which added least to your understanding? Why?

SET A   *Exercise 2 — Writing History*

Assume you are writing a paper that attempts to explain why Cromwell and his troops acted as they did in Ireland. The most important part of that paper will be the introduction. Read Writing Capsule 4 (below) and, using the passages above (including our brief description of the event) as your source materials, write a brief *introductory* paragraph to such a paper. In your introduction do two things: (1) provide the background information that you see as essential for a clear understanding of the events in question; and, (2) clearly state your major point, or thesis, indicating important supporting points. For instance, if your thesis is "Three factors in particular influenced Cromwell's actions in Ireland," be sure to list briefly what those factors were. It will be instructive to compare your paragraph with those of your colleagues in class.

WRITING CAPSULE 4

Essays: The Introduction

Just as a paragraph requires a clear and informative topic sentence, a history essay or paper needs a good introduction. The introduction, usually a paragraph or two, provides a gradual lead-in to the paper itself. And, make no mistake, writing a good introduction is not easy. You have to condense complex ideas and information into a few clear summary sentences. On one hand, a good introduction indicates the problem your paper is addressing, and the historical context of the events you are exploring. You cannot assume your reader is familiar with the period or event you are writing about so you must, briefly, summarize the necessary information.

In the introduction you should also unequivocally *state a thesis,* that is, the conclusion(s) you intend to support in the body of your paper. Your thesis, the basic interpretive generalization you intend to prove, is the cornerstone of any effective history paper, so you have to make sure it is clearly expressed.

Often a thesis is so broad that it needs a bit of elaboration before you proceed any further. If you claim, for example, that "Elvis Presley had a profound and lasting impact on American popular culture," you should summarize briefly the major reasons you think this is so. Later in the paper you will have to support these points with evidence; in the introduction it is sufficient to identify your points for the reader.

(For more on introductions see Chapter 12, Writing the History Paper, page 205.)

SET B   *Exercise 1 — Appeasement, 1933–38*

Few diplomatic policies have been as universally condemned as that called "appeasement" in the 1930s. So dramatic was the failure of appeasement that the policy became, in the words of one historian, "the most influential negative lesson for a whole generation of Western leaders" who came afterwards.

Appeasement refers to the attempts of the British and French, especially the British, to dampen the aggressive ambitions of Adolf Hitler's Nazi regime in Germany in the 1930s. Britain and France had been allies against Germany in World War I (1914–18) and, in the Treaty of Versailles, imposed upon the defeated Germans a set of military, economic, and territorial restrictions and penalties. The victors wanted to make sure that the Germans would not be able to seek revenge in the future. Adolf Hitler (1889–1945) became Chancellor of Germany in 1933 and immediately sought to overthrow the restrictions of the Versailles Treaty. He embarked on a campaign of rearmament and territorial expansion, which, within a short time, made Germany the most powerful country in Europe. Eventually Hitler's aggressive actions (the remilitarization of the German Rhineland in violation of the Treaty of Versailles, the annexation of Austria, the dismemberment and ultimate invasion of Czechoslovakia, and, finally, the invasion of Poland) led to the outbreak of World War II (1939–45).

From 1933 until 1938, the British argued that the best way to avoid war with a rearmed and aggressive Germany was to satisfy Hitler's territorial demands and ignore his violations of the Versailles Treaty. This was appeasement. The primary British proponent of appeasement was Neville Chamberlain, Prime Minister from 1937 to 1940. Chamberlain was the prime mover behind the September 1938 Munich Conference, which allowed Hitler to annex parts of Czechoslovakia without opposition. Munich was the most extreme example of the British determination to appease Hitler; it was dubbed by one critic as "one of the most disastrous episodes" in British history. Most historians have echoed that sentiment. For, rather than ensuring peace, appeasement led to war. J. W. Wheeler-Bennett writes: "It is a tragic irony of history that this very will for peace was among the most important contributory factors to the Second World War, for it is clear that early and bloodless victories convinced Hitler that Britain and France would never oppose him by force. . . ."[13]

All of this is very obvious to us now. Appeasement was a failure and the appeasers were shortsighted and naive. "The total upshot of their efforts," said one contemporary, "was to aid Nazi Germany to achieve a position of brutal ascendancy, a threat to everybody else's security or even existence, which only a war could end."[14] But are shortsightedness and naiveté enough of an explanation? No. Here, as elsewhere, the broader context is critical for an understanding of the attitudes and policies of the appeasers. The passages below (drawn from secondary sources) should help you understand the total environment in which the appeasers worked. Read each one carefully, and, in the spaces provided at the end of the exercise, note the *new pieces of information* each passage provides to help you understand why British policy makers and the British public were so committed to appeasement.[15]

Supplementary Information:

A. Appeasement rested on a number of assumptions. Perhaps its basic foundation was the conviction among the survivors of the First World War [1914–18] that Europe could not survive another such bloodletting. Every French town had its *monument aux morts* [war memorial] with its long list of the dead; no British village was without its war memorial. Even tiny villages displayed prodigious lists of casualties. Mutilated war veterans were conspicuous reminders, as was the arrival of the "hollow years" in the 1930s. Added to this were science fiction conceptions of the next war, with its aerial bombardments and poison gas. Millions of deaths were predicted. . . .

B. In the end, Chamberlain's critics were proven to be right, and the appeasement policy helped to bring on the war that the prime minister was seeking to avoid. This was not, however, due solely to his gullibility. Hitler's gifts of persuasion were con-

---

[13] J. W. Wheeler-Bennett, *Munich: A Prologue to Tragedy* (New York: Viking Press, 1965), 6.

[14] A. L. Rowse, *Appeasement* (New York: W. W. Norton, 1963), 118.

[15] Appeasement in general, and the Munich agreement in particular, would haunt and influence western diplomacy for decades after World War II. If ever there seemed to be a "lesson of history" that we should continue to heed, this seemed to be it. Surprisingly the Munich analogy continues to exert it influence well into the twenty-first century. In the summer of 2008 a military conflict broke out between Russia and neighboring Georgia, a state that had broken away from the collapsing Soviet Union in the 1990s. During the conflict the president of Georgia again raised the specter of Munich by comparing Georgia to Czechoslovakia in 1938. A *New York Times* writer covering the conflict wrote: "During a 10-day visit to Georgia in June, I heard the 1938 analogy again and again. . . ." (James Traub, "Taunting the Bear," *The New York Times*, August 10, 2008, "Week in Review"): 1.

siderable, and Chamberlain was not the only European statesman who was deluded by his ability to mask his true intentions until he felt strong enough to be able to disregard potential opposition.

C. One moral argument told strongly in Germany's favour: the argument which had been pressed, particularly by the Left, ever since the end of the first World War. The Treaty of Versailles had been presented as unjust, punitive and unworkable. Germany was entitled to equality in armaments and everything else. The Germans of Austria, Czechoslovakia, and Poland were entitled, like other nationalities, to self-determination, even if this meant an increase in German power. More broadly, Germany was entitled to a place in Europe and in the world commensurate with her greatness in population, economic resources, and civilisation.

D. The pressing economic problems created by the Great Depression also distracted the British and French. . . . The governments of both countries were reluctant to embark on rearmament programs that would be enormously expensive and would place a tremendous strain on the financial stability of their governments. Britain was especially sensitive to the wishes of the self-governing dominions [e.g. Canada, Australia, etc.], which also suffered from depression and wanted desperately to avoid war.

E. Since the inauguration of the League of Nations in 1920 Britain had taken very seriously the obligations incurred under the Covenant [of the League], more particularly those involving the reduction of armaments, and this tendency had been further encouraged with the increase of economic burdens. In an honest but fatal endeavour to achieve universal disarmament, successive Governments had reduced the armaments of Britain to a point at which many believed them to be no longer compatible with the demands of national defence, in the vain hope that others would be moved to emulate such an example of unilateral rectitude. . . . At this moment it was believed by all parties that the risk of financial disaster was far greater than the menace from any rival power.

F. The effects on foreign policy of the state of British armaments and strategic thinking were far-reaching. The fundamental problem was the disparity between Britain's commitments and her resources. The commitments were almost literally world-wide. The British Empire was at its greatest extent. The Dominions, though asserting their independence of the mother country, still relied on her for protection. . . . In 1937 the Chiefs of Staff produced a gloomy review of Britain's enemies: Japan in the Pacific, Italy in the Mediterranean, and Germany in western Europe. Their conclusion was that until rearmament was further advanced, it should be the first task of foreign policy to diminish the number of Britain's enemies. The policy of 'appeasement' should never be appraised without recalling this sternly realistic recommendation.

G. Originally "appeasement" did not mean surrendering to a bully's demands nor did it mean that nations must surrender their vital national interests in order to avoid war. Instead "appeasement" meant a reduction of international tensions between states through the removal of the causes of friction. It also meant concessions to disgruntled nations in the hope that the concessions would alleviate their grievances and lessen their tendency to take aggressive action. It was hoped that after the aggrieved nations had been pacified through appeasement, an era of confidence, peace, and prosperity would emerge.

H. In one sense it [appeasement] was Chamberlain's own policy, and a very personal one: but it rested on illusions which were very widely shared. Chamberlain's hatred of war was passionate, his fear of its consequences shrewd. He believed . . . that much could be accomplished by personal diplomacy in conference; that there "must be something in common" between different peoples since "we are all members of the human race;" that there was a human side to the dictators, which could be appealed to, especially in tête-à-tête [face-to-face] discussions.

Sources
    A. Robert O. Paxton, *Europe in the 20th Century*, 2nd ed. (San Diego: Harcourt, Brace Jovanovich, 1985), 428.
    B. Gordon A. Craig and Alexander L. George, *Force and Statecraft*, 3rd ed. (New York: Oxford University Press, 1995), 82.
    C. A. J. P. Taylor, *English History, 1914–1945* (Oxford: Clarendon Press, 1965), 417.
    D. Michael J. Lyons, *World War II: A Short History*, 4th ed. (Upper Saddle River, NJ: Pearson Prentice Hall, 2004), 53–54.
    E. J. W. Wheeler-Bennett, *Munich: A Prologue to Tragedy* (New York: Viking Press, 1965), 230–31.
    F. P. M. H. Bell, *The Origins of the Second World War in Europe*, 2nd ed. (London: Longman, 1997), 199–200.
    G. Keith Eubank, *The Origins of World War II*, 2nd ed. (Wheeling IL.: Harlan Davidson, Inc., 1990), 69.
    H. C. L. Mowat, *Britain Between the Wars* (London, Methuen, 1968), 590–91.

Questions

1. For each passage (A through H) note the specific *additional* pieces of information that enable you to put the British appeasement policy into a broader historical context.

Passage A: _____

Passage B:_____

Passage C:_____

Passage D: _____

Passage E: _____

Passage F: _____

Passage G: _____

Passage H: _____

2. The quoted passages help put the British appeasement policy into historical perspective by supplying: (1) information on the role played by specific individuals; (2) commentary on *immediate* political and economic realities (i.e., during the 1930s); (3) insights into the influence of Britain's *long-term* historical experiences; and (4) information about how contemporary Britons perceived reality and interpreted their world. Indicate by letter (A–H) the specific passage or passages that contain important information related to each of the general categories just listed. Multiple answers are possible, and you may use each letter more than once.

a. Specific individuals: _____

b. *Immediate* political/economic situation: _____

c. Britain's *long-term* historical experiences: _____

d. Perceptions of reality: _____

Discussion Topics:

1. Which passage or passages added *most* to your understanding of the 1930s appeasement policy? Why?

2. Which passage or passages added *least* to your understanding of appeasement? Why?

SET B *Exercise 2 — Writing History*

Assume that you are writing a paper that attempts to explain why British policymakers pursued the appeasement policy in the 1930s. The most important part of that paper will be the introduction. Read Writing Capsule 4 (on page 69), then, using the passages above as your source materials, write a brief *introductory* paragraph to such a paper. In your introduction do two things: (1) Provide the background information you consider essential for a clear understanding of the events in question; and, (2) clearly state your thesis, indicating important supporting points. For instance, if your thesis is "A number of factors help us understand the passion with which the British government pursued the appeasement policy," be sure to list briefly those factors. It will be instructive to compare your paragraph with those of your colleagues in class.

PART II: CONFRONTING THE HISTORICAL ACCOUNT

CHAPTER 6 LIBRARIES: REAL AND VIRTUAL

"Knowledge is of two kinds. We know a subject ourselves, or we know where we can find information upon it."

—Dr. Samuel Johnson (1709–1784)

"My library was dukedom large enough."

—William Shakespeare
(Prospero in The Tempest*)*

"What . . . will become of research libraries in the face of technological marvels such as Google?"

—Robert Darnton[1]

Revolutions change the course of history, and revolutionary leaders have long fascinated historians. Charismatic figures make good copy, whether they are popular orators (Sam Adams, Georges Jacques Danton, Rosa Luxemburg), politicians (George Washington, Nelson Mandela), conspirators (Maximillian Robespierre, V. I. Lenin), strategists and military leaders (Oliver Cromwell, Mao Zedong), or populist heroes (François Toussaint L'Ouverture, Che Guevara). Yet one of the most influential revolutionaries of the last two centuries was not a man of action. He defended no barricades, led no troops, and never held political office. He "totally lacked," in the words of one of his biographers, "the qualities of a great popular leader or agitator." Instead he was something of a bookworm, a man of ideas who spent "the greater part of his working life . . . in comparative obscurity in London, at his writing-table and in the reading-room" of Britain's national library.[2] His name was Karl Marx.

Libraries don't seem to us the sort of places where world-shaking events take place, but to the extent that ideas move individuals to act, we have to give libraries their due as among the most important institutions in a civilized society. Certainly Karl Marx (1818–83) proves the point. Marx was a journalist and political organizer whose radical activities and revolutionary writings (e.g., *The Communist Manifesto*) prompted his expulsion from Germany and then France in 1849. He spent the rest of his life in London, where he spent countless hours reading in the British Museum and writing many of the articles and books (e.g., *Das Kapital*) that became the founding texts of the international socialist and communist movements.

As an individual Marx was unkempt, irascible, and remote. A Prussian government spy wrote that Marx led a gypsy existence. "Washing, grooming and changing his

---

[1] Robert Darnton, "The Library in the New Age," *The New York Review of Books,* June 12, 2008, 72.
[2] Isaiah Berlin, *Karl Marx: His Life and Environment* (New York: Oxford University Press, 1963), 1.

linen are things he does rarely, and he is often drunk." But, though his work habits were irregular, he often worked day and night with tireless endurance.[3] The result was an immense body of work that was destined to change the world. His ideas were revolutionary in two senses: they inspired radical and revolutionary political movements in every corner of the globe, and they had a lasting impact on the way philosophy, economics, the social sciences, and history have been studied and understood ever since. (For more on Marx's vast influence see Chapter 13.) In the words of Sir Isaiah Berlin, "No thinker in the nineteenth century has had so direct, deliberate and powerful an influence upon mankind as Karl Marx."[4] Perhaps it's true that there is no weapon more powerful than a library card.

Karl Marx, 1818–1883.

It is certainly true that if Karl Marx were doing his research today, he would probably be doing it at home on a laptop computer, for the array of information accessible from a computer connected to the Internet is simply staggering. Still, it would be a mistake to think that libraries have become irrelevant. More than a hundred years after Marx's death, the library is still the most important educational resource on a college campus. Not only does the library house the books, journals, documents, films, videos, and sound recordings that serve as the lifeblood of learning, it can also provide access to a vast array of important electronic databases. Finally, don't overlook the library as a pleasant (and increasingly colorful) place to browse, study, think, and even socialize.

The only way to learn how to use a library properly is to use one. This is true even for seasoned scholars who may be quite ignorant of the sections of libraries (or library services) they rarely use. Jaroslav Pelikan, an eminent historian of Christian doctrine, once dumbfounded a Yale University library employee by asking where the periodicals room was. Pelikan explained that he knew where the rare books were, but since he never used recent magazines in his research, he had no idea where to find the periodicals room. Like Pelikan, you will learn how to locate library resources and use library services as the need arises. Be assured, mastering the skills of accessing library resources will be well worth your time in the long run. The faster you are able to collect your sources, the less time any research project will take.

First, play the role of a tourist in your own library. Ask for any available informational guides or pamphlets; then wander around and note especially the location of the main circulation desk, the reference area (printed encyclopedias, indexes,

---

[3] David McLellan, *Karl Marx: His Life and Thought* (New York: Harper Colophon, 1973), 280.
[4] Berlin, *Karl Marx*, 1.

dictionaries, map atlases, etc.), the reserve area, and the computer terminals where you can access the library catalog. Then, and this is very important, check out the myriad services and resources available on your library's Website.

The Classification System

Generally, print materials in college and university libraries will be shelved according to the Library of Congress classification system. Introduced around the turn of the twentieth century by the Library of Congress in Washington, D.C., this system uses twenty-one letters of the alphabet to designate general categories:

A.	General works	M.	Music
B.	Philosophy/Religion	N.	Fine Arts
C.	Auxiliary Sciences of History	P.	Language and Literature
D.	**UNIVERSAL HISTORY**	Q.	Science
E–F.	**AMERICAN HISTORY**	R.	Medicine
G.	Geography/Anthropology	S.	Agriculture
H.	Social Sciences	T.	Technology
J.	Political Science	U.	Military Science
K.	Law	V.	Naval Science
L.	Education	Z.	Bibliography/ Library Science

Subcategories are created by adding a second letter to the general designation. For instance:

D   History (general),
DA   Great Britain,
DB   Austria, Liechtenstein, Hungary, Czechoslovakia,
DC   France
Etc.

You don't have to memorize the entire system, but it is a good idea to know the designation(s) for your own field of study. Also, history students will often find a lot of useful material in sections other than "history." For instance, categories U and V (Military Science and Naval Science) will be indispensable for a project in military history or the history of warfare.

Initiating the Search[5]

Understanding your library's classification system will help you locate the relevant book collections, but to find specific works on specific topics you will have to turn to the catalog—the most important research tool in the library. For generations libraries

---

[5] Entire books are devoted to the techniques of finding sources for historical research. In this chapter we can only skim the surface of the subject. For more information consider Anthony Brundage, *Going to the Sources: A Guide to Historical Research and Writing,* 4th ed. (Wheeling, IL.: Harlan Davidson, Inc., 2008), or Jenny L. Presnell, *The Information-Literate Historian: A Guide to Research for History Students* (New York: Oxford University Press, 2007).

used card catalogs, but electronic catalogs have made the traditional card catalog obsolete. The catalog, which you can usually access from your home computer, will list all the materials held by your library.[6] With a computerized catalog you simply type an author's name, a title, a subject, or a key word, and the computer will show what is in the collection. When you see a promising title, a simple command will display an array of information on that source: the classification number, whether it is in the reference or general collection, the number of pages, whether it is illustrated, the date of publication, and, of great significance, *related subject areas.* You might also find out if it is already checked out or on order.

Looking up a specific title or the works of a given author is relatively easy, but finding *all* of the relevant books on a given subject or topic is not as simple. The electronic catalogs allow you to enter key words based on your subject, and you can combine key words in order to narrow the limits of your search. For instance, if you type in the word "war" you will get far more "hits" or matches than if you type in "Civil War." Using "United States Civil War" as the entry will narrow the list still further. To find primary sources look for qualifying words and phrases—e.g., "diaries," "sources," "early works to 1800," "correspondence," "personal narratives," and the like.

As convenient as all of this is, it can lead to overconfidence. If you have struck gold with a well-chosen subject or keyword entry, don't assume your search is complete. Try to think of additional subject headings that might yield results. To continue with our example of the U.S. Civil War, when we typed in the name "Abraham Lincoln," dozens more entries appeared, many of which were not included in the Civil War lists. Finally, it is very important to find out the official subject headings used by the Library of Congress. Whenever you access the listing of a book on your subject, look at the line that reads "**LC Subject**"—i.e., Library of Congress Subject. For instance, we found a listing in our library's catalog for a specialized study of the Battle of Gettysburg by historian Margaret Creighton: *The Colors of Courage: Gettysburg's Forgotten History: Immigrants, Women and African Americans in the Civil War's Defining Battle* (Basic Books: 2005). On the screen were listed a number of related Library of Congress subject headings. Under the LC subject *"United States—History—Civil War, 1861–1865* were three subheadings—*"Participation—Immigrant," "Women,"* and *"African Americans."* Additional LC subjects were *"Gettysburg, Battle of," "Immigrants—Pennsylvania—Gettysburg—History"* and similar listings for women and African Americans. By clicking on any of those headings more possibilities would be unearthed. In some cases you might discover books that are available electronically (i.e. "e-books") that you can read directly off the computer screen.

---

[6] Many libraries have cooperative sharing agreements with other libraries, so after you have searched for materials in your own library, you can broaden the search to include the network of cooperating institutions.

Author	Creighton, Margaret S., 1949-
Title	**The colors of courage : Gettysburg's forgotten history : immigrants, women, and African Americans in the Civil War's defining battle / Margaret S. Creighton.**
Published	New York : Basic Books, c2005.
Edition	1st ed.

Link to web version		
Table of contents		
LOCATION	**CALL NO**	**STATUS**
Webster Books 3rd Floor	E475.53 .C89 2005	AVAILABLE

Description	xxvii, 321 p. : ill., maps ; 25 cm.
Bibliog.	Includes bibliographical references (p. 237-308) and index.
Contents	The Gettysburg campaign, 1863 (chronology) -- Prologue : the lay of the land -- An afternoon in the badlands -- The season of disbelief -- Desolation's edge -- Flying thick like blackbirds -- Bold acts -- The wide eye of the storm -- The aftermath -- The seesaw of honor, or, How the pigpen was mightier than the sword -- Women and remembrance -- Making a living on hallowed land.
LC Subject	Gettysburg, Battle of, Gettysburg, Pa., 1863.
	Immigrants -- Pennsylvania -- Gettysburg -- History -- 19th century.
	Women, White -- Pennsylvania -- Gettysburg -- History -- 19th century.
	African Americans -- Pennsylvania -- Gettysburg -- History -- 19th century.
	United States -- History -- Civil War, 1861-1865 -- Participation, Immigrant.
	United States -- History -- Civil War, 1861-1865 -- Women.
	United States -- History -- Civil War, 1861-1865 -- African Americans.

This is an electronic catalog listing for Margaret Creighton's *The Colors of Courage*. Note the variety of Library of Congress (LC) subject headings that you can use to seek out additional source listings.

Reference Works: Print and Electronic

The catalog is only the first step in your search for information. Next you should try to find journal and other periodical articles on your subject,[7] and perhaps relevant books not currently in your library's collection. To do this you have to consult various indexes and bibliographies (i.e., lists of books and articles on a particular subject) found in your library's reference section. These indexes, bibliographies, and abstracts *do not* contain the actual historical information you are seeking (with the exception noted below); they are intended to help you find the books and articles that *do* contain the information you seek.

Many of the most useful resources are now available electronically, often through subscription databases provided by your library. You can tap into a number of these databases (see the list of resources on pages 85–87) by performing the same subject and keyword searches discussed earlier. In this way you will not only be able to find new materials in your own library, but also important books and articles that your library does not have. Of course, you may wish to order some of these materials through interlibrary loan, but increasingly you can download the full text of articles

---

[7] The word "periodicals" refers to a wide range of publications: scholarly journals, popular magazines, and newspapers. Newspapers are often published daily, and magazines monthly or weekly. Both are usually aimed at a broad popular audience. Journals are published less frequently and are written for scholars and specialists. Journal articles usually have source references and bibliographies of the sources used by the author. It is in such articles that you can find the most up-to-date research on your topic.

and books on your computer. A good general database offered by many libraries for history and humanities students is *Academic Search Premier* (Ebscohost).

As convenient as it is to use the electronic databases, a few words of warning are in order. Often the electronic databases don't go back further than the mid-twentieth century (e.g., the 1960s or 1970s), so you will miss important articles that were published earlier. In such cases you will still have to use the relevant print versions of the indexes and locate the print versions of the articles. One excellent database that *does* cover the entire run of the major English-language journals and allows full-text retrieval is *JSTOR*. What will be missing on *JSTOR* are the most recent issues of a given journal. Also, we need to mention that indexes of abstracts, like *Historical Abstracts* (covering world and European history from the Renaissance to the present) and *America: History and Life* (covering American history), do not always offer full-text retrieval. They do, however, provide brief summaries of the contents of the articles they index.[8]

You can narrow or broaden a keyword search by using "and" or "or" between search terms—e.g., "women or girls" to find a broad selection of titles on women's history, or "women and France" to narrow the search to materials on French history. You can also broaden your search by using a "wild card"—usually an asterisk (*) or exclamation point (!)—attached to the root of a key word. For instance, a search for "Scot*" would bring up materials on Scotland, Scots, Scottish but also, perhaps, articles on the "Scottsboro" trial in the United States, which would not be especially helpful if you were researching a topic in Scottish history. There is usually a simple command allowing you to eliminate the "Scottsboro" alternative, or "Scotch" whiskey, for that matter. Check the "Help" section of the database for specifics. Finally, some databases allow you to limit your search by historical time period.

This chapter ends with a list of indexes, bibliographies, and abstracts useful to the history student. Meriting special mention here are *Historical Abstracts* and *America: History and Life,* noted above. Also valuable are the *Readers' Guide to Periodical Literature* (to find article titles in popular magazines like *Time* or *Newsweek*) and the publication known variously as the *International Index* (to 1965), the *Social Sciences and Humanities Index* (to 1974), and now, separately, the *Social Sciences Index* and the *Humanities Index* (for articles that appear in the scholarly journals). A brief look at the key in the front of these volumes will help you understand the sometimes-confusing abbreviations they use to save space. These indexes are available electronically, but not every library will subscribe to the electronic back editions. The printed volumes will still be of use if electronic versions are not available.

In addition to these guides to books and articles, the reference section also has countless volumes that contain a wealth of actual historical information. Included in this group are historical dictionaries, encyclopedias, biographical dictionaries, atlases, collections of photographs, and statistical compilations. Somewhere in your reference collection there is a book that has the answer to just about any informational question you might have. Many of these are now available electronically, although you will be impoverishing your search if you rely only on electronic reference materials. The "old fashioned" book is still one of the most valuable resources for the novice researcher.

---

[8] For a more complete discussion see Brundage, *Sources,* 45–50.

> ## Tips for Searching Electronic Catalogs and Databases
>
> 1. Think of similar words and concepts for keyword searches to see which ones provide the most relevant source lists.
> 2. Pair terms using "and" or "or" to narrow or broaden the search.
> 3. Truncate key words with an asterisk (*) to broaden the number of results.
> 4. Limit the search by historical time period where possible—i.e. 1940s, 1880s, etc.
> 5. If you discover too many sources, narrow the search; if too few, expand it. You should try for perhaps thirty to forty *good* prospects.

Finally, and perhaps most important, when you are doing library research your best friends could be the reference librarians. They are not there to do your research for you, but their advice can be invaluable. If you need help, just ask for it.

Surfing Cyberspace: The Internet and the World Wide Web

As everyone knows, the last few decades have ushered in a revolution in information technology. The Internet made its first tentative appearance in the early 1970s, the Web (World Wide Web) dates from the 1980s, and the search engines that allow us to search through millions of Web sites (e.g., Yahoo and Google) date from the 1990s. So pervasive has the Internet become that most students begin their research projects by "Googling" their subject on their computer. The Internet presents history students with a world of research opportunities never before available. Original documents, scholarly articles, magazine and newspaper archives, images, and, increasingly, entire books are available in digital formats. But because there is so much material out there, the Internet is a mixed blessing for history students: the problem is not having too few resources on a given subject but too many. Further, since anyone with a computer can publish on the Internet, it is often difficult to evaluate the reliability of the information that you find. For instance, whereas the electronic databases discussed above (*JSTOR, Historical Abstracts,* etc.) provide materials reviewed and written by bonafide scholars, the Web contains everything from academically sound pearls of wisdom to absolute nonsense written by amateurs and members of the lunatic fringe. As a result, doing historical research on the Internet is often more difficult than doing it the old-fashioned way.

It is not our intention to write an in-depth primer on Internet use. There are plenty of them out there, and they often run to hundreds of pages.[9] In addition, the world of cyberspace changes so rapidly that anything written today may well be outdated tomorrow. Nonetheless, a few introductory points might be helpful. For our purposes, it is sufficient to note that students can access thousands of Web sites by

---

[9] For a brief, but comprehensive, overview see Andrew McMichael, *History on the Web: Using and Evaluating the Internet* (Wheeling, IL.: Harlan Davidson, Inc., 2005).

using search engines such as Google. The trick is to come up with a useable, *relevant* list of "hits."—i.e. Web addresses or URLs (Universal Resource Locators) with some mention of your subject. Too often a general keyword search will bring up thousands of possibilities, when what you need are thirty to forty good sources. To narrow your options it is often helpful to use plus (+) or minus (-) signs to force the search engine to include or exclude certain terms. For instance, searching for *Witchcraft* –(minus) *Salem* will eliminate all the sites that focus primarily on the Salem witch trials, clearing the way for a study of the European witch craze. Conversely, entering *Witch Trials* + (plus) *Salem* will provide the most relevant list for a research project on the Salem Trials of 1692. It might also be a good idea to explore the advanced search options in the search engine you are using.

Choosing the Best Sources

Once you have generated a list of relevant materials on your subject, you might ask yourself, "How do I select a usable and representative sample of sources from the vast mountain of information available?" Remember, if you have been conscientious in your search, you will have much more information than you need, and it will be necessary to choose the most appropriate materials. There are no hard and fast rules for doing so, but the following tips might prove helpful.

1. Don't let the perfect be the enemy of the good. It is better to have enough sources and get your assignment in on time than to try to read all the sources and never begin writing.

2. Making the proper selection usually requires a good deal of preliminary research and reading. You have to get to know a topic before you can discern the books and articles historians judge to be the most important.

3. In selecting books and articles (remembering there are exceptions to all that follows), choose the most up-to-date research over outdated works and choose works with substantive source references and bibliographies. Also, check book reviews to identify the most respected works in the field.

4. You must take special care to make sure that information taken off the Internet is trustworthy. Many new pages are being added to the World Wide Web every day, and anyone can place information on the Internet. Since no one filters this material or checks it for accuracy, it is your responsibility to make sure that any Internet resources you use for research are credible and academically sound. Your library will be able to provide you with guidelines for critically evaluating Internet resources.

5. As you become aware of scholarly controversies involving your topic, try to do justice to the differing interpretations by using sources written from more than one point of view in your research.

Evaluating Web Sites: Questions to Ask[10]

1. Where does the Web site originate? Look for sites ending in "edu," which usually indicates authorship by someone at a college or university.

2. Who is the author and what are his/her credentials? Is the person an authority in the field? Often you can find this information by doing a search on the author. Certainly, beware of anonymous postings.

3. Does the site include a bibliography? If so, how complete is it?

4. Does the site reflect an obvious bias or advocate a specific agenda?

A final note: Unless directed otherwise, do not base your research solely on digital (Internet) materials. There will likely be key print sources that are not available in an electronic format. No thorough research project should ignore the important books on your library's shelves.

Some Places to Begin*

The following section contains a selective list of reference works that will best serve you when you actually begin a research project. Reference works are increasingly available electronically. We indicate electronic availability in brackets, but you will always have to check with your library to find out what is or is not available in a digital format.

Indexes and Bibliographies: Finding Your Source Materials

America: History and Life [On-line]. Citations and abstracts (summaries) of periodical articles on the United States and Canada from prehistoric times to the present.

The American Historical Association's Guide to Historical Literature, 3rd ed. An excellent place to begin. The 3rd edition was published in 1995.

Book Review Digest. Contains brief excerpts of book reviews of important books. Useful in helping you decide which books are the best on your subject, and indispensable in helping you decide which complete book reviews to read. *ABC-Clio* and *Academic Search Premier* are also good sources for book reviews.

Harvard Guide to American History, Volumes 1 & 2. A bibliographical guide to the literature on American history. The opening chapter provides an excellent introduction to research methods and materials. There are many other specialized bibliographies for other regions of the world. Ask your reference librarian to help you find an appropriate subject bibliography for these areas.

(Continued)

---

[10] Based on McMichael, *History on the Web,* 42. For the full discussion see pages 38–46.

Historical Abstracts [On-line] Provides brief summaries of scholarly articles that have appeared in the world's periodical literature. Good for finding articles relevant to your research and also getting a preview of the content. The focus is world history excluding the United States and Canada.

JSTOR [On-line] An excellent source for the entire run of English-language journals. Allows full-text retrieval.

LexisNexis Academic [On-line] Full-text collection of newspapers and magazines for the last few decades.

The New York Times Index [On-line] Excellent source for the beginner. This is a thorough index of the articles that have appeared in *The New York Times* since 1851. It is important to follow the directions under each subject heading in order to find the full citation.

Reader's Guide to Periodical Literature [On-line] An excellent source; discussed above on pages 81–82. Note, however, that this index covers popular, non-technical magazines (e.g., *Time, Newsweek,* etc.) representing all the important fields of study.

Social Sciences Index [On-line] and the *Humanities Index* [On-line] (originally known as the *International Index* and then, as the *Social Sciences and Humanities Index*). Discussed above, pages 81–82. Excellent guides for the student of history and politics since these indexes concentrate on more scholarly, specialized periodicals.

Dictionaries and Encyclopedias: Finding General Information

The few titles listed below will help you get an initial overview of any topic you are researching. These sources are useful for getting started and for filling in the odd fact here and there; they are much too general, however, to serve as the core sources for your research. There are also electronic versions of certain dictionaries and encyclopedias.

In addition to the standard encyclopedias—*Britannica, Americana, Colliers*—the following reference works are often excellent resources for the student of history.

Dictionary of American Biography A multivolume collection of scholarly articles on prominent Americans who died before 1945. The articles have bibliographies that can serve as a guide to further research.

Dictionary of American History An eight-volume work with brief, signed, articles on aspects of American history. Each entry has a brief bibliography.

Dictionary of National Biography This is the British equivalent of the *Dictionary of American Biography.* The lack of any national designation often confuses American students. The DNB (as the former is known) was the first such biographical dictionary and everyone knew to which "nation" the title referred. British postage stamps, likewise the first in the field, also do not carry the name of the country of origin.

(Continued)

Encyclopedia of American History (Richard B. Morris, ed.) A condensed overview of the major events in American history. A good way to get a brief account of the events and chronology with which you are dealing.

An Encyclopedia of World History (William Langer, ed.) Does the same thing for world history that Morris does for American history.

International Encyclopedia of the Social Sciences [On-line] Articles in the realm of political science, economics, anthropology, law, sociology, and psychology. Much historical research touches on these related disciplines, and since history is the mother of the social sciences, it is quite appropriate to dip into such materials.

Oxford English Dictionary [On-line] A comprehensive, multivolume, English-language dictionary that traces the historical evolution of the meanings of words. When reading and interpreting documents from previous centuries it is important to know how the age under study understood certain words, rather than how we understand them today. To see what we mean, look up the word "enthusiasm" in the *OED*.

The Reader's Companion to American History (Eric Foner and John A. Garraty, eds.) Like many other standard, one-volume reference works, but with a larger dose of articles on social history—e.g., the history of the family, minorities, and women.

*This section has been compiled with the generous assistance of Webster University reference librarians Kathy Gaynor and Sue Gold.

EXERCISES

SET A   *Exercise 1 — The Search for Sources: The Catalog*

The catalog is the logical place to begin a search for research materials. But to get the full benefit of a catalog search, you should check a variety of possible subject headings, especially the headings established by the Library of Congress.

 For each of the topics below, list four or more *Library of Congress* subject headings under which relevant materials are listed. Don't guess! Go to your library's electronic catalog and check out the categories yourself. Start with a keyword search, and once you have found a book on your topic, click it and note other possible LC subject headings that appear in the display. Clicking on other book titles will yield still more possibilities. Note: Knowing the names of some of the important figures involved in each event/episode helps you expand the number of possible categories (e.g., Hernán Cortés in the example below).

Example:

```
Research Topic: The Spanish Conquest of Mexico (1500s)

Starting with a keyword search using "Spanish conquest" and "Ameri-
cas" or "Mexico" click on a likely book title and note the listed LC
catalog subjects.

Possible LC subject headings include:

Mexico—History—Conquest, 1519-1540
Indians of Mexico—First contact with Europeans (+ Sources)
America—Discovery and Exploration—Spanish
Latin America—History
Hernán Cortés
Aztecs—First contact with Europeans

Note: Many of the general categories (e.g., "Latin America—History)
have a number of thematic and chronological subheadings.
```

1. Topic: The Origins of World War I

World War I was fought during the years 1914–18, predominantly in Europe. The major contestants when the war broke out in August 1914 were Great Britain, France, and Russia on one side, and Germany and Austria-Hungary on the other. Italy, an ally of Germany and Austria-Hungary, remained neutral until joining the other side in 1915. Remember, the topic is the *origins* of World War I, hence your focus should be on the period *before* August 1914. For example, "Germany-History, 1871–1918," or "Europe-History, 1871–1914" would be two relevant catalog categories. Now find at least four more.

Possible Catalog Subject Headings:

_____   _____

_____   _____

_____   _____

2. Topic: Nat Turner's Rebellion

Nat Turner led a slave rebellion in Virginia in 1831.

Possible Catalog Subject Headings:

_____   _____

_____   _____

_____   _____

3. Topic: The American Women's Suffrage Movement (late 19th, early 20th century)

Possible Catalog Subject Headings:

_____   _____

_____   _____

_____   _____

4. Topic: The Collapse of the Soviet Union (1991)

Possible Catalog Subject Headings:

_____   _____

_____   _____

_____   _____

5. Topic: The Impact of the "Black Death" in the Middle Ages

The widespread epidemics of the bubonic plague in the fourteenth century (1300s) still rank as one of the greatest natural disasters in the history of the human race.

Possible Catalog Subject Headings:

_____   _____

_____   _____

_____   _____

SET A   *Exercise 2 — The Search for Sources: Reference Tools*

Using the reference collection in your library (i.e., books), the subscription electronic databases provided by your library (e.g. *JSTOR, Historical Abstracts*), and the Internet answer the following questions and list the specific source or location where you found each answer. Try to use print sources for at least 2–3 of your answers, and **do not** use the Internet (Google, Yahoo) for more than 2–3 of your answers. **You should not use** general encyclopedias, whether print or electronic (e.g., *Britannica, Wikipedia*[11]), but you may use specialized encyclopedias (e.g., *Encyclopedia of American History*). Finally, do not use any single source/database/Web site for more than one answer.

The object of this exercise is to acquaint you with a variety of possibilities. For each answer, list the source and indicate whether it was a printed volume, an electronic database, or an Internet site. You might want to review the list of possible references on pages 85–87.

The terms "where found" and "source" refer to the book, database, or Web site in which you found the information.

Questions

1. Locate a magazine or journal article written after 1990 (list the author, title, date, and the name of the periodical) about the Vietnam War. Locate another article on the same topic written before 1980.

Post-1990 Article:

_____

Pre-1980 Article:

_____

Where found:_____

2. What did the word "enthusiasm" mean in the 18th century?

_____

Where found: _____

---

[11] *Wikipedia*, the Internet encyclopedia, can be useful for getting some introductory information about a topic, but it should not be used as a final source in a paper or essay. Since users can edit the content, you can never fully trust the credibility of an entry.

3. List three places (no general encyclopedias) in which you can find a biographical sketch of Tecumseh, the Shawnee leader who tried to create an Indian confederacy in the early 1800s. Include the volume numbers (where relevant) and page numbers of the essays and/or complete Web addresses.

Source: _____

Source: _____

Source: _____

4. Locate a newspaper article about the British group the Beatles written in 2008 or later.

_____

Where found:_____

5. Locate a book review in a scholarly journal of Tony Judt's *Postwar: A History of Europe Since 1945* (2005). Simply provide the citation for the journal in which the review appeared, including the author of the review and the date.

_____

Where found:_____

6. Who wrote: "Power tends to corrupt and absolute power corrupts absolutely"?

_____

Source: _____

7. Find a solid Web site that would help you discover the best entertainment films about the European Middle Ages.

Title of Web site: _____

Web address (URL): _____

8. Locate a magazine (weekly or monthly) article on the Beatles' trip to the United States in 1964.

_____

Where found:_____

9. Locate a scholarly article on President Bill Clinton and the Irish Peace Process during the 1990s.

_____

Where found:_____

10. Find a review of a book about Tony Blair, British Prime Minister from 1997 to 2007. Give the author and title of the book, the name of the reviewer, and the journal or magazine in which it appeared.

_____

Where found: _____

SET A   *Exercise 3 — The Search for Sources: Web sites*

In the modern environment of computer-based research, it is important to distinguish between academically solid Internet Web sites and those that are more suspect. In this exercise your task is to compare two Web sites *on a single historical topic,* explaining why one is more trustworthy (or is *probably* more trustworthy) than the other. Choose a topic that interests you, or use a topic provided by your instructor. Review the points in the box titled: "Evaluating Websites: Questions to Ask" on page 85.

Web site #1: (URL/Web address) _____

What makes this Web site one you would trust?

Web site #2: (URL/Web address) _____

What makes this Web site questionable as a source?

SET A *Exercise 4 — Note Taking*

Gathering information in usable form requires well-developed note-taking skills, and, needless to say, effective note-taking skills are also extremely useful in the classroom or on the job. But note-taking skills aren't inborn; they must be learned.

Note-taking is not the same thing as copying; it requires active intellectual effort. A good note is not a literal transcript of a text or lecture, but a summary, written in your own words, that reflects your understanding of what you have read or heard. This requires thought and effort on your part, but the rewards are worth it. As Jacques Barzun and Henry Graff put it, "What you have accomplished is threefold: you have made an effort at thought, which has imprinted the information on your mind; you have practiced the art of writing by making a paraphrase; and you have at the same time, [if you are writing a paper], taken a step toward your first draft, for here and now these are your words, not a piece of plagiarism thinly veiled by a page reference."[12]

This exercise is designed to give you some experience in taking good notes. As you do the following segments, keep in mind that a good note summarizes the important points in your own words. Copying the original text or lecture verbatim is pointless. Before beginning, examine the following example of the right way and the wrong way to take notes.

Original Passage

"For most Americans . . . this was the deeply felt meaning of the Revolution: they had created a new world, a republican world. No one doubted that the new polities would be republics, and as Thomas Paine pointed out, 'What is called a republic, is not any particular form of government.' Republicanism meant more for Americans than simply the elimination of a king and the institution of an elective system. It added a moral dimension, a utopian depth, to the political separation from England—a depth that involved the very character of their society. 'We are now really another people,' exclaimed Paine in 1782." (Gordon S. Wood, *The Creation of the American Republic, 1776–1787* [New York: W. W. Norton, 1969], 47–48.)

---

[12] Barzun and Graff, *Modern Researcher,* 30.

I. Sample Note # 1:

```
G. Wood, Creation

Meaning of the Revolution

Most Americans felt Revolution had created a new, republican, world.
They wanted to create republics, but as Thomas Paine said, a republic
"is not any particular form of government." Republicanism meant to
Americans more than elimination of king and institution of an elec-
tive system; it had moral dimension and implied change in "the very
character of their society."

pp. 47-48
```

Comment

```
This note is OK as far as it goes. It records all the essentials, but
it is more a literal transcription than a summary. Such a note re-
quires very little work on the part of the researcher. Remember, a
good note should be a summary written in your own words. Now take a
look at another note based on the same passage.
```

II. Sample Note # 2:

```
Wood, Creation

Meaning of Am. Revol.

To Americans Revol. meant creation of a new world. A republic meant
elimination of king and use of elections, but Wood argues it also
meant a moral transformation of soc. itself. Quotes Paine: "We are
now really another people."

pp. 47-48
```

Comment

This note is much better. It is shorter (by more than a third) and it translates the key ideas into the words of the researcher. In this sort of note some true intellectual work has been done, in that the writer had to understand the passage fully in order to effectively summarize it in different language. When it comes time to write a paper, there will be no temptation to use the author's words (other than the quoted extract from Tom Paine) since the note already reflects the style and words of the student. Notice the use of abbreviations, a legitimate and timesaving practice. Also, the source and page numbers have been recorded along with a heading that indicates the general topic of the note.

For each of the passages below write a research note that summarizes the key ideas in your own words:

1. "Like most thinkers of his time, [black American civil rights pioneer and author W. E. B.] Du Bois hopelessly confused race, nationality and culture. He was also unclear about whether race was biological or cultural in nature. For the most part, he rejected the biological determinism of his time and stressed the historical and environmental factors in the formation of race. Yet at times he seemed to accept inherent racial differences and conflate biological and socio-historical factors. . . . Du Bois's idea of race drew upon the thinking of his Berlin teacher, Heinrich von Treitschke, and other German thinkers such as Johann Gottfried von Herder and Johann Gottlieb Fichte, all of whom lauded the contributions of different races to civilization. In 1897 Du Bois [pronounced "Due Boys"] could be described as a romantic racialist, a description that, as we have seen, fit many white abolitionists." (David W. Southern, *The Progressive Era and Race: Reaction and Reform, 1900–1917* [Wheeling, IL.: Harlan Davidson, Inc., 2005], 151.)

_____

_____

_____

_____

_____

_____

2. "Elizabeth [I of England (1558–1603)] had no intention of surrendering her powers, or acquiescing in men's views of women. She had a great longing, she said, 'to do some act that would make her fame spread abroad in her lifetime, and, after, occasion memorial for ever.' 'She seems to me,' wrote Feria, 'incomparably more feared than her sister [Queen Mary], and gives her orders and has her way as absolutely as her father [Henry VIII] did.' She kept matters of state very largely in her own hands, and generally consulted her councilors individually, on the principle of 'divide and rule.' " (J. E. Neale, *Queen Elizabeth I* [Garden City, NY: Doubleday Anchor, 1957], 67–68.)

_____

_____

_____

_____

_____

_____

_____

3. "In Colonial America, alcohol was vital to the myriad social and cultural expectations which colonists had brought with them from England and the Western world. It was universally honored as a medicine for almost every physiological malfunction, whether temporary or permanent, real or imagined. But even more, it was *aqua vitae*, the water of life, and 'the good creature of God'—in St. Paul's and then Increase Mather's cheerful phrases—a mystical integration of blessing and necessity. And so it had been for as long as men had recorded their fears or their satisfactions. 'Give strong drink unto him that is ready to perish,' reads the Book of Proverbs, 'and wine unto those that be of heavy hearts. Let him drink, and forget his poverty, and remember his misery no more.'" (Norman Clark, *Deliver Us from Evil: An Interpretation of American Prohibition* [New York: W. W. Norton & Co., 1976], 14.)

_____

_____

_____

_____

_____

_____

4. "Early Renaissance works of art which today we admire for their sheer representational virtuosity were part of a vigorously developing worldwide market in luxury commodities. They were at once sources of aesthetic delight and properties in commercial transactions between purchasers, seeking ostentatiously to advertise their power and wealth, and skilled craftsmen with the expertise to guarantee that the object so acquired would make an impact.

Take those Annunciations [religious paintings], for example. . . . These sacred works are fragments of the altarpieces which dominated the interiors of fifteenth-century chapels and churches. Those who commissioned them demonstrated thereby to the congregation at large their prominent position in the community, and the awe and respect to which they were entitled by birth or office." (Lisa Jardine, *Worldly Goods: A New History of the Renaissance* [New York: Doubleday, 1996], 19.)

_____

_____

_____

_____

_____

_____

_____

_____

SET B   *Exercise 1 — The Search for Sources: The Catalog*

The catalog is the logical place to begin a search for research materials. But to get the full benefit of a catalog search, you should check a variety of possible subject headings, especially the headings established by the Library of Congress.

For each of the topics below, list four or more *Library of Congress* subject headings under which relevant materials are listed. Don't guess! Go to your library's electronic catalog and check out the categories yourself. Start with a keyword search, and once you have found a book on your topic, click it and note other possible LC subject headings that appear in the display. Clicking on other book titles will yield still more possibilities. Note: Knowing the names of some of the important figures involved in each event/episode helps you expand the number of possible categories. For an example, see Set A, page 88.

1. Topic: The Japanese Attack on Pearl Harbor, December 7, 1941

Possible Catalog Subject Headings:

_____   _____

_____   _____

_____   _____

2. Topic: The Russian Revolution, 1917

Possible Catalog Subject Headings:

_____   _____

_____   _____

_____   _____

3. Topic: The History of African Americans in the South in the 1920s and 1930s

Possible Catalog Subject Headings:

_____   _____

_____   _____

_____   _____

4. Topic: Chivalry in the Middle Ages

Chivalry was the code of values and behavior (at least in theory) of the feudal aris-tocracy—the knights and members of the nobility—during the late Middle Ages (ca. 1100–1500) in Western Europe.

Possible Catalog Subject Headings:

_____   _____

_____   _____

_____   _____

5. The Feminist Movement in the United States during the 1960s and 1970s

Possible Catalog Subject Headings:

_____   _____

_____   _____

_____   _____

SET B *Exercise 2 — The Search for Sources: Reference Tools*

Using the reference collection in your library (i.e., books), the subscription electronic databases provided by your library (e.g. *JSTOR, Historical Abstracts*), and the Internet, answer the following questions and list the specific source or location where you found each answer. Try to use print sources for at least 2–3 of your answers, and **do not use** the Internet (Google, Yahoo) for more than 2–3 of your answers. **You should not use** general encyclopedias, whether print or electronic (e.g., *Britannica, Wikipedia*), but you may use specialized encyclopedias (e.g., *Encyclopedia of American History*). Finally, do not use any single source/database/Web site for more than one answer.

The object of this exercise is to acquaint you with a variety of possibilities. For each answer, list the source and indicate whether it was a printed volume, an electronic database, or an Internet site. You might want to review the list of possible references on pages 85–87.

The terms "where found" and "source" refer to the book, database, or Web site in which you found the information.

Questions

1. Locate a magazine or journal article written after 2000 (list the author, title, date, and the name of the periodical) about the Japanese attack on Pearl Harbor in 1941.

Article: _____

Where found:_____

2. List three places (no general encyclopedias) in which you can find a biographical sketch of W. E. B. Du Bois, the turn-of-the-century African American leader. Include the volume numbers (where relevant) and page numbers of the essays and/or complete Web addresses.

Source: _____

Source: _____

Source: _____

3. Find a book review in a scholarly journal of Linda Gordon's *Great Arizona Orphan Abduction* (1999).

_____

Where found: _____

4. Locate an article on Chinese revolutionary leader Mao Zedong, written before 1975 and appearing in a historical journal. Cite the title of the article, the author, the journal, and the date. Note: an earlier anglicized spelling of Mao's name was "Mao Tse-Tung."

Article: _____

Where found: _____

5. Find a credible Web site on the Scopes Trial (the "Monkey Trial") of the 1920s.

Title of Web site: _____

Web address (URL): _____

6. Who wrote: "A good book is the precious lifeblood of a master spirit"?

_____

Source: _____

7. Find an article in a scholarly journal about the Bosnian War of the 1990s.

_____

Where found: _____

8. Find a newspaper article about rock legend Bruce Springsteen written in 2007 or 2008.

_____

Where found: _____

9. Locate an article on the American civil rights movement written after 1980 and appearing in a scholarly historical journal. Cite the title of the article, the author, the journal, and the date.

Article: _____

Where found: _____

10. Locate and provide a citation for a book review of Jared Diamond, *Guns, Germs, and Steel: The Fates of Human Societies*, 1997. Simply provide the citation for the magazine or journal in which the review appeared, including the author of the review and the date.

_____

Where found: _____

SET B   *Exercise 3 — The Search for Sources: Web Sites*

In the modern environment of computer-based research, it is important to distinguish between academically solid Internet Web sites and those that are more suspect. In this exercise your task is to compare two Web sites on a single historical topic, explaining why one is more trustworthy (or is *probably* more trustworthy) than the other. Choose a topic that interests you, or use a topic provided by your instructor. Review the points in the box titled: "Evaluating Web sites: Questions to Ask" on page 85.

Web site #1: (URL/Web address) _____

What makes this Web site one you would trust?

Web site #2: (URL/Web address) _____

What makes this Web site questionable as a source?

SET B *Exercise 4 — Note Taking*

This exercise is designed to give you some experience in taking good notes. As you do the following segments, keep in mind that a good note summarizes the important points in your own words. Don't copy the original text or lecture verbatim. Before beginning, you may want to read the comments accompanying the example in Set A, Exercise 4.

For each of the passages below, write a research note that summarizes the key ideas in your own words. Before beginning, examine the example of note taking in Set A on pages 93–95.

1. "Undoubtedly this narration of Black Hawk's early life omits much that would help [us] understand his later attitudes and actions, but several clear indications of his personality and world view do emerge. He thought of himself as a traditional Sauk. He personified tribal rivalries throughout much of his life. Thus, because the Osages had been long-time enemies of the tribe they became his enemies. He practiced the ceremonies, dances, and mourning customs with determination, often going far beyond minimal expectations, as in mourning his father for five years instead of the usual six months. He grew to manhood during an era when the Sauks and their tribal neighbors still enjoyed a good degree of isolation and freedom from the demands of the European powers then trying to divide the continent among themselves." (Roger L. Nichols, *Black Hawk and the Warrior's Path* [Wheeling, IL.: Harlan Davidson, Inc., 1992], 18–19.)

_____

_____

_____

_____

_____

_____

_____

2. "Women of color coped [with the Depression of the 1930s] by using a strategy of downward mobility—that is, they took whatever jobs they could get. Rural black women often left their homes, migrating in larger numbers than black men to urban areas in search of employment. Urban black women also became small-scale entrepreneurs, peddling such goods as home-baked bread or home-raised vegetables on the streets or door to door. Urban black women also responded to economic hard times by gathering into so-called slave markets on street corners each morning, where they offered their labor to the highest bidder on an hourly basis, often for as little as

ten cents an hour. In New York City, an observer noted that hundreds of 'forlorn and half-starved girls were lucky to find a few hours' work one or two days each week.'" (Glenda Riley, *Inventing the American Woman: An Inclusive History,* 2nd ed., Vol. 2 [Wheeling, IL.: Harlan Davidson, Inc., 1995], 255.)

_____

_____

_____

_____

_____

_____

_____

3. "In Washington [in 1945], the battle over the future of American intelligence was growing fierce. The Joint Chiefs of Staff fought for a service firmly under their control. The army and the navy demanded their own. J. Edgar Hoover wanted the FBI to conduct worldwide espionage. The State Department sought dominion. Even the postmaster general weighed in.

General [John] Magruder defined the problem: 'Clandestine intelligence operations involve a constant breaking of all the rules,' he wrote. 'To put it baldly, such operations are necessarily extra-legal and sometimes illegal.' He argued, convincingly, that the Pentagon and State Department could not risk running those missions. A new clandestine service would have to take charge." (Tim Weiner, *Legacy of Ashes: The History of the CIA* [New York: Doubleday, 2007], 12.)

_____

_____

_____

_____

_____

4. "The clergy in France [in the late 1700s, just before the French Revolution] then numbered rather less than 100,000, yet they owned over one-tenth of the land, that is to say about 20,000 square miles. Despite these rich and rolling acres, most of the clergy were poor, for there existed in the Church a hierarchy quite as distinctly stratified as in the other orders of society. The bishops were all nobles, and canonries were often considered the perquisites of well-to-do bourgeois [middle class] families. Moreover, in many towns there were far more canons than there were hard-working parish priests. In Angers, for example, where Church buildings and gardens took up half the area of the town, there were seventy canons but less than twenty priests." (Christopher Hibbert, *The Days of the French Revolution* [New York: Morrow Quill, 1980], 30.)

CHAPTER 7   READING HISTORY

"Books are not made to be believed, but to be subjected to inquiry."

—UMBERTO ECO
(*William of Baskerville in* The Name of the Rose)

Historians are frequently asked to rate and rank American presidents. The presidents most frequently listed in the "top ten" include George Washington, Thomas Jefferson, Abraham Lincoln, and the two Roosevelts, Teddy and Franklin. Another perennial member of this elite circle is the man from Independence, Missouri, Harry S. Truman (1884–1972; president 1945–53).

Harry Truman would have seemed an unlikely candidate to be a great president to those who mourned the death of Franklin Roosevelt in 1945. Truman, Roosevelt's vice-president, was a short, bespectacled Midwesterner who spoke in a high, unimpressive voice, liberally salting his speech with "hells," "damns," and other colorful expletives. Politically Truman was relatively unknown, and his ties to the corrupt Kansas City political machine of Thomas Pendergast did little to inspire national confidence. With his rural Missouri roots and limited formal education he seemed quite a contrast to the patrician, Harvard-educated Roosevelt who had guided the nation through the Great Depression and World War II.

Truman's early years as president were difficult. His popularity in the polls dropped steadily in 1946 and 1947, and he was the object of many a nasty remark: "To err is Truman," "I'm just mild about Harry," "What would Truman do if he were alive." Yet, in the end, Truman's honesty, basic common sense, and ability to make tough decisions with conviction won him the election of 1948 and a perennial place on many great-president lists.

One of the things that misled Truman's contemporary critics was the widespread belief that Truman was relatively unsophisticated and unschooled. That impression was wrong. Though Truman had only a high school education, he was a passionate reader, intoxicated from an early age with a desire to learn. He grew up in a house filled with books, and as a young boy he read the Bible twice, had "pored over" *Plutarch's Lives,* and read an entire set of the works of Shakespeare. He spent many hours in the town library, vowing, along with his friend Charlie Ross, to read every one of the two thousand volumes (which they said they did). "I don't know anybody in the world that ever read as much or as constantly as he did," said his cousin, Ethel Noland.[1] Young Harry read everything he could get his hands on, but his greatest love was history. Truman's recent biographer, David McCullough, writes:

---

[1] David McCullough, *Truman* (New York: Simon and Schuster, 1992), 44, 58. Though Truman had no formal education beyond high school, that was a good deal more than most of his Independence, Missouri, contemporaries, most of whom did not even go to high school.

President Truman (right), his wife Bess (waving), daughter Margaret, and two unidentified men standing on the rear platform of the presidential train, Union Station, Washington, D.C., October 2, 1948. *U.S. National Archives, ARC Identifier 199961. National Park Service, Abbie Rowe, Courtesy of Harry S. Truman Library.*

History became a passion, as [Truman] worked his way through a shelf of standard works on ancient Egypt, Greece, and Rome. "He had a real feeling for history," Ethel [Noland] said, "that it wasn't something in a book, that it was part of life—a section of life or a former time, that it was of interest because it had to do with people." He himself later said it was "true facts" that he wanted. "Reading history, to me, was far more than a romantic adventure. It was solid instruction and wise teaching which I somehow felt that I wanted and needed."[2]

What Harry Truman discovered, and we need to remember, is that history is a reading subject. Our culture increasingly worships at the altar of visual images, but history remains a study firmly based on the written word. To learn history you have to read history—and a lot of it. Such being the case, it seems obvious that there are tangible rewards for those who become more effective readers. It is not the purpose of this chapter to turn you into a speed-reader with a photographic memory—a virtual impossibility in any case. We will, however, explore some techniques that will allow you to get the most out of the reading you do.

Historical accounts are, of course, reservoirs of factual information, but they also attempt to explain and interpret the past. And those interpretations and explanations often differ markedly from one account to the next. As we have seen, there is no single,

[2] McCullough, *Truman*, 58.

unanimously accepted version of any significant portion of the past. Instead there are many versions that often conflict with one another. As Dutch historian Pieter Geyl said, history is "an argument without end."

Certainly no student of history can ignore important pieces of information, for facts are the bricks out of which historical interpretations are built. But facts do not speak for themselves, and often the known facts will bear the weight of more than one interpretation. This is the primary reason historians keep rewriting the history of a single event or period. They are not writing simply to present facts that have already been recorded in other books. They are writing to explore alternative explanations (interpretations), firmly based on the evidence, of why and how things happened the way they did, and perhaps to introduce new evidence not included in previous studies. Or as the British wit Oscar Wilde put it: "The one duty we owe to history is to rewrite it."

Another reason for rewriting history is that as our perspectives and interests change over time, so do the questions we ask about the past. It was no accident that the explosion of interest in African American history and women's history paralleled the increased activism of both groups in the 1960s and 1970s. Nor should it be surprising that Americans became increasingly interested in the history of Southeast Asia during the Vietnam War, the history of the Balkans during the Yugoslav wars of the 1990s, or the history of the Middle East and Islam after the terrorist attacks of September 11, 2001.

The study of history, therefore, involves not only learning the events of the past, but learning (from written histories) what others before you have said about those events. However, a word of warning is in order. Even though all good history is interpretation, not all interpretation is good history. The fact that there is a subjective quality inherent in all historical interpretations should not be taken to mean that "one opinion is as good as another." As Francis Parkman, the eminent nineteenth-century American historian noted, "Facts may be detailed with the most minute exactness, and yet the narrative, taken as a whole, may be unmeaning or untrue."[3] Thus, while there is room for much honest disagreement among historians, in certain cases we must recognize that some interpretations fit the facts better than others, and interpretations based on shoddy scholarship or faulty reasoning should be exposed and rejected.

How to Read Historical Literature

Reading history cannot be done passively; it requires an alert mind critically engaged with the text. Unfortunately, no one has yet invented a labor-saving device to make the process effortless. You can save time and energy, though, if you know what to look for when reading history or other types of nonfiction.

Begin by remembering that when you read an article or book your main goal should be to understand the author's major interpretations and conclusions. You will come across much new information, and you should pay attention to the most important of the new facts. But it is more critical to master the author's *interpretation* of how the facts relate to one another. We all know that individual facts are

[3] Francis Parkman, *Pioneers of France in the New World* (1865), Introduction.

easy to forget. Once a noted expert on fish who became a college president vowed to memorize the name of every student on campus. He soon abandoned the effort, complaining, "I found that every time I learned the name of a student, I forgot the name of a fish." Many of us share the college president's forgetfulness for facts. We are, however, much better able (and it is much more important) to remember neatly summarized generalizations and conclusions.

The Thesis

When reading a book or article you should first try to ascertain the author's primary thesis, or major explanatory interpretations and conclusions. The factual information is, of course, important, but that information will be more easily assimilated if you understand the author's broader purpose in writing the account. It is an author's interpretation (thesis) that makes a book or article distinctive, and this thesis is the glue that ties together the disparate facts that can otherwise overwhelm the reader. In the late 1920s, for example, both Sidney Fay and Bernadotte Schmitt wrote lengthy studies of the origins of World War I (1914–18).[4] Both authors used essentially the same documentary evidence, but each interpreted that evidence in a different way. Schmitt assigned to Germany most of the responsibility for starting the war, whereas Fay minimized German war guilt by distributing blame more widely among a number of countries. Thus, the *topics* of the books were almost identical (the origins of World War I), but their *theses* (interpretations) were radically different.

Usually one can discover the thesis of a book quite easily.[5] If it's not immediately obvious, either the book is poorly constructed (not uncommon) or you missed something. Many times the author states the thesis explicitly ("My argument/thesis is . . . "); on other occasions you must do the work yourself. Most authors summarize their central arguments in a preface, foreword, introduction, or first chapter, and recapitulate the main points again at the end of a book or article. *These are the sections of a book you should read first.* In the case of an article, read the first few paragraphs and the last few in order to isolate the thesis. Don't be afraid to read the last chapter or section before those in the middle; a history book is not a murder mystery in which the reader needs to be kept in suspense until the end.

It is important to identify the thesis early. The facts in the book should support and illustrate the thesis, and if you have identified that thesis from the beginning, you will find it much easier to read the rest of the book. As you become increasingly familiar with a given topic, you will find it easier to master additional books on that topic. With the essential facts already at your command, you will be able to concentrate on the book's interpretation and how that interpretation differs from others you have read.

Finally, although the thesis is the most important single element in a book, you should by no means ignore the rest. As you read, take note of the important gener-

---

[4] Sidney B. Fay, *The Origins of the World War*, 2 vols. (New York: Macmillan, 1928); Bernadotte E. Schmitt, *The Coming of the War, 1914*, 2 vols. (New York: Scribners, 1930).
[5] We are indebted for the discussion of thesis-finding and selective-reading techniques to Norman E. Cantor and Richard I. Schneider, *How to Study History* (Wheeling, IL.: Harlan Davidson, Inc., 1967), especially Chapter Five.

Topic vs. Thesis

Don't confuse the topic of a book with the thesis. The topic refers to the specific subject matter the book covers. The topic is the *what* the author is writing about. The thesis refers to the distinctive *argument* the author is making about the topic—i.e., the interpretation. Many authors have written on the causes of the American Civil War (that is, they have written on the same topic), but they have presented different theses about the cause or mix of causes that led to the conflict. To some, the war was fought over slavery; to others it was a war that grew out of the economic differences between the South and the North; and still others have said the war was caused by a conflict over the issue of states' rights.

Remember:

The **topic** refers to the subject matter. When you say: "This book is *about* the origins of the Civil War," you are describing the topic of the book.

The **thesis** refers to the author's central argument about the topic under discussion: e.g., "The author *argues* that the Civil War was fought primarily over the issue of slavery." (No sentence can be a thesis statement unless it can be prefaced with the words: "The author *argues* that . . . ." or "I *argue* that . . . ." or a similar phrase.)

alizations made in each chapter or subsection of the book. You should also make a mental or written note of what factual material is covered in order to have a clear idea of what the book does and does not contain. That way, if you need a specific piece of information in the future, you will know where to find it.

Selective Reading

Reading a book is like mining for precious gems—the valuable stones must be separated from the surrounding rocks. A useful technique for "mining" historical accounts is selective reading. After you have read carefully to establish the thesis, the rest of the book can be digested more rapidly. A well-constructed book will contain regular patterns that you can use as shortcuts. For instance, an author's major points are usually summarized at the beginning or end (or both) of each chapter. Similarly, central ideas in individual paragraphs are often contained in a topic sentence, usually, but not always, the first sentence in the paragraph. Once you have established where a particular author tends to locate the key ideas, it becomes much easier to read the rest of the book. Be aware, however, that this technique is most valuable for books on topics about which you already know something. We do not recommend this technique when you are reading a book on an unfamiliar subject. Further, we are not talking here about speed-reading (a questionable and highly overrated technique) but about *selective* reading—the ability to discriminate between the sections of a book that you should read with relative care and those that you can read less intensively.

Authors' Choices and Hidden Agendas

"What I like in a good author," wrote American essayist and critic Logan Pearsall Smith, "is not what he says, but what he whispers." Indeed, the "whispers" in a work of history—what we can read "between the lines"—are frequently as important as the author's explicit statements. In every history book the author makes countless value judgments and decisions that, though not always explicitly identified, make that particular book different from all others. It is important, therefore, to try to identify the author's underlying assumptions and values. There is no absolutely foolproof way to do so. To some extent each book and each author is unique, and the historian-detective must use any and all clues to penetrate below the surface. At a bare minimum it might help to ask the following questions of every book you read:

- **Does the book reflect an identifiable bias or point of view, and how might the author's bias have influenced the book's subject matter or conclusions?** Books reflect—often unintentionally—the political, national, religious, or ideological values of their authors. As Arthur Schlesinger Jr. points out, "All historians are prisoners of their own experience."[6] For instance, in many cases books on the religious upheavals of the Reformation during the sixteenth century clearly reveal the religious convictions of the authors. Similarly, British accounts of the American Revolution often differ quite markedly from American accounts. Critical readers should look for clues to an author's values and biases in order to weigh more intelligently the arguments made in her or his book. A word of caution is necessary here. The intrusion of bias does not automatically discredit an author's thesis. The test of a historical interpretation—even one rooted in bias—is how well it conforms to the evidence.

- **How does the author approach the subject?** That is, which of the varieties or subcategories of history does the book represent? Most authors choose to emphasize some aspects of past experience more than others: e.g., economic relationships (economic history); politics (political/institutional history); individuals (biography); the role of groups (social history); ideas (intellectual history); war (military history); diplomacy (diplomatic history); everyday life (again, social history). The approach an author takes when writing about a subject reflects a conscious choice—perhaps to examine the subject from an economic as opposed to a political perspective—and you should always be aware of that choice.

- **How does the author organize the book?** The author also decides whether to organize an account chronologically (events discussed in order of occurrence) or topically (events discussed in thematic units). Actually, authors often combine the two, alternating the chronological narration of events with periodic analyses of specific issues or topics. Taken as a whole, though, most books will conform predominantly to one organizational scheme or the other. A look at the table of contents may help you determine whether a book is organized topically or chronologically. Usually, however, you will have to dip into the work itself to get a firm sense of how the author has organized the material.

- **What are the author's sources and how well are they used?** Here you are concerned with the author's research apparatus. Are there extensive source references

---

[6] Arthur Schlesinger Jr., "History and National Stupidity," *New York Review of Books* (April 27, 2006), 14.

Chronological vs. Topical Organization

Books organized *chronologically* present material the same way many college survey courses do—year-by-year or period-by-period. Books organized *topically* have chapters or sections based on thematically similar materials. Topically organized books might cover the same chronological periods again and again, but each time the actual "topic" under discussion will be different. A good example of a book organized topically is Clinton Rossiter's *The First American Revolution* (1956). While each chapter of Rossiter's book covers the same period of American history (the colonial period before 1776), each one focuses on a different aspect of the period—the economics, religion, politics, social structure, etc.

(footnotes, endnotes, or in-text citations)? Few? None? Is the bibliography long? Short? Missing altogether? This sort of information can give you a clue as to the seriousness and perhaps the credibility of the book, although it would be a mistake automatically to equate extensive source citations with quality. In addition, the lack of such research apparatus does not necessarily mean that the book is worthless. It could have been the author's intention to write an introductory study (like this one) intended for a general audience. You should also note what sources the author used. Are the sources appropriate to the subject matter? For instance, a history of American slavery using only material written by southern plantation owners would be highly suspect, as would a history of the labor movement based only on the observations of factory owners. Further, did the author use extensive primary (original) sources or was the book written on the basis of secondary literature? The answer to this question can help you discover whether the author was attempting to break new ground by examining original sources or attempting to synthesize the research findings of a number of other historians. (Primary sources—letters, diaries, government documents, newspapers, photographs, etc.—are the records created by those who lived through the events being investigated. Secondary sources are the books and articles written by historians, very often based on primary sources. See pp. 140–141 for a fuller discussion of the distinction between primary and secondary sources.)

• **Who is the author?** To answer all of the above questions it helps to know something about the author both personally and professionally. Is the author a scholar? Journalist? Politician? What is the author's political persuasion? Religion? Nationality? Gender? If a scholar, is the person a historian, political scientist, economist, sociologist, or a psychologist? What kind of reputation does the author have in academic circles? Many times you can find such information (or some of it) on jacket covers or in a brief biographical sketch in the book itself. It is also increasingly common to use the Internet to research an author's background. Finally, if you know of some other books the author has written, it might be helpful to read some reviews of those works.

• **When was the book first published?** This piece of information can provide many clues to the quality and orientation of a book. A history of World War II (1939–45) written in 1946 might be less objective and less substantive than one written in 1996 or 2006, although you should not automatically assume that. Certainly, though, the more recent authors would have had the opportunity to incorporate evidence unavailable to authors writing immediately after the war.

Writing Critical Book Reviews

The book review is one of the most common, and most commonly misunderstood, assignments in college. All too often students simply summarize the contents of a book, with little attempt to comprehend and comment critically on the author's major points. From what we have said above, however, it should be clear that a good book review provides critical commentary on the book in question: its purpose, major arguments, use of evidence, and presentation (organization and style). You should, of course, provide a brief summary of what the book is about, but it is more important to answer the question: "What unique ideas does this book present and is it worth reading?"

Use the following questions as a guide for writing critical book reviews. Do not try to answer each question in a mechanical way (some questions might not even be especially relevant to the book you are reading). Instead, ask yourself the following questions as you try to understand and evaluate the book. (Review as well the questions listed previously in the section on "Authors' Choices and Hidden Agendas," pp. 110–112.)

1. **What material does the book cover and what is the author's purpose in presenting that material?** Remember, there are almost no topics that haven't been considered before. Authors write books because they think they have something new or different to offer. Why does this author think another book on the subject is needed? At this point try to discern the author's approach to the subject (see p. 110)—i.e., is the book political history, economic history, religious history, social history, etc.?

2. **What is the thesis of the book and how does the author go about convincing you the thesis is valid?** Even if you disagree with the author's argument and conclusions, you should try to present the author's ideas fairly and sympathetically.[7] Discuss the book's thesis and central arguments in a way that would prompt even the author to say, "Yes, that's what I intended to say." In relaying the author's argument it is often helpful to tell your reader how the book is organized. Tell your reader why the book is organized the way it is. How does the organization reinforce the line of reasoning the author uses to advance the argument? If you have read other books on the same general topic, how does the interpretation (thesis) of this book differ from that of the others? Warning: be especially careful when thinking about the author's purpose and thesis (questions 1 and 2). If you are wrong on these points, your review won't make a lot of sense, nor will it be especially helpful to you or your readers.

---

[7] Thanks to our colleague Professor Kelly-Kate Pease for allowing us to incorporate some of the advice she gives her students about how to write book reviews.

3. **What sort of evidence does the author use to support the thesis?** Do not simply restate what the author says, but discuss the type(s) of evidence used: manuscripts, government documents, personal interviews, statistical data, memoirs, books by other authors, films, works of art, etc. Then ask, does the evidence effectively support the argument? Could the same evidence be used to support another conclusion? Did the author leave out evidence that might have weakened the case?

4. **How effective is the author's presentation?** Is the organization clear and helpful? Is the writing style interesting and engaging, or does the book read like a badly written insurance policy?

5. **What did the book add to your understanding of the subject? Did you enjoy the book?** Why or why not?

Again, these questions need not be answered in any specific order, but all of them should be addressed somewhere in the review. Finally, a book review, like any piece of writing, should observe the basic requirements of literary discourse. There should be an introduction (in this case an overview of your conclusions about the book you are reviewing—"This was a good book because . . . "), a middle section in which you develop your argument, and a brief conclusion. As always, clarity and grammatical precision are important if you want your reader to understand what you are saying.

EXERCISES

SET A　*Exercise 1 — Thesis-Finding*

Above, a distinction was made between the content of a book (the *topic*) and the interpretation or *thesis* of a book. The thesis will usually identify those forces, individuals, and relationships that the author considers most important for *explaining* the events in question.

Below are a number of brief book summaries written by the authors themselves, by editors, or reviewers. Some of the summaries emphasize the material the book covers (the topic or content); others talk more about the author's arguments (the thesis); still others discuss both content and thesis.

Identify those abstracts that primarily summarize the **C**ontent of the book by placing a "**C**" in the appropriate space. Identify those that emphasize the author's interpretation or **T**hesis by writing a "**T**." For passages that describe both **C**ontent and **T**hesis write "**CT**." For all passages labeled "T" or "CT," underline the sentence or sentences that best represent the author's central thesis. Before doing this exercise you might want to review the discussion of topic and thesis on page 108–109. The first item is completed for you as an example.

　__CT__　1. *Electoral Reform in War and Peace, 1906–1918* by Martin Pugh. London and Boston: Routledge & Kegan Paul, 1978.

The book is the first attempt to explain the major turning point of the Fourth [British] Reform Act which extended the vote to 13 million men and over 8 million women. It does so partly by examining the relationship between reform of the franchise and reform of the electoral system. In analyzing the prewar debate over proportional representation and the alternative vote it sheds new light on the Liberal-Labour relationship.

The book attacks the status traditionally accorded to the militant suffragettes and shifts attention to the role of the moderates. It demonstrates how reform grew out of prewar conditions and provides a salutory corrective to the assumption that twentieth-century warfare had a democratizing effect on British society.

Finally, wartime politics are reinterpreted as a struggle over the timing of the General Election, and the author explains how the Liberal and Labour parties exposed themselves to twenty years of Conservative hegemony under the mass franchise.

Comment

The first part of this passage describes content. You might have been tempted to consider this to be part of the thesis since it refers to the book's "attempt to explain the major turning point of the Fourth [British] Reform Act." But this passage never actually tells you what the explanation is. In the final two paragraphs, however, we find the author's argument, or thesis. Note how the second sentence, beginning "It demonstrates . . . ," can be attached to our test phrase: "The author argues that. . . ." Thus: "**The author argues that** reform grew out of prewar conditions, etc." Remember, if you can successfully splice this key phrase onto the beginning of a sentence or passage, the chances are good that you have found a thesis-type statement. In the last paragraph we find a direct reference to the author's [re]interpretation.

_____ 2. *Race, Ethnicity, and Class in American Social Thought* by Glenn C. Altschuler. Wheeling, Ill.: Harlan Davidson, 1982.

In this innovative study, Professor Altschuler argues that the origins of the modern liberal state can be found in the responses to important social issues after the Civil War. The questions raised by emancipation and the new role of blacks in American society was a key issue that would be superseded by the concerns over the "new immigration" in the 1880s. Despite many retreats, a new progressive synthesis slowly emerged to challenge nativism and Social Darwinism—a development that ushered in a new era in American social thought.

_____ 3. *The Uncivil Wars: Ireland Today* by Padraig O'Malley. Boston: Beacon Press, 1990.

Praised as being the most comprehensive analysis of the troubles in Northern Ireland, *The Uncivil Wars* brings this tangled and tragic conflict into sharp, dramatic focus. Padraig O'Malley has interviewed all the key players: Catholics, Protestants, Loyalists, Republicans, Unionists, and nationalists whose clashing backgrounds, ideas, and hopes fuel the conflict. Their words, more than anything else, tell the extent of the impasse. In this updated edition, O'Malley chronicles and analyzes the developments that have occurred since the controversial Anglo-Irish Agreement.

_____ 4. *The Russian Revolution* by Richard Pipes. New York: Vintage Books, 1990.

Ground-breaking in its inclusiveness . . . *The Russian Revolution* draws conclusions that have already aroused great controversy in this country—and are certain to be explosive when the book is published in the Soviet Union. Richard Pipes argues convincingly that the Russian Revolution was an intellectual, rather than a class, uprising; that it was steeped in terror from its very outset; and that it was not a revolution at all but a coup d'etat—"the capture of a governmental power by a small minority."

_____ 5. *Lincoln at Gettysburg: The Words That Remade America* by Garry Wills. New York: Simon and Schuster, 1992.

The power of words has rarely been given a more compelling demonstration than in the Gettysburg Address. Lincoln was asked to memorialize the gruesome battle. Instead, he gave the whole nation "a new birth of freedom" in the space of a mere 272 words. His entire life and previous training, and his deep political experience went into this, his revolutionary masterpiece.

By examining both the address and Lincoln in their historical moment and cultural frame, Wills breathes new life into words we thought we knew, and reveals much about a president so mythologized but often misunderstood. Wills shows how Lincoln came to change the world and to effect an intellectual revolution, how his words had to and did complete the work of the guns, and how Lincoln wove a spell that has not yet been broken.

_____ 6. *World on Fire* by Amy Chua. New York: Anchor Books, 2003.

In this investigation of the true impact of globalization, Yale Law School professor Amy Chua explains why many developing countries are in fact consumed by ethnic violence after adopting free market democracy. Chua shows how free markets have often concentrated starkly disproportionate wealth in the hands of a resented ethnic minority. These "market dominant minorities"—Chinese in Southeast Asia, Croatians in the former Yugoslavia, whites in Latin America and South Africa, Indians in East Africa, Lebanese in West Africa, Jews in post-communist Russia—become objects of violent hatred. At the same time, democracy empowers the impoverished majority, unleashing ethnic demagoguery, confiscation, and sometimes genocidal revenge.

American civil rights leader and author, W. E. B. Du Bois, 1868–1963. Du Bois was one of the founders in 1909 of the committee that became of the National Association for the Advancement of Colored People (NAACP) in 1910. *Library of Congress, Prints & Photographs Division, (LC-USZ62-16767).*

SET A   *Exercise 2 — Book Analysis: Getting a Head Start*

In the discussion on reading historical literature (pp. 108–109) we note that authors tend to summarize their central arguments in a preface, foreword, introduction, or first chapter. Accordingly, it is important that you begin a book by reading carefully the introductory section(s). Once you have a working overview of the book's thesis and organization, understanding the rest will be much easier.

Below is the Introduction and condensed Table of Contents to David W. Southern's book *The Progressive Era and Race: Reaction and Reform, 1900–1917.* (Harlan Davidson, 2005. Reprinted by permission of Harlan Davidson.) Your task is to learn as much about this book as possible (thesis, major points, organization, etc.) relying only on these sections. Read the Table of Contents and Introduction and answer the questions that follow. You might want to look at the questions before you begin reading.

From David W. Southern, *The Progressive Era and Race: Reaction and Reform, 1900–1917* (Wheeling, IL: Harlan Davidson, Inc., 2005).

CONTENTS

INTRODUCTION

¶1 When the Progressive Movement swept across the United States in the early twentieth century, oppressed African Americans saw the exuberant impulse toward liberal reform as a glimmer of hope. Led by middle-class, moralistic reformers, the Progressive Movement was a stunningly broad and diverse effort to harness industrialization for the good of the people. Progressive crusaders broke up monopolies, regulated big business and railroads, established the Federal Reserve banking system, legislated progressive taxes, enacted pure food and drug laws, campaigned against vice and corruption, and ushered in women's suffrage and Prohibition. They carried out reforms in virtually every aspect of American life, from the boardroom to the playground. Championing human rights over property rights, progressives spoke fluently the Jeffersonian idiom of egalitarianism and lamented the "betrayal of democracy" that corporate forces had allegedly imposed on the nation. Young, energetic, well-educated progressives believed they had loosed a new interest in social justice and helping the downtrodden. William Allen White, the revered progressive journalist from Kansas, said that his kind felt compelled to reach out to the "have-nots . . . because we felt that to bathe and feed the under dog [sic] would release the burden of injustice on our conscience."

¶2 But for all the talk about removing injustices and realizing the democratic promise of America, progressive interest almost always stopped short of the color line. During the Progressive Era the nation was in fact caught up in a powerful tide of white supremacy at home and imperialism against people of color abroad. Looking back, it is clear that race was the major blind spot of the progressives. Progressive thinkers and politicians became ensnared in a web of "scientific racism." Incredibly, the best science of the time told them that blacks were innately inferior and deserved to remain at *the* bottom of society as a despised caste. Even those whites who believed in black rights often became defeatist on the race issue because of the overwhelming opposition to racial equality.

¶3 Indeed, Americans in the Progressive Era were obsessed with race. Race explained historical development and human society not only for white-supremacist intellectuals such as Theodore Roosevelt and Woodrow Wilson but also for black leaders such as W. E. B. Du Bois. White progressives used their belief in the racial inferiority of blacks to justify the exclusion of African Americans from American democracy. One can even trace the racial sentiment that militated against the inclusion of blacks in the thinking of two future liberal icons in the Progressive Era: Franklin D. Roosevelt and Harry S. Truman. As a Harvard student and young Democratic legislator, Roosevelt referred to blacks as "semi-beasts" and wrote in the margin of one of his political speeches, "story of a nigger." In a 1911 letter to his future wife, Truman expressed the limits of his democratic sentiments by saying, "I think one man is just as good as another so long as he's honest and decent and not a nigger or a Chinaman." On the other end of such attitudes, Du Bois declared in 1900, "The problem of the twentieth century is the problem of the color line. . . ."

¶4 If academics today insist that race is a mere social construct with no biological meaning, early twentieth-century reformers believed that race was a palpably real biological fact that had ultimate importance. The ideas of race and color were powerful, controlling elements in progressive social and political thinking. And this fixation on race explains how democratic reform and racism went hand-in-hand in the Progressive Era. The most progressive politicians in the South, where almost 90 percent of African Americans lived from 1900 to 1917, led campaigns for legal segregation and disfranchisement of blacks and even vowed to lead lynch mobs against black men accused of raping white women. For their part, the great bulk of northern progressives acquiesced in the consolidation and maintenance of southern white supremacy.

¶5 In *The Negro in American Life and Thought: The Nadir 1877–1901* (1954), the black historian Rayford W. Logan placed the low point of black life in the post-Reconstruction period. In a later edition of his book, however, Logan extended the concept of the "nadir" into the Progressive Era. Rightly so. It was particularly dispiriting for the most oppressed group in the nation to be excluded from a reform movement that espoused democracy and social justice. The emotions of African Americans boiled because white progressives seemed so indifferent to, even supportive of, the racial staples of the Progressive Era: segregation, disfranchisement, peonage, lynching, and race riots. Nothing aroused the anger of blacks more than the racist policies of the federal government, such as President Woodrow Wilson's segregation of the federal bureaucracy. As the historian Richard Weiss summed it up, "[A]s the Progressive movement reached its peak, and the nation prepared to embark on a war to save the world for democracy, the black man found himself more threatened, more despised, and more discriminated against in his own land than at any time since emancipation."

¶6 One of the reasons for so much belligerent anti-black discourse and action in the Progressive Era was the advent of the "New Negro." E. L. Doctorow described one of the new militants, Coalhouse Walker, in his celebrated novel *Ragtime* (1975). The fictional Walker was a dapper young jazz musician who proudly owned a shiny new Ford. Resentful white firemen in the area soiled the seats of Walker's prized car with human excrement and forbade him to pass on the road. Doctorow conveyed the black man's thoughts as follows, "He was not unaware that in his dress and as the owner of a car he was a provocation to many white people." The novelist added that the defiant Walker "had created himself in the teeth of such feelings." Not surprisingly, the reaction of Walker to rampaging racism was dramatic and explosive—the stuff of novels and movies. But Walker's steadfast resolve to achieve and advance was emblematic of the New Negro of the Progressive Era. And the specter of such a black man proved exceedingly provocative to whites, thus explaining the pervasive racial violence of the time.

¶7 The history of African Americans always has two sides. One side relates what whites have thought about and done to blacks, as much of this book does. The other side traces the aspirations and strivings of blacks to make a life for themselves in a hostile white world. If one focuses only on the first aspect, blacks appear as no more than victims. As the black scholar Cornel West observed, "While black people have never been simply victims, wallowing in self-pity and begging for white giveaways, they have been—and *are—victimized* [emphasis in original]." The guidelines of this series do not, for considerations of length, permit me the space to discuss all the social and cultural ways that blacks avoided victimization and carved out a social harbor for themselves in church, education, music, fraternal orders, sports, and the like, but Chapter Five demonstrates in some detail how African Americans forged their own Progressive Movement and fought doggedly and courageously against the ideology and practice of white supremacy.

¶8 In this study I have chosen as the chronological boundaries of the Progressive Era the years 1900 to 1917. Some historians place the start of the era in the late nineteenth century, usually at 1890, where progressivism obviously had its roots. I use the more traditional starting date of 1900, for I believe that the Progressive Movement did not achieve any significant cohesion or momentum until early in the twentieth century; indeed, there was little or no sense of a Progressive Movement before 1900. In 1914 the journalist Walter Lippmann said, "The adjective 'progressive' is what we like, and the word is new." Others would extend the Progressive Era through World War I to 1920, for which a good case can be made. But I end my story with the entry of the United States into World War I as, again, the allotted space does not allow an adequate discussion of the racial impact of the military conflict and its ghastly aftermath. I have only hinted at the racial implications of the postwar period in the Epilogue. Finally, I would like to alert the reader that I sometimes use the word "liberal" in this book to distinguish the small minority of progressives who were pro—civil rights from the majority who were either demonstrably racist or indifferent to blacks.

1. **Topic** of the book? (i.e., the subject matter; the material the book covers):

_____

_____

2. Central **thesis**? (the author's interpretation or argument):

_____

_____

_____

_____

Note: Indicate paragraph number(s) where the thesis is most clearly summarized.

3. **Major sub-points** that support the thesis? Indicate relevant paragraph numbers. (You may not need to use all the answer lines):

    a. *Example:* In this period Americans both white and black were obsessed with race. (¶ 3)

    b. _____

    c. _____

    d. _____

    e. _____

    f. _____

4. Predominant mode of **organization**? (topical/analytical or chronological/narrative):

_____

_____

Explain your choice: _____

_____

_____

_____

_____

5. **Author's "approach"** to the subject? (i.e., is the emphasis on political history, intellectual history, cultural history, social history, etc.?)

_____

_____

Explain your choice: _____

_____

_____

_____

_____

6. **Author's use of sources?** (You can't answer this question using only the Introduction. However, if you were writing a critical review of the book as a whole you should include a discussion of the type of sources the author used and the thoroughness of the documentation—i.e., source references):

SET A   *Exercise 3 — Writing the Précis*

Read Writing Capsule 5 (below), and write a brief précis (no longer than one-half page, typed or word-processed, double spaced) of the Introduction you read above.

WRITING CAPSULE 5

The Précis

A précis is a critical summary of a book, chapter, article, or essay. The purpose is to convey briefly, and as clearly as possible, the central points made by the author of the piece you have read—whether or not you agree with what the author says. The précis should not focus on your opinions; rather it should attempt to do full justice to the points the author considers important. A précis should not merely list isolated points. It should be written as an essay that discusses the thesis and major points of the author in a narrative fashion. If you have the space available, it is appropriate to insert a personal observation or two—but only after you have explained what the author had to say.

Writing a précis can be a very effective way of determining how well you understand the material you read. It is very difficult to summarize a lengthy piece of writing unless you truly understand the thesis and major arguments of the author. Further, it provides a useful reminder that our first obligation when reading an author's work is to understand the author's ideas in a fair and open-minded way before we go to the next step of critiquing those ideas, which is the task of the book review discussed earlier in the chapter.

SET B   *Exercise 1 — Thesis-Finding*

Above, a distinction was made between the content of a book (the *topic*) and the interpretation (or *thesis*) of a book. The thesis will usually identify those forces, individuals, and relationships that the author considers most important for *explaining* the events in question.

Below are a number of brief book summaries written by the authors themselves, by editors, or reviewers. Some of the summaries emphasize the material the book covers (the topic or content); others talk more about the author's arguments (the thesis); still others discuss both content and thesis.

Identify those abstracts that primarily summarize the **C**ontent of the book by placing a "**C**" in the appropriate space. Identify those that emphasize the author's interpretation or **T**hesis by writing a "**T**." For passages that describe both **C**ontent and **T**hesis write a "**CT**." For all passages labeled "T" or "CT," <u>underline the sentence or sentences that best represent the author's central thesis</u>. Before doing this exercise you might want to review the discussion of topic and thesis on pages 108–109. For an example see Set A, Exercise 1, Number 1 on pages 113–114.

_____ 1. *War in European History* by Michael Howard. London, Oxford, and New York: Oxford University Press, 1976.

This is a study of warfare as it has developed in Western Europe from the Dark Ages until the present day. In it I show not only how the techniques of warfare changed, but how they affected or were affected by social, economic, and technological developments in the societies that employed them. I trace the growth and decay of the feudal organization of Western Europe for war; the rise of mercenary troops and their development into professions as the framework of the state became strong enough to keep them permanently employed; the connection between war and the development of European trade overseas; and the impact of the French Revolution on the military system of the ancien régime. I go on to show how the development of industrial technology and the social tensions within industrial states culminated in the two world wars, and end by summarizing the military situation of a continent kept at peace by a balance of nuclear terror.

_____ 2. *In Command of France: French Foreign Policy and Military Planning, 1933–1940* by Robert J.Young. Cambridge, MA.: Harvard University Press, 1978.

This work, based extensively on recently released archival material in Britain and France, is one of the first to combine a detailed survey of French foreign policy during the Nazi period with an examination of France's corresponding military planning and preparation. This combination of diplomatic and military perspectives has led the author to a revisionist interpretation of the French response to Nazi Germany, an interpretation which credits the civilian and military command in France with more vision, more determination, more competence than generally has been recognized. Rich in unpublished material and new in interpretation, the work also introduces the reader to some of the leading personalities of the day, soldiers and statesmen whose names have come close to fading from our view.

_____ 3. *The Coming Plague: Newly Emerging Diseases in a World Out of Balance* by Laurie Garrett. New York: Penguin Books, 1995.

Unpurified drinking water. Improper use of antibiotics. Local warfare. Massive refugee migration. Changing social and environmental conditions around the world have fostered the spread of new and potentially devastating viruses and diseases—HIV, Lassa, Ebola, and others. Laurie Garrett takes you on a fifty-year journey through the world's battles with microbes and examines the worldwide conditions that have culminated in recurrent outbreaks of newly discovered diseases, epidemics of diseases migrating to new areas, and mutated old diseases that are no longer curable. She argues that it is not too late to take action to prevent the further onslaught of viruses and microbes, and offers possible solutions for a healthier future.

_____ 4. *Head and Heart: American Christianities* by Garry Wills. New York: The Penguin Press, 2007.

The struggle within American Christianity, Garry Wills argues, now and throughout our country's history, is between the head and the heart: between reason and emotion, Enlightenment and Evangelicalism. Why has this been so? How has the tension between the two poles played out, and with what consequences, over the past four hundred years? How "Christian" is America, after all? Garry Wills has brought a lifetime's worth of thought about these questions to bear on a magnificent historical reckoning that offers vitally needed perspective on some of the most contentious issues of our time.

_____ 5. *The Rise of the Nazis* by Conan Fischer. Manchester: Manchester University Press, 1995.

Conan Fischer examines the history of the Nazis in Germany. Beginning with an overview of the historical context within which Nazism grew, Fischer considers the foreign relations, politics and society of Weimar [1919–33] as well as the role of the elites in the rise of Nazism. He analyzes the anatomy of Nazism itself. What lent its ideology coherence and credibility? What distinguished the Nazis' program from their competitors' and how did they project it so effectively? How was Hitler able to put together and fund an organization so quickly and effectively that it could launch a sustained assault on Weimar? Who supported the Nazis and what were their motives? Where, precisely, does Nazism belong in the history of Europe? In concise, readable chapters, the book offers an essential rethinking of these complex issues.

SET B   *Exercise 2 — Book Analysis: Getting a Head Start*

See Set A, Exercise 2. A good alternative would be to have students use the same format to analyze a scholarly article as assigned by the instructor.

SET B   *Exercise 3 — Writing the Précis*

See Set A, Exercise 3.

[The historian must have] "the power to embody ghosts, to put flesh and blood on dry bones, to make dead men living before our eyes."[1]

—THEODORE ROOSEVELT, 1913

"Artists certainly have the right—and possibly the obligation—to step in and reinterpret the history of our times."[2]

—OLIVER STONE, 1991

On December 8, 1941, President Franklin Roosevelt declared to Congress that December 7, the day of the surprise Japanese attack on the U. S. naval base at Pearl Harbor, was "a date which will live in infamy." With that, the United States entered World War II, a titanic struggle that would require the mobilization of millions of American men and women into the armed services.

War is rarely popular, especially in modern democracies. So one of the most urgent tasks faced by the military was to convince an increasingly educated citizenry—especially those involuntarily drafted into the army—that the cause they were fighting for was a just one. At first the army tried lecturing the inductees about the reasons for the war, highlighting the nobility of the Allies' cause (America was now fighting in tandem with Great Britain and Russia against Germany and Japan) and the iniquity of the enemy's cause. The lectures were a total failure. The troops were bored and unresponsive.

At this point the army chief of staff, General George Marshall, decided to try something different: film. In the 1930s the German film *Triumph of the Will* (1935) showed the world the effectiveness of film as a propaganda tool, and Marshall, decided to fight fire with fire. He asked the already-famous Hollywood director Frank Capra (whose films at the time included *It Happened One Night* and *Mr. Smith Goes to Washington*) to make a series of film documentaries to show Americans what they were fighting for—and against. Capra, a Sicilian-born immigrant who passionately believed in the American dream, was reluctant at first, but he finally agreed to make "the best damned documentary films ever made."[3] The result was the *Why We Fight* series, seven films that told the story of the war up to that point in time: *Prelude to*

---

[1] Theodore Roosevelt, *History as Literature and Other Essays* (New York: Charles Scribner's Sons, 1913), 16.

[2] Oliver Stone, "Who Is Rewriting History?" *The New York Times*, December 20, 1991, A35.

[3] John Dower, *War Without Mercy* (New York: Pantheon, 1986), 15. On the making of the films see David Culbert, "'Why We Fight': Social Engineering for a Democratic Society at War," *Film and Radio Propaganda in World War II*, ed. By K. R. M. Short (London: Croom Helm, 1983), 173–191.

War, The Nazis Strike, Divide and Conquer, The Battle of Britain, The Battle of Russia, The Battle of China, and *War Comes to America.*

The series was successful beyond General Marshall's wildest hopes. Capra used animated Disney maps, witty narration, and miles of graphic war footage—often captured from the enemy—to appeal to the emotions of his audience. The series was based on a strategy of truth: "Let the enemy," said Capra, "prove to our soldiers the enormity of his cause—and the justness of ours."[4] The films were so good that they were shown in public theaters as well as on military bases, and they ultimately were distributed worldwide, with translations in Russian, French, Chinese, and Spanish. The power of the films is most poignantly conveyed by Alfred Kazin, a son of Russian immigrants, who described the affect of seeing *The Battle of Russia* at an army camp in southern Illinois in 1944. "It was a physical shock," recounted Kazin thirty-five years later, "walking out of the theater in the gray dripping twilight, watching the men plodding back to their barracks in the last slant of light, to realize how drained I was, how much I had been worked over, appealed to. In the end, as so often happened to us after a terrific American movie, we were stupefied.[5]

Kazin's experience in 1944 captures perfectly the power of film both to inform and move us deeply. History, as we have seen, is a discipline primarily based on the written word, and in Kazin's day, history on film was something of a novelty. Not so today. Increasingly people are turning to movies and television for their entertainment and information, and often what people think they know about history is as likely to have been learned from films and television as from books. This is not altogether a bad thing, given the growing body of respectable historical video and film produced in recent years (e.g., Ken Burns's series on the Civil War). However, it is not entirely a good thing either.

Whether the trend is welcome or not is immaterial. History films are here to stay, and history instructors have recognized this by incorporating a variety of films and videos into their classes.[6] And, as they continue to do so, the debate over the legitimacy of history on film becomes more passionate and, of course, relevant. Traditional historians regularly point out the myriad deficiencies of such films, for there are many things that written history can do that films cannot. On the other hand, film has its own set of advantages. One historian goes so far as to argue that rather than being defective versions of written history, history films constitute a valid alternative to books and articles. "However we think of it," says Robert Rosenstone, "we must admit that film gives us a new sort of history, what we might call history as vision. . . . Film changes the rules of the game and creates its own sort of truth, creates a multilevel past that has so little to do with language, that it is difficult to describe adequately in words."[7] Oliver Stone, the controversial director of a number of history films would agree: "artists certainly have the right—and possibly the obligation—to step in and reinterpret the history of our times."

Few historians would go as far as Rosenstone on this point, but with the ubiquity of film histories on television and in local movie theaters, students of history need

---

[4] Dower, *War Without Mercy,* 16.
[5] Culbert, "Why We Fight," *Propaganda,* 185–86.
[6] The term "history films" is used by historian Robert Rosenstone to denote all works that "consciously try to recreate the past," whether documentary or dramatic films. *History on Film/Film on History* (Harlow, England: Pearson Education Ltd., 2006), 3.
[7] Rosenstone, *History on Film,* 160.

to become as adept at "reading" and analyzing history films as they are at evaluating the more traditional written historical accounts. In this chapter we will provide a brief introduction to the critical analysis of film documentaries as well as more mainstream Hollywood-type dramatic films. (Although there are technical and perceptual differences between videotape and film, we include both media in our references to "film.") Although space limitations prevent us from doing more than scratching the surface of this immense topic, interested readers will find more detailed guidance in the sources listed in the footnotes of this chapter.[8]

Films vary widely in character, and historians use films in quite distinctive ways. Before viewing and analyzing a film, it is important to understand the type of film you are viewing. To begin it is important to distinguish between film as record, film as representation, and film as cultural artifact.

Film as Record

On the most basic level, film can provide a visual record of an event. Taped footage on the nightly news, amateur videos/films of important events (e.g., Abraham Zapruder's Super-8 film of the Kennedy assassination, the myriad video clips found on the Internet, some of them recorded by cellphones), and the raw footage taken by documentary filmmakers can provide the historian with an invaluable visual record of the personalities and events that have shaped our lives. At this level, film is the equivalent of a primary source—the raw material out of which historians construct their accounts of the past.

Nonetheless, even when dealing with "actuality footage," historians must not let down their guard, for cameras can indeed lie. First, every piece of film is shot from a specific location, showing some things but not others. Therefore, the historian must always consider what wasn't in the viewfinder. Furthermore, it is a rare piece of film that hasn't been edited (cut) to fit time constraints, eliminate unwanted material, or conform to a censor's mandate.[9] Taped television interviews are often edited down from hours of footage to the few minutes that are actually broadcast. In the 1930s and 1940s there was a tacit agreement among news professionals not to show that President Franklin Delano Roosevelt was confined to a wheelchair due to an earlier bout with polio. When FDR's disability was filmed, that footage was edited out before the newsreels were released to the public.[10] Finally, visual evidence can be (and has

---

[8] The amount of scholarship devoted to history in films and television programs is growing exponentially, and a single chapter in a book such as this can do no more than provide a few flimsy guideposts for those who want to think more seriously about the merits and drawbacks of moving-image history. In addition to the Rosenstone book noted above, students and instructors could benefit from reading some of the essays published in John E. O'Connor, *Image as Artifact: The Historical Analysis of Film and Television* (Malabar, FL: Robert E. Krieger Publishing Co., 1990), and in Steven Mintz and Randy Roberts, eds., *Hollywood's America: United States History Through Its Films* (St. James, NY: Brandywine Press, 1993). For instructors a place to begin would be John O'Connor and Martin A. Jackson, *Teaching History with Film* (Washington, DC: AHA, 1974).

[9] Even in countries that value freedom of the press, there are societal and institutional constraints that have the end result of limiting and coloring what is presented to the public in the mainstream media. For an analysis of the ability of political and economic elites to manage the media, see Daniel Hellinger and Dennis Judd, *The Democratic Facade*, 2nd ed. (Belmont, CA.: Wadsworth Publishing Co.: 1994), Chapter 3, "Political Elites and the Media."

[10] Robert E. Herzstein, "News Film and Documentary as Sources for Factual Information," in O'Connor, *Image as Artifact*, 180.

Lyman H. Howe was a traveling showman who promoted "high-class moving pictures" in the late nineteenth century. This 1898 poster shows an audience watching a filmed infantry attack from the Spanish-American War. *Library of Congress, Prints & Photographs Division, (LC-DIG-ppmsca-05941).*

been) falsified. The advent of digital computer technology has made this easier to do today than ever before.

Film as Representation: Documentaries and Dramatic Films

More complex are those films crafted by filmmakers to represent real people and real events. Whether documentaries or dramatic films, they are carefully scripted historical reconstructions, and, as such, are the visual equivalent of secondary sources. These films attempt to narrate and explain events in a manner analogous to books and essays. Historical documentaries, such as Ken Burns's *The Civil War* (1990) and *Baseball* (1994), often use actual film footage and photos interlaced with interviews to tell their story. Dramatic films, on the other hand, attempt to recreate a segment of the past using actors and modern movie-making magic. Some of these films try—sometimes successfully, sometimes not—to tell a "true" story. *Glory* (1989), *Elizabeth* (1998), *The Longest Day* (1962), *JFK* (1991), *Malcolm X* (1992), *Schindler's List* (1993), and the HBO miniseries *John Adams* (2008), are good examples. We would also include in this category films that, though essentially fictional, attempt to present a defensibly accurate portrait of a piece of the past—*Platoon* (1986) the Vietnam War, *Das Boot* [The Boat] (1981) submarine warfare during World War II, *Titanic* (1997), *The Grapes of Wrath* (1940) the Dustbowl migrants during the Great Depression, and *Saving Private Ryan* (1998) the 1944 D-Day invasion and the Battle of Normandy.[11]

Many dramatic films play fast and loose with the facts, and therefore need to be evaluated carefully and critically. We are, however, more willing to accept documentaries at face value, since they use original film footage, photographs, and interviews with participants, eyewitnesses, and academic experts. But even documentaries must be scrutinized with the same skepticism as Hollywood potboilers. Documentaries are still constructions that present a filmmaker's point of view (e.g., Al Gore's Oscar-winning 2006 documentary *An Inconvenient Truth*), and are as much in need of critical analysis and commentary as any written version of history.

Film as Cultural Mirror

Finally, films of all types—whatever their historical content—can be viewed as reflections of the era in which they were made. They can teach us something about the values, behaviors, preoccupations, and myths of the time in question. Here we have come full circle. Just as raw documentary footage can be considered a primary

---

[11] Historical films have become so popular that various historical journals now feature regular film review sections. The historical accuracy of over seventy such films is discussed by a variety of historians, in Mark Carnes, ed., *Past Imperfect: History According to the Movies* (New York: Henry Holt and Co., 1995). Robert Brent Toplin provides an in-depth analysis of eight films about American history in *History by Hollywood* (Urbana: University of Illinois, 1996). A book to be used with care, but worth consulting at the beginning of a film-based project is Joseph Roquemore, *History Goes to the Movies: A Viewer's Guide to the Best (and Some of the Worst) Historical Films Ever Made* (New York: Broadway Books, 1999). Roquemore seems concerned primarily with the literal accuracy of historical dramas, and he often pans films that actually have some broader historical merits—e.g., *The Crucible* (1996), *Michael Collins* (1996), and Oliver Stone's immensely controversial *JFK* (1991).

source, *all films*, whether made to educate or entertain, are primary sources when used as evidence for the cultural conditions and attitudes of the societies that made and viewed the films. For example, D. W. Griffith's *Birth of a Nation* (1915), which portrays the post–Civil War South and the rise of the Ku Klux Klan, would be a secondary source if we were interested in how it represented the Reconstruction period of American history. It would be a primary source, however, if we were viewing it a cultural artifact useful for measuring Americans' attitudes in 1915 toward race relations and the Reconstruction period.

Thinking about Historical Films

Films have a language all their own, a language that is in some ways similar to the written language of books but unique enough to require very different interpretive and analytical skills on the part of those who want to "read" films as easily as they do books.[12]

Film has certain advantages over the written word. It can communicate the look of people, places, and events in ways that even the best-written descriptions cannot. Also, film creates an emotional intensity and immediacy that captures audiences in ways that writers can only envy. Theodore Roosevelt was arguing that historians should strive to give their accounts the qualities of literature when he said historians must have "the power to embody ghosts, to put flesh and blood on dry bones, to make dead men living before our eyes," but he might as well have been lauding the powers of modern cinema.[13] In short, film can make the past come alive.

On the other hand, the emotional power of film is, from the historian's perspective, not always a good thing. Film is inherently manipulative, using clever editing, calculated lighting and camera angles, emotion-laden sound tracks, and special effects of various kinds to create illusions that appeal less to our intellects than our emotions. In fact, film's often non-linear narrative style (think of the rapid-fire presentation of changing, often unrelated, images in many television commercials) might be said to be antithetical to the very enterprise of history. Good historical writing is based on linear thinking. Historians must lead their readers in a logical sequence from one event to another, or make a systematic argument using linear logic—if A, then B, therefore C. Film need not communicate in this way, leading us to wonder if the meaningful, objective study of history will be possible for people who grow up with a nearly constant exposure to the nonlinear visual syntax of moving images.

In comparing words and images, two other points should be made. First, written or spoken language is a medium of intercommunication in which an ongoing dialogue is possible. This is not true of film. According to James Monaco, "Cinema is not strictly a medium of intercommunication. . . . Whereas spoken and written languages are used for intercommunication, film, like the nonrepresentational arts in general . . . , is a one-way communication" [between the artist and the viewer].[14]

---

[12] The image here is taken from one of the best summaries of the history and nature of film: James Monaco, *How to Read a Film*, rev. ed. (New York: Oxford University Press, 1981). See also Art Silverblatt, *Media Literacy: Keys to Interpreting Media Messages*, 3rd ed. (Westport, CT.: Praeger Publishers, 2007).

[13] Or, as Pierre Sorlin, put it, "Film can open our minds to another, more vivid and human, less literary understanding of the past." ("Historical Films as Tools for Historians," in O'Connor, *Image as Artifact*, 50.)

[14] Monaco, *How to Read a Film*, 132.

Additionally, it is much more difficult to check on a film's use of source materials than it is to evaluate the evidence used in a piece of written history. The source citations in history books can be checked for accuracy and contextual legitimacy, but the relationship between content and sources in a film is often difficult to discover. How, for instance, can we find out whether the film footage and interviews in a documentary do justice to the original uncut footage and interviews? How do we discover where writers of dramatic films get their facts and interpretations? Often the answer is, we can't. For the most part, we must use existing written histories to test the credibility of historical films.

Asking Questions of Film

When trying to "read" a film, the old cliché still applies: The more you know, the more you will get out of it. And the questions you should ask are the same ones you should ask when analyzing a written document or a history book: What does the content tell us? How was the film produced? How was it received?[15]

Content

Analysis of content is still the heart of the historical enterprise and applies to both the written word and to film. Every documentary or film drama has a distinctive point of view and often, especially in the case of documentaries, contains an identifiable thesis. Once you identify the point of view and thesis, consider the following: Is the reconstruction accurate? What does the filmmaker want the audience to think about the events being presented? What does the filmmaker want the audience to feel? Are the film's "conclusions" defensible in the light of what is already known about the event in question? You should also ask yourself how particular techniques—lighting, use of camera position, sound, color, editing—have contributed to the overall message of the film. (See the insert on film language.)

Dramatic films pose challenges all their own. Like history books they are historical reconstructions. However, the historian's primary responsibility is to the evidence, whereas the filmmaker's priorities are artistic and financial. Television productions and films must be artistically coherent and entertaining in order to score well in the Nielsen Ratings or succeed at the box office. As historians James Davidson and Mark Lytle comment:

> For filmmakers, far different principles of construction are paramount. They involve questions of drama, not fidelity to the evidence. Does the screenplay move along quickly enough? Do the characters 'develop' sufficiently? Does the plot provide enough suspense? These matters dominate the making of a film even when that oft-repeated claim flashes across the screen: Based on a True Story.[16]

---

[15] The triad of Content, Production, and Reception is based on a number of the essays in O'Connor's *Image as Artifact.*

[16] Davidson and Lytle, *After the Fact,* 4th ed., Vol. II, 368. The chapter on "History and Myth in the Films of Vietnam," provides an excellent introduction to the analysis of historical films.

Clearly, then, filmmakers exercise a great deal of artistic license in their quest to make entertaining films. There is no way to make a fully accurate film about even the simplest historical episode. (The same, of course, is true of written history!) But it would be a major mistake to judge historical films strictly by the criterion of literal accuracy. This is so because films (like good historical novels) can communicate two kinds of truth—literal truth and a larger, human, truth that we still recognize as good history. The Civil War film *Glory* (1989) provides a good example. *Glory* dramatizes the experiences of Col. Robert Gould Shaw's 54th Massachusetts African American regiment and its assault on Fort Wagner in 1863. Although Shaw was a real person, the soldiers are fictional composites and there are many fictional elements in the film. For instance, in the film most of the black troops are portrayed as former slaves, a blatant factual inaccuracy. In fact, most of the African American soldiers at Fort Wagner were free Blacks. Yet, since most of the African Americans who volunteered for the Union army as a whole *were* ex-slaves, we would argue that the film fairly represents that larger historical truth. As Civil War historian James McPherson has written: "Not only is [*Glory*] the first feature film to treat the role of Black soldiers in the American Civil War, but it is also one of the most powerful and historically accurate movies ever made about that war."[17]

A final word about content: though it is important to determine the accuracy of historical films, even inaccuracies can tell us something about a society's cultural myths. As one commentator wrote, "historians who tried to list the historical inac-

---

[17] Quoted in Rosenstone, *History on Film*, 40. For an extended discussion of *Glory* see pages 39–46.

The storming of Fort Wagner, the climactic episode in the film *Glory*. (Kurz and Allison print, ca. 1890). *Library of Congress, Prints & Photographs Division, (LC-DIG-pga-01949).*

curacies in *Birth of a Nation* would be ignoring the fact that their job should not involve bestowing marks for accuracy but describing how men living at a certain time understood their own history."[18] While we think it is important to consider the accuracy of a film, we agree that even misrepresentations of history can provide invaluable insights into the minds of those who originally made and viewed a film.

Production and Reception

Effective analysis of a book requires that we know something about the times in which the book was written as well as something about the author's values, background, and intent. The same is true of film analysis. *Platoon,* for example, did the same thing for the American experience in Vietnam that *Glory* did for the African American experience in the Civil War. Using fictional characters, it captured the larger truth about the war better than most of the other Vietnam War films. Why does *Platoon* stand out? Knowing something about its context helps us understand.

Platoon was made at a time (1986) when Americans were finally willing to confront the agonies and traumas of the Vietnam experience, which helps us understand why the film could portray American soldiers less as mythic heroes (a common approach in dramatic films about World War II) than as frightened, confused, sometimes callous young men who didn't want to be in a war they didn't understand. It is also helpful to know that the film was made by Oliver Stone, a twice-wounded Vietnam veteran, many of whose films (such as *Born on the Fourth of July* and *JFK*) display a gut-level bitterness about the war as well as a distrust of the U.S. government and military.[19] Stone's worldview explains not only the convincing realism of *Platoon* but its antiwar message.

The *popularity* of a film or television show also tells us a good deal about the time in which it was made. This is especially important information if we are studying the film as a cultural artifact—i.e., as evidence for social and cultural history. One could hardly argue that a given television show accurately reflected American tastes if no one watched it, or if it was taken off the air after a few episodes. Similarly, a popular historical film, even if more myth than fact, can tell us how people at the time viewed (or wanted to view) their own history.

Conclusion

History films are here to stay. The danger is not that we find it enjoyable to watch the magical images, but that we do so casually and uncritically. When the lights go down it is too easy to turn off the brain and wait to be entertained. But what we see on the screen must be analyzed, discussed, and challenged if we are to avoid becoming passive receptacles for whatever messages are broadcast in our direction. The critical skills discussed in this book must be used to examine all serious ideas, whatever the medium of their transmission.

---

[18] Daniel Leab, "The Moving Image as Interpreter of History," in O'Connor, *Image as Artifact,* 89.

[19] This discussion of *Platoon* is based largely on Davidson and Lytle, *After the Fact,* 4th ed., 388–92.

A Primer on Film Language

Students interested in historical film should know something about film language. Below are a few important terms and concepts used in much formal film analysis.[20]

Shot, Scene, Sequence

The basic unit of a film is the single shot. A series of shots make a scene, and connected scenes form a sequence. Some commentators suggest that shot, scene, and sequence can be equated to sentence, paragraph, and chapter in written language. Others find the analogy inaccurate and overly simplistic. Whether or not the analogy is appropriate, reasoned critiques of historical films must begin with an analysis of the individual shots (*mise-en-scène*) and how the shots are edited into scenes and sequences (*montage*).

Mise-en-scène

Mise-en-scène (French for "putting together") is a commonly used term in film criticism for the contents and photographic "look" of a single unbroken shot, no matter how long its duration. In evaluating a historical film you should consider the accuracy of the set and costumes, and take notice of how the scene is photographed. Important photographic elements in a single shot are:

• *Duration,* or the length of time a shot is on the screen. A shot can be short and simple or quite long and complex. In tracking shots the camera moves while filming, often going from a distance shot to a close-up, or even following an actor or sequence of events without any editorial cutting. Directors occasionally try to enhance a sense of naturalistic realism by filming tracking shots with hand-held cameras.

• *Lighting and Color* The intensity and direction of the lighting and the colors that compose each shot can be powerful evokers of emotion. Dark shadowy images, for example, convey a sense of danger and apprehension. Colors have psychological correlates (red=anger; blue=sadness) as well as culturally significant symbolic meanings.

• *Camera Position* In this category we include a number of elements that film buffs treat independently—composition, camera angle, camera movement. Composition refers to the arrangement of objects and people on the screen, camera angle to how high or low the camera is placed, and camera movement speaks for itself. All of these elements can play a role in influencing the emotions of the viewer. The single variable of camera angle, for instance, can influence greatly the audience's reading of a film. Leni Riefenstahl, the film genius responsible for the Nazi propaganda film *Triumph of the Will* (1935), often photographed Hitler, his entourage, and German soldiers with a high tilt, or from below to make them appear heroic and larger than life.

Montage

Montage, another French term, refers to film editing—that is, the sequencing of the individual shots. If mise-en-scène refers to the modification and manipulation of space, montage refers to the filmmaker's manipulation of time. Since history is the systematic study of events as they happened in time, historians should pay close attention to how filmmakers manipulate emotions through the editing process. *Hearts and Minds,* a 1974 documentary critical of U.S. involvement in Vietnam, includes an interview with U.S. General William Westmoreland in which he states that Asian people don't respect life the same way Westerners do. During this section of the interview the filmmaker, Peter Davis, undercut Westmoreland's credibility by inserting a scene of a Vietnamese woman weeping over the grave of a loved one. Skillful editing can also telescope or compress time in a way that can compromise the historical "truth" of a given sequence or film.

Sound

Sound is one of the most important weapons in the filmmaker's arsenal of artistic tools. To appreciate this point, compare the emotional impact of the same film viewed with and without the soundtrack. When analyzing a historical film, pay conscious attention to the soundtrack and the feelings it creates.

---

[20] For a more in-depth discussion see Monaco, *How to Read a Film,* Ch. III, "The Language of Film: Signs and Syntax," or O'Connor, *Image as Artifact,* Ch. V, "An Introduction to Visual Language for Historians and History Teachers."

EXERCISE

Films can be a component of any segment of a history course. There are no specific exercises for this chapter, but we suggest that you think of classroom films as something more than mere entertainment. You can use the categories below to analyze films used as part of a traditional history course.

A Note on Film Research

A legitimate question is: "Where do I go to find out background information on a specific historical film?" A good place to start would be with newspaper and magazine reviews written at the time of the film's release. Also, consult Mark C. Carnes's, *Past Imperfect,* John O'Connor's *Image as Artifact,* Steven Mintz's and Randy Roberts's *Hollywood's America,* Robert B. Toplin's *History by Hollywood,* Robert Rosenstone's *History on Film,* as well as the bibliographies in each book. Especially noteworthy is the section in O'Connor's bibliography entitled, "Sources on the Connections between History and the Moving Image." The journal *Film & History* is a valuable source, and, as noted earlier, a number of historical journals have begun to review pertinent films and publish articles on the use of film in the classroom.

Film Analysis:

Name of Film: _____

Release Date: _____

Type of Film (documentary or drama): _____

Analysis of Content

Thesis (documentary) or Central Historical Message (drama):

Major Points:

Context

Information about director/producers/writers:

What does the film reveal about the period in which it was made?

How was it received then or later?

Visual Analysis

(Here you should note those elements of film language that contributed significantly to the overall "message" or impact of the film—editing, sound, camera placement, set, costumes, etc. Refer to the insert on film language on page 134.)

The "Look" of the Film (mise-en-scène):

Editing (montage):

Sound:

Overall Conclusions

How does the film hold up as a piece of history?

PART III: DOING HISTORY

CHAPTER 9 EVIDENCE

"The documents are liars."

—T. E. LAWRENCE

"We don't simply forget; we re-remember. Memory is a rewritable CD that is constantly being rewritten. And rewritten in a particular way: one that both makes sense of the story to us and makes it more comfortable for us."

—TIMOTHY GARTON ASH

The famous soldier-scholar T. E. Lawrence (Lawrence of Arabia) once wrote a friend: "The documents are liars. No man ever yet tried to write down the entire truth of any action in which he has been engaged."[1] Lawrence exaggerated, but he certainly had a point. Not all documents "lie," but they do not always tell the unalloyed truth either. There exists, says historian Simon Schama, a "teasing gap separating a lived event and its subsequent narration,"[2] and it is that gap which creates a treacherous problem for those who try to wring the truth out of the records of the past.

That "teasing gap" between events and how they are remembered and narrated is familiar to any close observer of courtroom testimony. Witnesses, to the dismay of judges and juries, remember events in very different ways. As historian Timothy Garton Ash notes above, "We don't simply forget; we re-remember."[3] A startling example of this occurred in an obscure village in the south of France more than four hundred years ago. The story so strains credibility that it is tempting to dismiss it as a piece of fiction; yet it is true.

The outlines of the story are quite simple. A relatively prosperous peasant, Martin Guerre, one day left his wife and child and village without explanation, and was for years what we would call a missing person. Somehow another man, Arnaud du Tilh, learned of this and, claiming that he was Martin Guerre, one day appeared to reclaim his wife, property, and place in the community. The village, after overcoming some initial suspicions, welcomed the new Martin, and, remarkably, so did his long-suffering wife, Bertrande. A few years later, after a period of apparent domestic happiness, Bertrande and members of her family charged that the new Martin was an impostor. Bertrande said she had been duped. The false Martin was arrested and tried. Just when the judges were about to rule in the imposter's favor—he was an eloquent witness in his own defense—the real Martin reappeared. The game was up, and Arnaud du Tilh was condemned by the court and executed in 1560.[4]

---

[1] Barzun and Graff, *Modern Researcher*, 50.
[2] Quoted in James Atlas, "Stranger Than Fiction," *The New York Times Magazine*, June 23, 1991, 22.
[3] Timothy Garton Ash, "On the Frontier," *New York Review of Books*, Nov. 7, 2002, 60.
[4] Natalie Zemon Davis, *The Return of Martin Guerre* (Cambridge, MA.: Harvard University Press, 1983).

Natalie Zemon Davis, one of America's (and Canada's) most respected historians, is the author of the classic study, *The Return of Martin Guerre* and was the historical adviser for the award-winning French film *Le Retour de Martin Guerre*. She is an emeritus professor at Princeton University. *Photograph by Rino Bianchi.*

The soap-opera qualities of this story are evident, and the tale has been told many times in books, plays, novels, and in an operetta. The award-winning French film, *Le Retour de Martin Guerre* (1982) and historian Natalie Zemon Davis's book, *The Return of Martin Guerre* (1983), introduced the story to modern audiences.[5] Both film and book pose the question, "how, in a time without photographs, with few portraits, without tape recorders, without fingerprinting, without identity cards, without birth certificates, with parish records still irregular—if kept at all—how did one establish a person's identity beyond doubt?"[6] The answer is that the court had to rely on eyewitness testimony. They had to ask the villagers what they remembered of the original Martin Guerre and if they thought the man who returned was the man they remembered twelve years earlier. In the first trial (there were two) about forty-five of the witnesses said that the prisoner was not Martin Guerre; thirty to forty said that "the defendant was surely Martin Guerre; they had known him since the cradle." About sixty witnesses refused to identify him one way or the other.[7]

Let this story serve as an object lesson about the nature of evidence. Even with 150 "witnesses," the court that tried the case of Martin Guerre was left uncertain of the truth. The same uncertainty accompanies events for which we have ample written documents to study. But, whatever the imperfections in the evidence, such documents along with other surviving artifacts are all we have. They are the basic raw materials of history. In this chapter we will consider the types of sources historians use to learn about the past and to write history. We will also examine some of the techniques used by the historian to evaluate and interpret the raw data of the past.

---

[5] *Sommersby* (1993) was an American adaptation loosely based on the 1982 French film. So much of the original story was changed, however, that *Sommersby* must be considered fiction, not history.
[6] Davis, 63.
[7] Davis, 67–68.

The Sources: Primary and Secondary

The problem of weighing evidence is never an easy one, but the difficulty can be eased by an appreciation of the various types of sources historians rely upon in their work.

A *primary source* (also called an original source) is a piece of evidence written or created during the period under investigation. Primary sources are the records of contemporaries who participated in, witnessed, or commented on the events you are studying. They are the documents and artifacts—letters, reports, diaries, government records, parish registers, newspapers, business ledgers, photographs, works of art, buildings, and a host of others—that make the writing and study of history possible. A note of caution: even though an eyewitness or participant writes down memories many years after the event, the commentary is still a primary source. In sum, a primary source is to the historian what a mountain is to the geologist: the surviving record of events that took place a long time ago.

A *secondary source* is an account of the period in question written after the events have taken place. Often based on primary sources, secondary sources are the books, articles, essays, and lectures through which we learn most of the history we know. Historians take the raw data found in primary sources and transform it into the written histories that attempt to explain how and why things happened as they did.[8]

The distinction between primary and secondary sources is not always as clear as the above definitions imply. For instance, newspapers are definitely primary sources for the periods in which they were published. But parts of newspapers—especially news stories and editorials—also share many characteristics with secondary sources. Very often journalists are not eyewitnesses to the events they write about. Like historians, journalists must interrogate witnesses—in this case directly—and read pertinent documents in order to construct the story, the "history," that appears in the paper.

Another problematic source is the personal memoir or autobiography written by a politician, military officer, or movie star. Such memoirs often straddle the line that separates primary from secondary sources. While memoirs and autobiographies are first-person narrations of events, their authors rarely rely totally on their memories, as the term "memoir" implies. Authors often "recollect" the events of their public life with the help of a variety of documents, or with previously published accounts of friends and colleagues. In this case the memoir writer is functioning like any other historian, so the memoir must be considered, at least in part, a secondary source.

Also confusing is the fact that many sources can be categorized either as primary or secondary *depending on the subject being studied.* An example is Charles Beard's famous book, *An Economic Interpretation of the Constitution,* published in 1913. Beard's controversial thesis was that the delegates to the Constitutional Convention in Philadelphia designed the Constitution to protect their own personal economic

---

[8] Textbooks and similar works represent a special category of "tertiary" source. Most general survey texts are not based on research into primary sources so much as they reflect the findings of a wide variety of secondary sources—that is, other history books. An author who attempted to cover American history from pre-Columbian times to the present could not in a lifetime read all the necessary primary sources. Such an author has to rely on books and articles written by other scholars (i.e., secondary sources) in order to complete the project. Thus textbooks are a step or two further removed from the original sources than are most secondary works.

interests. For scholars studying the origins of the Constitution, Beard's book is a secondary source, and its central thesis has been long debated. However, the book would be a primary source for anyone studying the ideas of Charles Beard himself. That is, if *Charles Beard and his ideas* were the subject of the study, *An Economic Interpretation of the Constitution* would be a primary source; if the origins of the Constitution were the subject, Beard's book would be a secondary source. Finally, many primary sources have been published in book form. In spite of their resemblance in form to secondary sources, these materials remain primary. Remember, the basic question to ask is: When did the materials originate? Not: When were they published or reprinted? *The Declaration of Independence* printed in the back of a textbook is still a primary source for the revolutionary period of American history, even though the textbook itself is a secondary source.

Using Primary Sources

However inadequate the surviving store of records related to a specific historical episode, so many documents and artifacts have survived (especially from the more recent centuries) that the task of historians is truly daunting. Before historians can use any body of evidence, they must thoroughly sort and sift it. Evidence is found in mixed-up bundles, with relevant and irrelevant information thrown together like kernels of grain and their husks. Only a small part of the existing evidence will be relevant to a particular investigation, and the historian must separate the wheat from the chaff.

Equally daunting is the task of coaxing the truth from the sources. Sources can be seductive or coldly aloof. They can mislead, lie, or lure you into a false sense of security. They can be written in the obscure languages or the incomprehensible jargon of the modern bureaucrat. They can lead the researcher into blind alleys, false turns, and dead ends. For all the frustrations, however, unlocking the secrets of the records of the past can be a fascinating task. The historian is the detective, the primary sources are the clues.

Since most primary sources are in written form, historians typically limit themselves to the study of that segment of the past for which we have written records. (The study of preliterate or prehistoric cultures and societies is the domain of cultural anthropologists and archeologists.) Not all primary sources, however, are documents. Remember our definition: A primary source is something that came into existence during the period that the historian is studying. From this perspective, just about anything that has survived (including your Aunt Edna) is a potential primary source—buildings, tools, works of art, weapons, coins, and, more recently, photographs, films, and recordings.

Not all types of written primary evidence are equally "primary." That is, some primary sources are inherently less useful and less trustworthy than others. Admittedly newspapers are indispensable primary sources, but we have seen that press accounts are frequently written by journalists who are not themselves eyewitnesses to the stories they write. Journalists, like historians, have to piece together stories from many sources, and such stories are often somewhat "distanced" from the events they describe. Also problematical are the memoirs and autobiographies we discussed above. They are often written years after the events they describe; and vanity, personal bias, or failing memory can influence the tale an author has to tell. Even someone who is determined to provide a balanced and accurate account rarely remembers the same event in precisely the same way that someone else does.

Often the most revealing sources are those that were never intended to be made public. "The most primary source of all," says historian Barbara Tuchman, "is unpublished material: private letters and diaries or the reports, orders and messages in government archives."[9] But even here the situation is ambiguous because public figures are now very conscious that history will judge them. Thus, what they write or say often reflects their desire to leave a positive "legacy." (You will find more on these sources later in the chapter.)

Primary Sources and Critical Method

The most challenging task of the historian-detective is to draw testimony from the records of the past. Here the historian has two aims, neither of them simple: (1) to determine if a source is authentic and, (2) to establish the meaning and believability

---

[9] Tuchman, *Practicing History*, 19.

Deposition of Captain John Parker concerning the Battle of Lexington, April 25, 1775. *U.S. National Archives, Record Group 360, ARC Identifier 595246.* See Set A, Exercise 4.

of the contents. The first is accomplished through external criticism; the second through internal criticism.

External criticism, in the words of one historian, "authenticates evidence and establishes texts in the most accurate possible form."[10] Many historical records lack precise dates or correct attribution (i.e., who wrote them). Many texts, for various reasons, are inaccurate, and forgeries are not uncommon. Highly specialized techniques are required to authenticate documents and artifacts: carbon dating, linguistic analysis, chemical analysis, and the like. Extensive knowledge of the period in question is also a prerequisite. Beginners rarely have either the background knowledge or the specialized skills for such criticism, so we need not dwell on this aspect of critical method. For present purposes, assume that the documents in the exercises and the sources you might be using in a class are authentic.

Once the authenticity of a document has been established, the historian faces the far more important challenge of reading and interpreting the contents. This is called *internal criticism,* and the techniques involved are much less mysterious. More than anything else, the process requires a healthy skepticism. We have an innate tendency to believe anything if it is written down, and, the older the document or more ornate the script, the more we tend to believe it. Therefore, it is important to remind ourselves that our venerable ancestors could lie, shade the truth, or make a mistake, just as we can.

Documents do not reveal their secrets easily. You must learn to question the evidence like an attorney in a courtroom—from different angles, from different perspectives, relentlessly, suspiciously. Even an account written by an individual of unimpeachable honesty can be marred by error and half-truth. What sort of questions should you ask of the evidence? Below is a partial list of some of the most important.[11]

1. What exactly does the document mean?

Often the literal meaning differs from the real meaning. Diplomatic communications, for example, are notorious for veiling harsh international disagreements in extremely polite language. Diplomats are trained to phrase messages in such a restrained fashion that even an impending war can be made to sound no more threatening than a neighborly disagreement over the backyard fence. At one point in the 1930s the Soviet [Russian] dictator Josef Stalin wrote to the British Ambassador: "The Soviet Union would take all measures to prevent the reestablishment of the old balance of power in Europe." As diplomat/historian Henry Kissinger comments, "In diplomatic language, 'all measures' usually embraces the threat of war."[12] Therefore, the historian must become familiar with the conventions of diplomatic correspondence in order to understand the real meaning of the dispatches.

Another problem facing the historian is that words can change meaning from one age to the next. A nineteenth-century reference to a "gay" person means something quite different from a similar reference in twenty-first century. Likewise, the word "enthusiasm" meant something quite different in the eighteenth century, when the

---

[10] R. J. Shafer, ed., *A Guide to Historical Method* (Homewood, IL.: Dorsey Press, 1969), 100.
[11] These questions are based on those printed in Shafer, *Guide to Historical Method,* 137–38.
[12] Henry Kissinger, *Diplomacy* (New York: Simon and Schuster, 1994). 359.

connotations were largely pejorative. To discover these sorts of differences, you have to know as much as possible about the cultural and political context of the period you are studying.

2. *How well-situated was the author to observe or record the events in question?*

Here there are a number of subsidiary questions. What was the author's physical location? Was he or she a direct eyewitness or did the information come from someone else? What was the author's *social ability* to observe? That is, might the person's social or economic position in the society have influenced *how* he or she observed an event or situation? A middle-class English woman, for example, would view the agitations of the early-twentieth-century suffragettes quite differently than the male Members of Parliament, who were convinced that women lacked the capacity to be trusted with the right to vote. Finally, did the witness have specialized knowledge that might enhance the credibility of the testimony? A lawyer's report of a murder trial might be far more insightful than that of a casual observer in the audience. On the other hand, the casual observer might be able to report on things the lawyer missed.

3. *When, how, and to whom was the report made?*

Obviously, the longer the time between the event and the report, the greater the chance a witness's memory will play tricks. In addition, you should ponder the intended purpose of the report. An army officer reporting to a superior may tell what the commander wants to hear rather than a more disappointing truth. The number of casualties inflicted by American soldiers on the enemy during the Vietnam War (1961–75) was constantly exaggerated as field commanders turned in unrealistically high "body counts" to please their superiors at headquarters.

4. *Is there bias that must be accounted for?*

Personal bias can be the enemy of truth on two levels. It is, of course, common for a piece of testimony to be colored by an author's personal beliefs and convictions. In the same way, however, your own biases can often blind you to much that the sources reveal. Knowing as much as possible about the person who left the account will help you recognize and compensate for the first sort of bias. Knowing yourself is the only way to insure that your own biases don't get in the way of understanding.

5. *What specialized information is needed to interpret the source?*

Many times you will have to look up names, places, dates, and technical terms to get the full meaning of a statement.

6. *Do the reported actions seem probable in the light of informed common sense?*

Here the significant words are "probable" and "informed common sense." We can never get absolutely conclusive answers for many questions in history. The test of the believability of a given piece of testimony is the inherent probability of its being true. The issue is not whether a version of events is possible (just about anything is at least possible) but whether, given all the evidence, it is *probable.*

In this process the historian's most important tool is simple common sense, seasoned with appropriate relevant information. In the end, the credibility of testimony must be judged in the light of our understanding of how people behave. But there are pitfalls. Our "common sense" may deceive us unless we also have all the special knowledge necessary to make it work. Reports of eighteenth-century armies marching great distances in short periods of time violate our "common sense" notion of what infantrymen can accomplish. Yet such reports are too numerous to have been fabricated. Clearly, we must supplement our native intelligence with solid information.

7. Is there corroborating testimony?

No document can stand alone. Even asking all of the preceding questions can't insure that you won't be fooled. You must seek other witnesses—what lawyers call corroborating testimony—to reinforce and substantiate the first account. Just as corroboration is necessary in the courtroom, it is essential to good history.

This list is not definitive. When evaluating evidence you have to be infinitely imaginative and critically alert. The more you know about the period in question, human behavior, and the workings of the natural world, the better off you will be.

Inference and Historical Method

We have seen that there are always gaps in the historical record, and historical documents cannot speak for themselves. Even when there is a great deal of evidence on a specific topic or period, we cannot always find definitive answers to many historical questions—especially the more interesting ones. Did President Harry Truman really have to drop the atomic bomb on Japan in order to bring World War II to a speedy end? Was the assassination of John F. Kennedy the work of a lone assassin or a conspiracy? Could the United States have won the Vietnam War? Was President George W. Bush's decision to invade Iraq justified? These are questions historians still debate, in spite of the survival of mountains of evidence related to each of them.

Such doubt is inevitable in history because historians cannot just "lift" the answers off the pages of the documents they read. In order to move from the "facts" contained in the records to the explanatory generalizations that constitute the heart of written history, historians must make *inferences.* Inferences are conclusions or deductions based on evidence, and, even though inferences are often "notoriously unreliable,"[13] the making of legitimate inferences is central to all historical reasoning.

Inference-making skills are especially valuable when you attempt to learn things by reading between the lines, that is, when you try to find out things that the records weren't intended to reveal. As Arthur Marwick argues, "a primary source is most valuable when the purpose for which it was compiled is at the furthest remove from the purpose of the historian."[14] Italian merchants during the Renaissance period (ca. 1300–1600), for example, were pioneers in developing modern accounting practices.

---

[13] Robin Winks, ed., *The Historian As Detective* (New York: Harper Colophon, 1970), xvi.
[14] Arthur Marwick, *The Nature of History* (New York: Knopf, 1971), 177.

They created account books to keep track of their debtors and creditors. Historians, however, can use these records to learn many fascinating things about the evolution of modern banking and business techniques, the state of the Italian economy in the fifteenth century, or the ways in which certain segments of the population earned a living. These are things the original documents were never meant to communicate.[15] Historians, then, cannot function without making inferential "leap[s] of faith,"[16] and because of that, historical accounts will always contain a mixture of the speculative, the probable, and the things we know for certain.

EXERCISES

SET A   *Exercise 1 — Primary Sources*

As noted on page 141, historians make a distinction between primary and secondary sources. Below are sources you might consult if you were preparing a paper on President Harry S. Truman's controversial decision to drop the atomic bomb on Japan at the end of World War II. Truman had to make the decision shortly after he unexpectedly became president in April 1945. The first atomic bomb was tested in New Mexico on July 16, 1945, and less than three weeks later, on August 6, another bomb was dropped on the Japanese city of Hiroshima. In the spaces provided indicate whether the sources should be classified "Primary" ("**P**") or "Secondary" ("**S**"). If you think a source shares both primary and secondary characteristics, write "**PS.**" The dates in parentheses indicate the year(s) of publication.

_____ 1. Harry S. Truman, *Memoirs,* Vol. I, Year of Decisions [1945] (1955).

_____ 2. Margaret Truman, *Harry S. Truman* (1973). [Margaret was Harry Truman's daughter, born February 17, 1924.]

_____ 3. Herbert Feis, *The Atomic Bomb and the End of World War II* (1966; orig. 1961).

_____ 4. Leslie R. Groves, *Now It Can Be Told* (1964). [Groves was the commanding general of the bomb project in New Mexico.]

_____ 5. U.S. Atomic Energy Committee, *In the Matter of J. Robert Oppenheimer: Transcript of Hearing Before Personnel Security Board* (1954). [Oppenheimer was one of the scientists who built the bomb.]

_____ 6. Barton J. Bernstein, "The Atomic Bombings Reconsidered," *Foreign Affairs* (January/February, 1995).

_____ 7. *Presidential Papers: Harry S. Truman,* 1945, I.

_____ 8. *The New York Times,* 1945.

_____ 9. Joseph M. Siracusa, editor, *The American Diplomatic Revolution: A Documentary History of the Cold War, 1941–47* (1977).

---

[15] Another example of creative inference-making can be found in *Salem Possessed* (Cambridge, MA., 1974), by historians Paul Boyer and Stephen Nissenbaum. They used detailed town plans and income records to show how the Salem witch trials, in part, grew out of social, economic, and geographic divisions within the community. Boyer and Nissenbaum saw in these relatively sterile and "uninteresting" records things that the original record keepers had no intention of revealing. They milked unintended testimony from documents created for dramatically different purposes.

[16] Winks, *Historian as Detective*, xv.

_____ 10. Henry L. Stimson, "The Decision to Use the Atomic Bomb," *Harper's Magazine* (February, 1947). [Stimson was Secretary of War and Chairman of the Interim Committee on the Atomic Bomb.]

_____ 11. Alice Kimball Smith, "The Decision to Use the Atomic Bomb, 1944–45," *Bulletin of the Atomic Scientists* (October, 1958).

SET A   *Exercise 2 — Types of Primary Sources*

There are many types of primary sources, and each type has its characteristic strengths and weaknesses. This exercise requires that you use your imagination (actually your critical intelligence) since we have not discussed the potential values and hazards inherent in each type of primary source. Below, indicate what you think *might be the potential weaknesses* of each type of evidence. Accept as a given here that each type of source can be extremely valuable depending, of course, on the topic being investigated. For this exercise we are asking you to consider the potential traps that might await the unwary researcher who attempts to use a particular piece of evidence. In what ways might each of the following pieces of evidence mislead the researcher? We have answered the first item to give you a start.

1.   Memoirs/Autobiographies:

Sample Comments: *Possible weaknesses include (a) potential bias on the part of the author (i.e., the author is writing about his or her own life), and (b) potential memory lapses on the part of the author.* (Note: A key word here is "potential." These are potential problems since an author may be quite objective and accurate, or biased but correct. Whether the memoir is trustworthy or not is a judgment that needs to be made only after you have done further research to corroborate or question what a memoir writer says.)

Possible weaknesses

2. Newspapers: _____

_____

3. Political Speeches: _____

_____

4. Public Opinion Polls: _____

_____

5. Diplomatic Communications (from one government to another): _____

_____

_____

6. Records of a Government Agency:

_____

_____

SET A   *Exercise 3 — Inference*

Inference, as previously noted, is a major tool in the interpretation of evidence. Because the questions that interest historians are often quite different from the objectives of those who created various pieces of primary evidence, historians constantly have to make logical deductions that may not be provable in any absolute sense.

Below are a number of short statements followed by some possible inferences. After reading a statement, indicate for each inference whether it is a "**V**alid" inference ("**V**"), an invalid or "**F**alse" inference ("**F**"), or an inference for which we have Insufficient **D**ata ("**ID**") to determine its validity or invalidity. If you label an inference "**F**" (False/Invalid), indicate your reasons on the lines provided at the end of each unit. *For an inference to be labeled "False" (F) there must be clear evidence in the passage that contradicts the inference.*

For the purposes of this exercise assume that the statements reflect the best judgment of the speaker or writer. Also assume that for any statement of fact there exists corroborating evidence. The first unit is already completed as an example.

A. Statement of Dr. Victor C. Vaughan comparing his medical experiences during the Spanish-American War with those during World War I (1914–18; U.S. participation, 1917–18). Quoted in Paul Starr, *The Social Transformation of American Medicine* (1982).

> I served in the war with Spain in 1898, and I went time and time again to a division officer and made certain requests or offered certain advice. As a rule, I was snubbed and told by action, if not by words, that I was only a medical officer, and that I had no right to make any suggestions, and it was impudent of me to do so.
>
> The commanding general at Chickamauga [a Spanish-American War army camp], when we had an increasing number of cases of typhoid fever, would every day ostentatiously ride up to a well which had been condemned and drink of this water to show his contempt. But in the late war [World War I] I had a different experience. I never went to a line officer with a recommendation but that he said, 'Doctor, it will be done. . . .'

Possible Inferences (V=Valid; F=Invalid/False; ID=Insufficient Data):

___V___ 1. Doctors were not treated with much respect in the military during the Spanish-American War.

___V___ 2. There was a change in the attitude of the military towards medical doctors between 1898 and 1918.

___ID___ 3. Dr. Vaughan was a good physician.

___F___ 4. The commanding general at Chickamauga camp believed that the well water caused typhoid. (See comments below.)

___ID___ 5. Typhoid was not as serious a problem in World War I, as it was in the Spanish-American War.

Comments

```
Remember, you are to assume that corroborating evidence exists for
statements of fact made in each excerpt. 1 and 2 are, then, valid
inferences. We labeled 3 and 5 "ID" ("Insufficient Data") because,
though perhaps true, neither inference is addressed at all in the ex-
cerpt. Number 4 is false in that the general's behavior (drinking the
well water) suggests he believed no such thing.
```

B. A soldier's account of his experiences in the Vietnam War. From Philip Caputo, *A Rumor of War* (1978).

To keep the troops from becoming complacent, the company gunnery sergeant, a broad-chested cheerful man named Marquand, would send them to their positions with prophecies of impending attacks. 'They're gonna hit us tonight. I gar-untee you. We're gonna get hit.' But nothing happened. Our role in the alleged counteroffensive was limited to making detailed reports of whatever firing we heard forward of our respective platoon sectors. I am not sure who did what with that information, but I think it helped the battalion intelligence officer plot what is known in the jargon as a 'sitmap'—a map showing the dispositions of friendly and enemy forces.

Possible Inferences:

_____ 1. Boredom was a problem for many soldiers in Caputo's unit.

_____ 2. The information collected for the "sitmap" was used for planning future military operations.

_____ 3. Caputo thought the counteroffensive accomplished little of value.

_____ 4. Sergeant Marquand was well liked by his troops.

_____ 5. This unit experienced a lot of action during this period.

Reasons for "F" Labels:

_____

_____

C. Journalist Henry Mayhew's account of "Shilling Day" (i.e., bargain admission day) at London's Great Exhibition of 1851. The Great Exhibition was the first "world's fair." From E. Royston Pike, *Golden Times: Human Documents of the Victorian Age* (1972).

And inside the Great Exhibition the scene is equally different from that of the first week or two. The nave is no longer filled with elegant and inert loungers—lolling on seats, and evidently come there to be seen rather than to see. Those who are now to be found there [the "shilling folk" or workers and their families] have come to look at the Exhibition, and not to make an exhibition of themselves. There is no air of display about them—no social falsity—all is plain unvarnished truth. . . . The shilling folk may be an 'inferior' class of visitors, but at least, they know something about the works of industry, and what they do not know, they have come to learn. . . .

For many days before the 'shilling people' were admitted to the building, the great topic of conversation was the probable behavior of the people. Would they come sober? Will they destroy things? . . . But they have surpassed in decorum the hopes of their wellwishers.

Possible Inferences:

_____ 1. Mid-nineteenth-century Britain was a society marked by significant class divisions.
_____ 2. At the time this passage was written there was a widespread fear of class conflict in Britain.
_____ 3. The people who first attended the Exhibition were members of the upper classes and they were not especially interested in the exhibits.
_____ 4. At least some members of the upper classes thought better of members of "inferior" classes after their good behavior on shilling day.
_____ 5. Mayhew's statement is evidence that the gap between classes was becoming narrower in the 1850s.
_____ 6. There was no vandalism at all during the entire run of the Great Exhibition.

Reasons for "F" labels:

_____

_____

D. Recollection of Ben Simpson, a former slave. From B. A. Botkin, ed. *Lay My Burden Down* (1945).

Boss, I's born in Georgia, in Norcross, and I's ninety years old. My father's name was Roger Stielszen, and my mother's name was Betty. Massa Earl Stielszen captures them in Africa and brung them to Georgia. He got kilt, and my sister and me went to his son. His son was a killer. He got in trouble there in Georgia and got him two good-stepping hosses and the covered wagon. Then he chains all the slaves round the necks and fastens the chains to the hosses and makes them walk all the way to Texas. My mother and my sister had to walk. Emma was my sister. . . .

Massa have a great, long whip platted out of rawhide, and when [someone] fall behind or give out, he hit him with that whip. . . . Mother, she give out on the way, 'bout the line of Texas. Her feet got raw and bleeding, and her legs swoll plumb out of shape. Then Massa, he just take out he gun and shot her. . . . Boss, you know that man, he wouldn't bury mother, just leave her laying where he shot her at. You know, then there wasn't no law 'gainst killing . . . slaves.

Possible Inferences:

_____ 1. The events related above occurred before the end of the Civil War.
_____ 2. Ben Simpson could read and write.
_____ 3. The interviewer was an African American.
_____ 4. Ben Simpson's father had died before the family was moved to Texas.
_____ 5. Ben Simpson changed his name after the slaves were freed.

Reasons for "F" labels:

_____

_____

The First Blow for Liberty. Battle of Lexington, April 1775. *Copy of a print by A.H. Ritchie after F.O.C. Darley. John K. Hillers Collection, U.S. National Archives, ARC Identifier 559250.*

SET A   *Exercise 4 — Analysis of Evidence*

Lexington Green, April 19, 1775
The first shots of the American Revolution were fired on April 19, 1775. At Lexington Green colonial militiamen confronted British troops on their way to destroy colonial military stores in nearby Concord. Shots rang out and military hostilities began.

Since neither the British nor the American colonists wished to appear the aggressor, both sides denied firing the first shot. Below are five brief accounts of the event.

In this exercise your task is not to determine who fired the first shot, but to examine the reports with the critical eye of the historian. Instead you should try to note any facts about each piece of evidence that would help you assess its believability. Make pertinent observations concerning the authorship, circumstances of composition, content, and potential believability of each piece of evidence. To do so you should ask of each piece of evidence the following questions:

1. Are there any problems in understanding the literal meaning of the document, or parts of the document? That is, are there words you have to look up? Phrases you don't understand? Etc.
2. Who made the report, and under what circumstances?
3. When was the report made?
4. How well placed was the witness to observe and record the event?
5. Is bias present? (ideological, class, personal?)
6. Might your own biases influence your interpretation of the evidence?
7. Is specialized information necessary to understand the document? If so, what information is required?

For a discussion of these questions, review pages 144–146.

1. The official deposition of the commander of the colonial militia, John Parker:[17]

Lexington, April 25, 1775

I, John Parker, of lawful age, and commander of the Militia in Lexington, do testify and declare, that on the nineteenth instant, in the morning, about one of the clock, being informed that there were a number of Regular [British] Officers riding up and down the road, stopping and insulting people as they passed the road, and also was informed that a number of Regular Troops were on their march from Boston, in order to take the Province Stores at Concord, ordered our Militia to meet on the common in said Lexington, to consult what to do, and concluded not to be discovered, nor meddle or make with said Regular Troops (if they should approach) unless they should insult us; and upon their sudden approach, I immediately ordered our Militia to disperse and not to fire. Immediately said Troops made their appearance, and rushed furiously, fired upon and killed eight of our party, without receiving any provocation therefor from us.

John Parker

[17] Excerpts 1 and 2 are taken from the Peter Force, ed., *American Archives* (New York: Johnson Reprint Corp., 1972), Fourth Series, II, 491. Excerpt 3 is from Peter S. Bennett, ed., *What Happened on Lexington Green* (Reading MA.: Addison-Wesley, 1970), 16–17. Excerpts 4 and 5 are from Allen French, *General Gage's Informers* (New York: Greenwood Press, 1968), 53–54; 55.

Analysis:

Sample Comment: *Parker was an American and might tend to blame the British for firing the first shot.* (Note: This is only one of a number of possible comments you might make on this passage. Add some observations of your own. See the seven guide questions above.)

_____

_____

_____

_____

2. Deposition of John Robbins, colonial militiaman:

Lexington, April 24, 1775

I John Robbins . . . do testify and say, that . . . the Company under the command of Captain John Parker being drawn up (sometime before sunrise) on the green or common, and I being in the front rank, there suddenly appeared a number of the King's Troops, about a thousand, as I thought, at the distance of about sixty or seventy yards from us, huzzaing and on a quick pace towards us, with three officers in their front on horseback, and on full gallop towards us; the foremost of which cried, "Throw down your arms, ye villains, ye rebels;" upon which said Company dispersing, the foremost of the three officers ordered their men, saying "Fire, by God, fire; at which moment we received a very heavy and close fire from them, at which instant, being wounded, I fell, and several of our men were shot dead by one volley. Captain Parker's men, I believe, had not then fired a gun.

Analysis: _____

_____

_____

_____

3. Robert Douglass, who had been at Lexington, swore to the following deposition on May 3, 1827:

In about fifteen minutes after we entered the tavern, a person came to the door and said the British were within half a mile. I then heard an officer (who I afterwards learned was Captain Parker) call his drummer and order him to beat to arms. I paraded with the Lexington company between the meeting-house and the tavern, and then marched to the common near the road that leads to Bedford; there we were ordered to load our guns. Some of the company observed, "There are so few of us, it would be folly to stand here." Captain Parker replied, "The first man who offers to run shall be shot down." The Lexington company began to break off on the left wing, and soon all dispersed. I think no American was killed or wounded by the first fire of the British, unless Captain Parker might have been. No one of Captain Parker's company fired on the British, to my knowledge, that morning, and I think I should have known it, had they fired. I knew but two men of the Lexington company, and I never heard any person say that the Americans fired on the British that morning at Lexington.

After the British marched toward Concord, I saw eight men who had been killed. . . .

Analysis: _____

_____

_____

4. British commander Major John Pitcairn's official report to General Gage:

I gave directions to the Troops to move forward, but on no account to Fire, or even attempt it without orders; when I arrived at the end of the Village, I observed drawn up upon a Green near 200 of the Rebels; when I came within about One Hundred Yards of them, they began to File off towards some stone Walls on our Right Flank—The Light Infantry observing this, ran after them—I instantly called to the Soldiers not to fire, but to surround and disarm them, and after several repetitions of those positive Orders to the men, not to Fire &c—some of the Rebels who had jumped over the Wall, Fired Four or Five Shott at the Soldiers, which wounded a man of the Tenth, and my Horse was Wounded in two places, from some quarter or other, and at the same time several Shott were fired from a Meeting House on o[u]r Left—upon this, without any order or Regularity, the Light Infantry began a scattered Fire, and continued in that situation for some little time, contrary to the repeated orders both of me and the officers that were present—It will be needless to mention what happened after, as I suppose Col. Smith hath given a particular account of it. I am sir

Boston Camp
26th April, 1775

Your most humble Servant,
John Pitcairn

Analysis: _____

_____

_____

5. Personal account of British ensign Jeremy Lister written in 1782:

> However to the best of my recollection about 4 oClock in the Morning being the 19th of April the 5 front [companies] was ordered to Load which we did, about half an hour after we found that precaution had been necessary, for we had then to unload again [i.e., fire] . . . and then was the first Blood drawn in this American Rebellion. It was at Lexington when we saw one of their [Companies] drawn up in regular order Major Pitcairn of the Marines second in Command call'd to them to disperce, but their not seeming willing he desired us to mind our space which we did when they gave us a fire they run of[f] to get behind a wall. we had one man wounded of our [Company] in the Leg his Name was Johnson also Major Pitcairns Horse was shot in the Flank we return'd their Salute, and before we proceeded on our March from Lexington I believe we Kill'd and Wounded either 7 or 8 men.

Analysis: _____

_____

_____

For Discussion:
1. Which pieces of evidence do you find most convincing? Which do you find least convincing? Why?
2. On which "facts" does there seem to be general agreement?
3. What are the central points of disagreement?

SET A *Exercise 5 — Essay*

Based on the evidence above, write a paragraph-length account of the confrontation on Lexington Green. In your paragraph take a position on the question at issue: Who fired first? In your paragraph you might want to help the reader understand (1) what can be established beyond doubt (assume the excerpts above are all the sources you have available to you), (2) what is *probable* given the above evidence, and (3) what cannot be established with certainty. In your account, include direct quotations from the documents. Read Writing Capsule 6 (next page) before you begin.

WRITING CAPSULE 6

Integrating Quotations

Since writing is a way for you to express your ideas, you should use your own words to paraphrase your sources. Quotations should be used sparingly. Some use of quotations, however, especially from primary sources, is certainly justified. Letting contemporaries speak on the issues being examined can help bring history to life and help you convince a reader that your interpretation of the evidence is correct.

If quotations are to enhance the impact of your writing they have to be integrated smoothly into the narrative. They should not hang alone, wrenched out of their context. Therefore, always preface a quotation with a "signal phrase" that identifies the author and prepares the reader for the quotation.[18] For example, a sentence in the Exercise 5 essay might look something like this:

According to John Parker, commander of the colonial militia, "upon their sudden approach, I immediately ordered. . . ." (The signal phrase appears before the quotation marks.)

• If you leave out sections of the quotation, indicate the omitted words with an ellipsis (three periods separated by spaces). The remaining fragment must make sense and fit grammatically with the rest of the passage. Example:

Parker testified that on April 19 he decided not to "meddle or make with said Regular Troops . . . unless they should insult us; . . . . (The fourth period is exactly that: a period.)

[18] See Hacker, *A Writer's Reference*, 5th ed., Section MLA-3.

SET B *Exercise 1 — Primary Sources*

As noted on page 141, historians make a distinction between primary and secondary sources. Below are sources you might consult if you were preparing a paper on the origins of World War II in Europe. Adolf Hitler became Germany's Chancellor in 1933 and war in Europe broke out in September 1939, when Germany invaded Poland, and Britain and France declared war to stop this latest of Germany's aggressions. In the spaces provided indicate whether the sources should be classified "Primary" ("P") or "Secondary" ("S"). If you think a source shares both primary and secondary characteristics, write "PS." The dates in parentheses indicate the year(s) of publication. Remember, your hypothetical paper deals with the *origins of the war*, not the war itself.

_____   1. *Documents on German Foreign Policy, 1918–1945*, Series D, Vols. I–VII (September, 1937–1939).

_____   2. Gerhard Weinberg, *Germany, Hitler, and World War II* (1995).

_____   3. Konrad Heiden, *Hitler* (1936).

_____   4. *The Goebbels Diaries*, edited by Louis P. Lochner (1948). [Joseph Goebbels was one of Hitler's original followers and became Nazi propaganda minister in 1933.]

_____ 5. A. J. P. Taylor, *The Origins of the Second World War* (1961).
_____ 6. *The Speeches of Adolph Hitler, 1922–29*, edited by Norman H. Baynes, 2
           vols. (1942).
_____ 7. Hugh Trevor Roper, *The Last Days of Hitler* (1947).
_____ 8. *The Times* (London), 1933–39.
_____ 9. Adolf Hitler, *Mein Kampf* [My Struggle], 1939.
_____ 10. Winston Churchill, *The Second World War*, Vol. I, *The Gathering Storm*
           (1948). [Churchill was a member of the British Parliament when the
           war broke out and in 1940 became Britain's prime minister.]

SET B   *Exercise 2 — Types of Primary Sources*

See Exercise 2 in Set A.

SET B   *Exercise 3 — Inference*

Inference, as we noted, is a major tool in the interpretation of evidence. Because the questions that interest historians are often quite different from the objectives of those who created various pieces of primary evidence, historians constantly have to make logical deductions that may not be provable in any absolute sense.

Below are a number of short statements followed by some possible inferences. After reading a statement, indicate for each inference whether it is a "**Valid**" inference ("**V**"), an invalid or "**False**" inference ("**F**"), or an inference for which we have **Insuf-ficient Data** ("**ID**") to determine its validity or invalidity. If you label an inference "F" (False/Invalid), indicate your reasons on the lines provided at the end of each unit. *For an inference to be labeled "False" (F) there must be clear evidence in the passage that contradicts the inference.*

For the purposes of this exercise assume that the statements reflect the best judgment of the speaker or writer. Also assume that for any statement of fact there exists corroborating evidence. For a completed sample see Item A, Set A, Exercise 3, pages 149–150.

A. *Declaration of Sentiments* from the women who met at the Seneca Falls Conven-tion in 1848. (Reprinted in David Burner, et al., eds., *America Through the Looking Glass*, Vol. I, Prentice-Hall, 1974, 280–81.)

> When, in the course of human events it becomes necessary for one portion of the family of man to assume among the people of the earth a position different from that which they have hitherto occupied, but one to which the laws of nature and of nature's God entitle them, a decent respect to the opinions of mankind requires that they should declare the causes that impel them to such a course.
>
> We hold these truths to be self-evident: that all men and women are created equal; that they are endowed by their Creator with certain inalienable rights; . . .
>
> The history of mankind is a history of repeated injuries and usurpations on the part of man toward woman, having in direct object the establishment of an absolute tyranny over her. To prove this, let facts be submitted to a candid world. [There follows a specific list of grievances.]

* * *

In entering upon the great work before us, we anticipate no small amount of misconception, misrepresentation, and ridicule; but we shall use every instrumentality within our power to effect our object. We shall employ agents, circulate tracts, petition the State and National legislatures, and endeavor to enlist the pulpit and press in our behalf.

Possible Inferences:

_____ 1. The authors of this document probably were middle- and upper-class women.

_____ 2. The women who wrote this were extreme radicals who were willing to resort to violence to achieve their ends.

_____ 3. The authors were familiar with the events of the American Revolution.

_____ 4. Political activism among women was unusual at this time.

_____ 5. This protest resulted in a number of important reforms.

Reasons for "F" labels:

_____

_____

_____

B. General Dwight Eisenhower's reflections on his World War II experiences. From Dwight Eisenhower, *Crusade in Europe,* (1948).

Except during World War I, the U.S. public has habitually looked upon Europe's quarrels as belonging to Europe alone. For this reason every American soldier coming to Britain was almost certain to consider himself a privileged crusader, sent there to help Britain out of a hole. He would expect to be treated as such. On the other hand, the British public looked upon itself as one of saviors of democracy, particularly because, for an entire year, it had stood alone as the unbreakable opponent of Nazism and the European Axis. Failure to understand this attitude would of course have unfortunate results.

Possible Inferences:

_____ 1. Eisenhower feared U.S. and British troops would not get along.

_____ 2. Eisenhower feared that arrogance in American troops would create conflicts with the British public.

_____ 3. Eisenhower saw no reason why Americans and Britons could not get along well.

_____ 4. Eisenhower had studied American history at some time in his life.

_____ 5. There were many conflicts between British troops and American troops during the latter stages of World War II.

Reasons for "F" labels:

_____

_____

C. Robert Conquest's account of a conversation with a Russian he met in St. Petersburg. From Robert Conquest, *Reflections on a Ravaged Century* (New York: W. W. Norton, 2000).

> A Russian in that city once said to the present writer, in late Soviet times [probably the 1980s]:
>
> "Our roads are bad."
>
> ". . . Yes. Why is that?"
>
> "It's our weather—an isotherm [temperature boundary] runs down the Finnish border."
>
> "And seriously?"
>
> "They are built by the state."
>
> "Yes, but we have roads in England which were built by the Roman state nearly two thousand years ago, and some of them are still sound."
>
> "Ah, but then the centurion would check that the six layers of stone had been laid down. Here, the inspector asks the foreman if they have been laid down and is answered with a bottle of vodka."

Possible Inferences:

_____ 1. The author is an American.
_____ 2. The Russian blames the shoddy state of Russian roads on the weather.
_____ 3. The Russian is a member of a government bureaucracy.
_____ 4. The author thinks that corruption was a serious problem in Russia during the Soviet era.
_____ 5. The author is a historian.

Reasons for "F" labels:

_____

_____

D. A scholar's statistical summary of the role of women in American medicine in the nineteenth century. From Paul Starr, *The Social Transformation of American Medicine* (1982).

> By 1893–94, women represented 10 percent or more of the students at 19 coeducational medical schools. Between 1880 and 1900, the percentage of doctors who were women increased nationally from 2.8 to 5.6 percent. In some cities the proportion of women was considerably higher: 18.2 percent of doctors in Boston, 19.3 percent in Minneapolis, 13.8 percent in San Francisco. With more than 7,000 women physicians at the turn of the century, the United States was far ahead of England, which had just 258, and France, which had only 95.

Possible Inferences:

_____ 1. In the United States a higher percentage of women studied medicine than in western Europe during the twenty years after 1880.

_____ 2. Women had an easier time becoming doctors in the United States because women's rights were more widely recognized in America than in Europe.

_____ 3. American women were smarter than European women.

_____ 4. A lower percentage of American women was studying medicine in the United States in the 1970s than in 1900.

_____ 5. More women could study medicine in the United States (as opposed to Europe) because there were more medical schools in the United States.

Reasons for "F" labels:

_____

_____

SET B   *Exercise 4 — Analysis of Evidence*

The Kent State Incident, May 4, 1970

One of the most tragic and controversial events in Vietnam era America was the violent confrontation between the Ohio National Guard and a large group of students at Kent State University on May 4, 1970. On that day four students were killed and nine wounded. What exactly happened at Kent State, and why, will never be known with absolute certainty. In spite of reams of testimony, Kent State remains a highly controversial subject.

The late 1960's were a time of increasing unrest on America's college campuses. The Vietnam War spurred student protests all over the country, and radical student political groups (like the SDS—Students for a Democratic Society) proliferated on many campuses. Student outrage over the U.S. failure to get out of Vietnam peaked when President Richard Nixon announced, on April 30, 1970, that he had ordered U.S. troops into Cambodia, thus apparently expanding the war.

The next four days were marked by escalating student unrest on the campus of Kent State University and in the town of Kent itself. On Friday, May 1, there were disorders in the city; on Saturday a group of students burned the campus ROTC building and the authorities requested troops from the National Guard; on Sunday the first confrontations between the Guard and the students took place; on Monday, the fateful day, the accumulated tensions climaxed with the killings that shocked and aroused the nation.

How could such a thing happen? This question led to newspaper investigations, grand jury proceedings, civil suits, the creation of a government commission on student unrest, and many books and articles. It is not our purpose to answer that question. But by examining some of the eyewitness testimony we can get a better idea of how the historian "questions" evidence. The evidence below relates to one very specific question that many investigators tried to answer after the shootings: was the National Guard endangered by the student mob on May 4? Was the Guard justified in firing at the students in self-defense?

In this exercise your task is not to determine whether or not the students threatened the National Guard. Instead you should try to note any facts about each piece of evidence that would help you assess its believability. Make pertinent observations concerning the authorship, circumstances of composition, content, and potential credibility of each piece of testimony. Use the seven questions on pages 144–146 as a basis for your analysis.

The Evidence

1. Statement of General Robert Canterbury, Assistant Adjutant General of the Ohio National Guard, to the President's Commission on Campus Unrest, August 25, 1970. (From *The Report of the President's Commission on Campus Unrest, 1970*, 269–70.)

As the troop formation reached the area of the Pagoda near Taylor Hall, the mob located on the right flank in front of Taylor Hall and in the Prentice Hall parking lot charged our right flank, throwing rocks, yelling obscenities and threats, 'Kill the pigs,' 'Stick the pigs.' The attitude of the crowd at this point was menacing and vicious.

The troops were being hit by rocks. I saw Major Jones hit in the stomach by a large brick, a guardsman to the right and rear of my position was hit by a large rock and fell to the ground. During this movement, practically all of the guardsmen were hit by missiles of various kinds. Guardsmen on the right flank were in serious danger of bodily harm and death as the mob continued to charge. I felt that, in view of the extreme danger to the troops at this point, that they were justified in firing.

Analysis: _____

_____

_____

2. Observations of Charles Brill, a Kent State professor, as reported in *Time*, May 18, 1970.

"They are shooting blanks—they are shooting blanks," thought Kent State Journalism Professor Charles Brill, who nevertheless crouched behind a pillar. "Then I heard a chipping sound and a ping, and I thought, 'My God, this is for real.'" An Army veteran who saw action in Korea, Brill was certain that the Guardsman had not fired randomly out of individual panic. "They were organized," he said. "It was not scattered. They all waited and they all pointed their rifles at the same time. It looked like a firing squad." The shooting stopped—as if on signal. Minutes later, the Guardsmen assumed parade-rest positions, apparently to signal the crowd that the fusillade would not be resumed unless the Guardsmen were threatened again.

Analysis: _____

_____

_____

3. Testimony of Claudia Van Tyne, a 20-year-old junior at Kent State at the time of the shootings. (From *The Middle of the Country: The Events of May 4th As Seen By Students and Faculty at Kent State University,* ed. by Bill Warren, June, 1970, 119–121.)

> For what occurred on Kent State University's campus I can only give one term-murder. . . .
> The area was filled with students in the middle, many spectators on the outskirts and the pigs
> were lined-up waiting. I don't like the expression 'pig' but it is the only word I shall ever use
> again to refer to law officials. . . . The pigs then informed us that we must disperse over their
> bull horn. In our response, we informed them that they, not us, should get off our campus and
> we began to chant 'Power To The People—Off The Pigs' etc., etc. They then began making their
> advance and everyone walked, telling others not to run but to walk, up the hill. We were all
> choking and sputtering because the tear gas (pepper pellets) had already been shot. . . . The pigs
> advanced, came up the hill and marched down into the old football practice field behind Taylor
> Hall (architecture building) where they gassed us again. Many of us picked up the cannisters and
> tossed them back. Finding themselves out of teargas, the pigs retreated followed by jeers and a
> few rocks. I was next to the architecture building, about twenty feet away from them, when sud-
> denly they turned and fired. I was stunned to say the least. We all were. No one expected it. . . .

Analysis: _____

_____

_____

4. Testimony of unnamed Guardsman—a 23-year-old, married machinist. (Reported in a Special Report by the *Akron Beacon Journal,* May 24, 1970. Quoted in I. F. Stone, *The Killings at Kent State,* 1970, 125.)

> Q. —Did you shoot to save your life?
>
> A. —No. I didn't feel that. Because, like it was an automatic thing. Everybody shot, so I shot. I
> didn't think about it. I just fired. . . .
>
> Q. —Did you feel threatened?
>
> A. —No. I didn't think they'd try to take our rifles, not while we could use the bayonets and
> butts. . . . The guys have been saying that we got to get together and stick to the same story, that
> it was our lives or them, a matter of survival. I told them I would tell the truth and couldn't get
> in trouble that way.

Analysis: _____

_____

_____

5. Testimony of Richard Schreiber, Assistant Professor of Journalism. Schreiber had been in the army and was a life member of the National Rifle Association. (From James Michener, *Kent State: What Happened and Why*, 1971, 359.)

> I went out on the south porch of Taylor with my binoculars and saw something which has caused a lot of discussion. While the Guard was pinned against the fence, the students kept throwing rocks, but they were rather far away and most of the rocks were falling short. I happened to have this one Guard in my glasses and I saw him raise his revolver and bang away. I've fired many hundreds of rounds with a .45 and I know a shot when I see one. There can be no question but that he fired the first round of the day. But the damnedest thing happened. Even while he was firing, some student ran up with a gas grenade and threw it at him. Where could he have possibly got it? Didn't look like the ones the Guards had been using. One of the Guardsmen, foolishly I thought, picked up the grenade and threw it back. It seemed like horseplay, so I turned away.

Analysis: _____

_____

_____

For Discussion

1. Which pieces of evidence do you find most convincing? Which do you find least convincing? Why?
2. On which "facts" does there seem to be general agreement?
3. What are the central points of disagreement?

SET B   *Exercise 5 — Essay*

Based on the evidence above, write a paragraph-length account of the incident at Kent State. In your paragraph take a position on the question at issue: Were the National Guardsmen or the students most responsible for the violence? In your paragraph you might want to help the reader understand (1) what can be established beyond doubt (assume the excerpts above are all the sources you have available to you), (2) what is *probable* given the above evidence, and (3) what cannot be established with certainty. In your account, include direct quotations from the documents. Read Writing Capsule 6 (on page 157) before you begin.

CHAPTER 10 ORAL HISTORY AND STATISTICS

"We have agencies aplenty to seek out the papers of men long dead. But we have only the most scattered and haphazard agencies for obtaining a little of the immense mass of information about the more recent American past—the past of the last half century—which might come fresh and direct from men once prominent in politics, in business, in the professions, and in other fields; information that every obituary column shows to be perishing."

—ALLAN NEVINS (1938)[1]

"Historians deal with a universe not of absolutes but of probabilities, and for a world conceived in these terms statistics are the appropriate tool."

—WILLIAM O. AYDELOTTE[2]

Richard Goodwin, a White House advisor and speechwriter during the early 1960s, related an unforgettable episode when he wrote his political memoir, *Remembering America*. In April of 1964 he got a call from his colleague, Bill Moyers, saying "Come on, Dick, the president wants to see us."

"In his office?" Goodwin replied.

"Nope, in the pool. He's swimming and so are we."

"I don't have a bathing suit."

"You don't need one."

At that Goodwin says he realized he had been summoned for a skinny-dip with the president. "We entered the pool area," Goodwin continued, "to see the massive presidential flesh, a sun-bleached atoll breaching the placid sea, passing gently sidestroke, the deep-cleft buttocks moving slowly past our unstartled gaze. Moby Dick, I thought, being naturally inclined to literary reference." The president called across the pool: "Come on in, boys. It'll do you good." Goodwin and Moyers stripped on the spot and joined the president, circling the pool in the buff, with the president discussing his plans for the future of the country.[3]

The president was, of course, Lyndon Baines Johnson (1963–69), surely one of the most colorful, larger-than-life individuals ever to play on the stage of American politics. Johnson was a big man from a very big state. In the words of one writer he "seemed like the quintessential Texan to many Americans: big, loud, brash, friendly,

---

[1] *Gateway to History*, 1938. Quoted in Louis Starr, "Oral History," *Oral History: An Interdisciplinary Anthology*, David K. Dunaway and Willa K. Baum, eds. (Nashville, Tenn,: American Association for State and Local History, 1984), 8.

[2] Quoted in Robert P. Swierenga, ed., *Quantification in American History* (New York: Atheneum, 1970), xi.

[3] Richard N. Goodwin, *Remembering America* (New York: Harper and Row, 1988), 267–68.

Lyndon B. Johnson, President 1963–1969.
*Library of Congress, Prints & Photographs Division,
(LC-USZ62-13036).*

informal, folksy, pushy, vulgar, and combative."[4] He was also intelligent, superhumanly energetic (he once gave twenty-two campaign speeches in a single day), and a temperamental and uncompromising taskmaster who worked his staff until they were ready to drop. "I don't have ulcers," he said. "I give 'em!"[5] By many measures Lyndon Johnson was an effective president (his administration passed much landmark social and civil rights legislation), but he was never popular. Even before the Vietnam War destroyed his presidency, he had failed to "connect" with most Americans. Many were repelled by his folksy country manner, uninspiring speaking style, and penchant for the outrageous—e.g., showing reporters his scar from a gall bladder operation, and racing them around his ranch in his car at ninety miles an hour while sipping beer from a can.

Johnson, like other modern presidents, was very conscious that his reputation was ultimately in the hands of historians. In contrast, we know that much important information from the Johnson years has effectively been lost forever. Johnson was a master of political persuasion, and as he tried to build Congressional majorities for his programs he spent countless hours on the telephone. Johnson, Richard Goodwin notes, "labored, often far into the night, telephone constantly in hand, to persuade, seduce, coerce congressional leaders, committee chairmen, and, it seemed, most of an entire membership. . . ."[6] What historian wouldn't love to have transcripts of those calls.[7]

---

[5] Quoted in Boller, *Presidential Anecdotes*, 309.

[6] Goodwin, *Remembering America*, 260.

[7] As it turns out, long after President Johnson left office the public learned that many of his private phone conversations had not been lost after all. For years, even before he became president, LBJ kept records of his phone calls, first by having an aide take shorthand notes, and then by tape recorder. Johnson originally intended that the recordings be locked away until the year 2023, but they were released early. See Michael Beschloss's *Taking Charge: The Johnson White House Tapes, 1963–1964* (Simon and Schuster, 1997) and *Reaching for Glory: Lyndon Johnson's Secret White House Tapes, 1964–1965* (2001). These tapes actually dramatize the point made above: they are a very rare exception to the reality that the great majority of phone messages are lost to historians forever. And, if LBJ had had his way, no historian would have listened to those tapes until well into the twenty-first century.

The Challenge

"Countless federal records are being lost to posterity because federal employees, grappling with a staggering growth in electronic records, do not regularly preserve documents they create on government computers, send by e-mail and post on the Web. Federal agencies have rushed to embrace the Internet and new information technology, but their record-keeping efforts lag far behind. . . . This confusion is causing alarm among historians, archivists, librarians, Congressional investigators and watchdog groups that want to trace the decision-making process and hold federal officials accountable."

Robert Pear, "In Digital Age, Federal Files Blip into Oblivion," *The New York Times,* September 13, 2008, A1.

Johnson's desire to save every piece of paper for future historians, and his constant use of the telephone to get things done illustrate some of the frustrating ambiguities faced by historians of the twentieth and twenty-first centuries: on one hand there is too much information, and, on the other, there is too little. We generate and save so much information that no mortal has time to read it all. At the same time, much information that used to be written down is now communicated by phone, text message, or e-mail, and, unless someone has made a point of preserving this material, it may be lost to the historian forever.

If the twentieth century has presented historians with new challenges, it also has given them some powerful new tools. In the last chapter we discussed the analysis of documentary evidence, the most traditional and important type of evidence used by historians. Yet two other types of evidence—oral interviews and statistics—have become increasingly important in recent decades, giving rise to oral history on the one hand and quantitative history (i.e., history grounded in numbers and statistics) on the other. Ironically, oral history is as old as quantitative history is new, but both owe their prominence to the emergence of technologies that didn't exist a century ago: the tape (and later video) recorder and the computer. Even if you never try to do either type of history, you should be aware of the strengths and potential pitfalls of each.

Oral History

Oral history is older than the practice of writing about the past and, at the same time, a true child of the last half of the twentieth century. Historians have always interviewed living witnesses, as any reader of Herodotus or Thucydides can testify. Yet, as an organized enterprise, oral history dates from the government-sponsored interview projects of the New Deal and from Allan Nevins's 1938 plea (quoted at the beginning of this chapter) for the collection of the living memories of important individuals.

Oral history weds the ancient practice of interviewing witnesses to the modern technology of the tape and video recorder. Defined as "recorded interviews which preserve historically significant memories for future use,"[8] oral history provides the contemporary historian with a wealth of source materials that simply did not exist sixty or seventy years ago.

Oral history refers to the source materials—the evidence—not the final product created by the historian. Recorded interviews, even if transcribed, are oral documents roughly equivalent to the printed and manuscript sources that have for generations been the basis of historical scholarship. Historians must sift, analyze, and interpret oral sources in precisely the same manner they would scrutinize diaries, letters, or government documents. After all, as historian Barbara Tuchman noted, "The memories of the living . . . are no more reliable or free of wishful recollection and the adjustments of hindsight than the memoirs of the dead."[9] Thus, when students do an oral history project, they are (1) collecting sources in the interviewing process and (2) actually doing history when they critically evaluate those sources and write a narrative or commentary.

In the beginning oral history projects targeted the prominent individuals who had always been the objects of historical scholarship: politicians, intellectuals, business leaders, generals, etc. But it was not long before historians realized that the magic of the tape recorder opened up dramatic new possibilities. Now one could tape the remembered experiences of the not-so-famous people who had previously slipped through history's net: the poor, the illiterate or uneducated, marginalized members of minority groups, women, workers who rarely wrote journals or diaries, the anonymous soldiers and sailors who usually bear the brunt of war—in short, people like most of us.

Critics have argued that the quest to interview anyone who would sit still in front of a microphone has created a mountain of trivia of questionable accuracy and merit that few historians will ever use. While there is some truth to the charge, the influence of the telephone and rapid air travel make oral sources increasingly important to historians of the twentieth and twenty-first centuries. Whereas political leaders in the past wrote lengthy letters and kept extensive diaries, today they pick up the phone, send an email, or fly a few hours to have a person-to-person conference. Oral history, then, necessarily replaces the manuscript sources that have become increasingly scarce in our high-technology age. Further, oral history is something in which even novice historians may participate. It is personally satisfying and can render a valuable community service.

Doing Oral History: Interviewing

Oral history involves much more than turning on a tape (or digital) recorder in front of an interviewee. In this section we will attempt to single out the most important considerations fledgling oral historians should keep in mind. For a more detailed discussion of the process of oral history, however, and for project suggestions, we

---

[8] Dunaway and Baum, *Oral History,* xix.
[9] Barbara Tuchman, "Distinguishing the Significant from the Insignificant," in Dunaway and Baum, *Oral History,* 76.

recommend that you turn to one of the many guides written to help teachers and students get started.[10]

The scouting motto, "be prepared," is triply relevant for oral history. After making sure that your recorder works (are the batteries fresh?), you have to (1) choose with care the people you intend to interview, (2) do background research on your subject and prepare for the interview, and (3) familiarize yourself with the legal and ethical constraints that responsible interviewers observe.

1. Choosing Narrators

Almost anyone, young or old, can be a good source for the oral historian, depending on the subject under investigation. Still, you will want to select interview subjects with care. Choose individuals who have good memories (to the extent that can be determined) and who have the potential of making a valuable contribution to your particular study. Build a list of prospects by soliciting suggestions from parents, friends, and teachers. If you are studying events a few decades in the past, inquire at retirement centers, local churches, and nursing homes. Excellent possible sources are members of your own family, whose testimony might be incorporated into a family history project.[11]

2. The Interview

Never conduct an interview unless you have done some preliminary research on the topic in question. It is difficult to ask meaningful questions about the Vietnam War, an industrial strike, or Hurricane Katrina unless you know something about the events prior to conducting the interview. Background reading allows you to test the generalizations you find in textbooks against the individual experiences of the people you interview.

You should also prepare yourself to be an effective interviewer. One expert notes, "The interviewer's paramount objective is to help the narrator reconstruct his/her personal history with as much accuracy and vivid detail as possible."[12] To accomplish this it is wise to prepare some questions in advance. Then, at the interview itself:[13]

- Ask provocative questions—Who? What? Where? When? How? Why? Keep questions broad and general to encourage interviewees to respond with more than "yes" or "no" answers.
- Try to get the interviewee to evoke specific events or experiences by asking questions such as: "Why did you vote as you did in the 2000 election?" "Where

[10] For example, Cullom Davis, Kathryn Back, and Kay MacLean, *Oral History: From Tape to Type* (Chicago: American Library Association, 1977); Thad Sitton, George L. Mehaffy, and O. L. Davis, Jr., *Oral History: A Guide for Teachers (and Others)* (Austin: University of Texas Press, 1983); James Hoopes, *Oral History: An Introduction for Students* (Chapel Hill: University of North Carolina Press, 1979). Section V ("Oral History and Schools") of Dunaway and Baum, *Oral History* (1984) is also valuable. The bibliography of this work lists a number of additional oral history manuals.

[11] See David E. Kyvig and Myron A. Marty, *Your Family History: A Handbook for Research and Writing* (Wheeling, IL.: Harlan Davidson, Inc., 1978).

[12] Davis, et al., *Oral History*, 20.

[13] These questions were drawn from lists suggested in Davis, et al., *Oral History*, 20–21, and William Bruce Wheeler and Susan D. Becker, *Discovering the American Past: A Look at the Evidence*, Vol. II (Boston: Houghton Mifflin, 1986), 228.

were you when you watched the telecast of the first moon landing?" "What was it like to work on the Ford assembly line in the 1940s?"

- Elicit emotions. Ask the person to recall actual feelings about the events and experiences you are discussing.
- Ask your narrator to reconstruct specific conversations and physical locations. Asking for such concrete details often helps people recall a wealth of interesting particulars.
- Don't argue with the person you are interviewing. You are there to solicit their experiences and opinions, not to question the accuracy of their recollections or to convert them to your way of thinking.
- Save controversial issues until the end of the interview. By that time the narrator may feel more comfortable talking with you about sensitive matters.
- Make sure you have written down all pertinent personal information: name, age, educational and family background, occupation at time of events being investigated, etc.
- Make sure the interviewee signs a proper release form.

3. Ethical and Legal Considerations

At some point in the interviewing process, preferably at the beginning, it is necessary to obtain the interviewee's signature on a legal release. The legal release "acknowledges the legal (and legitimate) rights of interviewees to shield themselves from public ridicule or the betrayal of confidences. Generally, legal releases either give complete access to an interview or stipulate the conditions under which all or portions of the interview will be released."[14] Without such a signed release you do not have the legal right to allow others to have access to the collected materials. There are other rules that, though not mandated by law, are dictated by common sense and good manners. The Oral History Association, founded in 1967, encourages practitioners to "recognize certain principles, rights and obligations for the creation of source material that is authentic, useful and reliable." Individuals pursuing an oral history project should review these guidelines before beginning.[15] A final warning: In some colleges and universities "Institutional Research Boards" (IRB's), originally set up to monitor potentially dangerous or harmful biomedical research using human subjects, are also insisting on approving oral history projects. Since doing oral history does not involve such medical risks to interviewees, historians have argued that oral history projects should not be subject to IRB approvals. Still, it is best to check on the expectations at your institution.

Doing Oral History: The Narrative

Oral testaments are pieces of evidence—not history as we have defined it in this book. The most important goal of an oral history project is to use your newly created sources to write some history. The length and nature of what you write depends on

---

[14] Sitton, et al., *Oral History*, 78. For a sample release form see Appendix C.
[15] A copy of the Oral History Association guidelines is reprinted in Dunaway and Baum, *Oral History*, 415–416.

individual classroom circumstances, but something should be written, however brief or tentative. It is at this point that you actually do the work of the historian, and it is the most meaningful phase of the project.[16] That said, have fun.

History by the Numbers: Quantitative History

Like oral testimony, historians have always used quantitative (i.e., numerical) evidence in their work. They tell us how many soldiers died in the battle of Waterloo, what percentage of the population voted for the Republicans in the presidential election of 2008, and how many people lived in Great Britain in 1871. They tell us how Congress voted on the Compromise of 1850, how much steel was produced at the turn of the nineteenth century, and how many immigrants from Ireland came to North America after the Irish potato famine of the 1840s. On the other hand, the most casual glance at the average history book will show that numerical evidence usually takes a distinct back seat to literary or written evidence. Historians, and students of history, are generally more comfortable with words than with numbers.

There are those who argue, however, that in this age of the computer, history should become much more quantitative (number oriented). Numerical data and statistics are necessary, they say, if history is to become more rigorous, systematic, and "scientific"; quantification will help us move beyond the vague and impressionistic style that characterizes so much traditional historical writing.

To this, many traditionalists have reacted with barely controlled outrage. The historian Oscar Handlin lamented that "we have long known the danger of depending on translators; we must now learn the danger of depending on programmers." The eminent intellectual historian Jacques Barzun said that when people examine a chart [of numbers], they are "not *reading history*."[17]

The details of the debate between the quantifiers and traditionalists need not detain us. However, it is important to understand both the advantages and disadvantages of using numbers in history. After all, graphs, tables, and opinion polls have become such common currency in our day that individuals who desire to understand the world in which they live must be able to interpret simple numerical data.

On the positive side, numerical evidence can make history much more precise. Historians mention quantities all the time, but often in a vague and shapeless manner. We talk about majorities who support such-and-such a proposition; about social classes growing in strength (the "middle classes were on the rise"); about a rising tide of antigovernment opinion, and the like. Our history would be much more convincing if, when possible, we could attach some precise numbers to such statements—a 54 percent majority; a middle class that numbered 37 percent of the population; 63 percent opposed the government on a specific measure.

---

[16] Another important aim of oral research projects is to catalog and store the oral histories (often in written transcriptions) for the use of future historians. Given the nature of this book, these elements have not been discussed. See the resources in Note 10 for further information.

[17] Quotations are from Richard E. Beringer, *Historical Analysis: Contemporary Approaches to Clio's Craft* (New York: John Wiley and Sons, 1978), 193–94. As far back as the 1940s the British historian R. G. Collingwood wrote: "Statistical research is for the historian a good servant but a bad master. It profits him nothing to make statistical generalizations, unless he can thereby detect the thought behind the facts about which he is generalizing." *The Idea of History*, 228.

Statistical data and computer calculations are useful in other areas of historical study. Many issues in modern social history—the study of people as groups, not individuals—can be approached only if we have some meaningful numbers with which to work. Quantification is essential if we are to find answers to such questions as: At what age did people get married in England in the seventeenth century? What was the average life expectancy in Boston, New York, and Charleston in 1850? What percentage of the population lived on family farms in the pre–Civil War South? Were illegitimate births a serious problem in pre-industrial France?

In asking these questions we are trying to understand the history of the great mass of people—people like most of us—who lived and died without leaving a written legacy. And we cannot answer such questions by studying individuals one by one. We can begin to get answers only when we use parish records, census data, and court records to count heads and compile a collective portrait of a group of people at a given time and place. We can never know these people as individuals, but statistics can provide countless clues to the very real lives they lived.

On the other hand, "history by the numbers" should not be embraced uncritically. Three objections to quantification in history are worth noting here. First, most historical evidence is still in the form of written records. Since quantifiable evidence is simply not available for many questions, most history will still have to be based on the written record.

Second, many important historical questions cannot be answered with numbers or statistics. American historian Arthur Schlesinger, Jr., pointed out in 1962: "Most of the variables in an historical equation are not susceptible to commensurable quantification." Further, said Schlesinger, "almost all important questions are important precisely because they are *not* susceptible to quantitative answers."[18] Thus, while quantification can provide many valuable insights, it is necessary to know when such evidence is and is not appropriate to the subject being studied.

Finally, numbers can be seductively misleading. Given the scientific bias of our age, many people have a tendency to trust numbers over more literary formulations. Statistics carry weight in debates and discussions, and effective politicians, journalists, and social reformers are quick to cite relevant figures in support of their positions. The problem for the historian is that numbers do not speak for themselves. Like all other forms of evidence, numerical evidence must be analyzed and interpreted by the historian. Note the difference between saying that "one-quarter of southern white families owned slaves in 1860," versus saying that "*only* one-quarter of those families owned slaves." The first statement is more-or-less neutral while the second includes a very clear judgment that slave holding was concentrated in a small minority of families.[19] And notice what a different impression would be created if we said, "*fully* one-quarter of Southern white families owned slaves." In each case 25 percent carries a different connotation.

It is also useful to pay attention to the source of the numbers you are reading. The way numbers are presented can influence the way they are interpreted, or, in the case of modern opinion polls, the wording of the questions can have a significant impact

---

[18] Quoted in Beringer, *Historical Analysis*, 195.
[19] See Peter J. Parish, *Slavery: History and Historians* (New York: Harper and Row, 1989), 28.

Lies, Damned Lies and Statistics

Custom suggests that British Prime Minister Benjamin Disraeli said: "There are three kinds of lies: lies, damned lies and statistics." He had a point. Joel Best, a sociology professor at the University of Delaware, discovered the repeated use of the statistical claim that "Every year since 1950, the number of American children gunned down has doubled." Nominating this statement as "the worst—that is, the most inaccurate—social statistic ever," Best pointed out that if, in 1950, there was one child gunned down in America, by 1995, when the claim appeared in a journal article, the number of children gunned down *each year* would exceed 35 trillion! (Try it. Starting with one, double the number each year for 45 years.) When Best tracked down the source of the statistic he found that the original claim was that between 1950 and 1994 the total number of children killed by guns had doubled, and even that was not a dramatic increase since the American population had almost doubled in the same period. Note how radically different are the two claims. This dramatizes the need to *think* about the numbers you read.

(Joel Best "Telling the Truth about Damned Lies and Statistics," *The Chronicle of Higher Education,* May 4, 2001, B7.)

on the answers people give. And, sad to say, sometimes people lie to polltakers for a variety of reasons. The point is, quantitative information that appears in books and in the press should never be accepted uncritically.

To see how the presentation of data can influence its interpretation, compare the two (fictitious) graphs in Figure A. Both show the identical information: that the unemployment rate for the State of Clio went up 3 percent in a six-year period (1995–2001). Graph I uses a percentage scale that begins at 0 percent and ends at 8 percent; Graph II, however, uses an expanded amount scale and grounds the graph at the original 3 percent unemployment rate. Note how much more severe the rise in unemployment appears in Graph II. Yet the "numbers" are identical. How might unwary readers react differently to the two graphs?

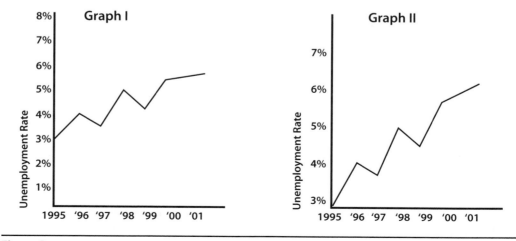

Figure A

In sum, quantification in history is here to stay. Computers and statistical techniques have enriched and will continue to enrich our understanding of the human past. On the other hand, instead of eliminating the need for historians to draw "legitimate inferences" from the raw, undigested evidence, numerical data demands even more sophisticated inference-making skills.

EXERCISES

SET A   *Exercise 1 — History by the Numbers*

Although history remains a discipline primarily grounded in a literary tradition, a significant number of historians use numerical and statistical evidence in their work. Moreover, since much of the history and journalism read by the general public is accompanied by tables, graphs, opinion polls, and statistical assertions, it is important for students of history to be able to read and interpret evidence that comes in numerical form.

It is not our aim to provide an in-depth immersion in the techniques of quantification and the interpretation of numerical evidence, but the exercise below will provide a taste of the sort of reasoning and analysis that the use of statistical evidence requires. The tables below do not represent primary sources in the purest sense. The historian who drew up the charts, John Demos, has culled the information from many original documents and has done the counting for you. Moreover, the organization of the information reflects the questions that Demos wished to investigate.[20] Nevertheless, the charts do represent raw data that does not "speak for itself": the numbers must be interpreted by the historian.

The tables printed below categorize by age, sex, and marital status those people who, during the infamous Salem witchcraft trials in 1692, were either accused of being witches or who accused others of witchcraft. On the basis of the evidence presented, what general conclusions can you make concerning the "types" of people most likely to be accused of witchcraft (group I) compared with the "types" of people who accused others of witchcraft (group II)?

I. Persons accused of being witches.

Age	Male	Female	Total
Under 20	6	18	24
21–30	3	7	10
31–40	3	8	11
41–50	6	18	24
51–60	5	23	28
61–70	4	8	12
Over 70	3	6	9
Total	**30**	**88**	**118**

Marital Status	Male	Female	Total
Single	8	29	37
Married	15	61	76
Widowed	1	20	21
Total	**24**	**110**	**134**

---

[20] John Demos, "Witchcraft in Seventeenth-Century New England," *American Historical Review* LXXV (June 1970), 1311–26. ©The American Historical Association, 1970. Statistical tables (pp. 1315–16) reprinted by permission of the publisher, the University of Chicago.

II. Persons who accused others of witchcraft.

Age	Male	Female	Total
Under 11	0	1	1
11–15	1	7	8
16–20	1	13	14
21–25	0	1	1
26–30	0	1	1
Over 30	0	4	4
Total	**2**	**27**	**29**

Marital Status	Male	Female	Total
Single	5	23	28
Married	0	6	6
Widowed	0	0	0
Total	**5**	**29**	**34**

1. General characteristics of persons in group I:

_____

_____

_____

_____

2. General characteristics of persons in group II:

_____

_____

_____

_____

SET A *Exercise 2*

Refer back to the tables on the accusers and accused in the Salem witch trials. Using the letters A, B, C, indicate whether each statement below:[21]

   A. Can be *proved* using the data in the tables.
   B. Can be *neither proved nor contradicted* using the data in the tables.
   C. Can be *contradicted* using the data in the tables.

Be prepared to defend your answer orally.

---

[21] The inspiration for this exercise came from Horace T. Morse and George H. McCune, *Selected Items for the Testing of Study Skills and Critical Thinking* (Washington, D.C.: National Council for the Social Studies, 1964).

Statements:

_____ 1. Most of the men accused of being witches were over forty years old.
_____ 2. Most of the men accused of witchcraft were economically well off.
_____ 3. A majority of all those accused were between the ages 41 and 60.
_____ 4. Three times as many women as men were accused of witchcraft.
_____ 5. The young women who accused other women of witchcraft were envious of the status and power of the older women.
_____ 6. Men made accusations of witchcraft almost as often as women did.
_____ 7. Most of those accused of witchcraft were married.
_____ 8. Most people in Salem believed that witches made pacts with the devil.
_____ 9. Twenty-four of those accused of witchcraft were teenagers.
_____ 10. The accusers tended to be very religious people.

SET A   *Exercise 3 — Oral History (Optional)*

Even a modest oral history project can be very time consuming, so many instructors may decide to pass it by. If circumstances permit, however, the following exercise can be an interesting introduction to doing history from the ground up.

Oral history is written from the recorded interviews of people who actually witnessed and experienced the history later generations can only read about. Obviously, to do oral history you have to interview people who are still alive, which limits your pool of interviewees to those from relatively few generations.

To do oral history even moderately well you have to prepare thoroughly and allot sufficient time. Therefore, begin this exercise by rereading the information on pages 168–171. A full-fledged oral history project involves the collection, transcribing, editing, dissemination, and storage of the interviews.[22] For the purposes of this exercise we will limit the activity to interviewing subjects and disseminating the findings in a written paper or oral report.

Oral history projects take many forms, but for this exercise we suggest that you attempt an oral history of a significant theme or local or national event—a natural disaster, an election campaign, experiences during a war (at home or abroad), etc.[23] After making the preparations outlined in this chapter, you should record an interview with at least two individuals who can comment on your chosen event or theme. The interviews will constitute the evidence from which a paper, as assigned by the instructor, will be written.

An abbreviated exercise could take the form of (1) a group interview (in the classroom) of a person who has useful firsthand knowledge to share, or (2) an oral autobiography assignment in which each student is expected to prepare an account based on an interview with another student in class. In both cases questions and expectations would have to be thoroughly discussed beforehand. Both of these options allow students to practice, and instructors to critique, interviewing skills.

---

[22] See Davis, et al. (1977).
[23] For a list of many oral history project options, see Sitton, et al. *Oral History: A Guide for Teachers (and Others)* (1977), Ch. 2. To do your project as family history, see Kyvig and Marty, *Your Family History* (1978).

SET B *Exercise 1 — History by the Numbers*

Although history remains a discipline primarily grounded in a literary and humanistic tradition, a significant number of historians use numerical and statistical evidence in their work. Moreover, since much of the history and journalism read by the general public is accompanied by tables, graphs, and statistical assertions, it is important for students of history to be able to read and interpret evidence that comes in numerical form.

It is not our aim to provide an in-depth immersion in the techniques of quantification and the interpretation of numerical evidence, but the exercise below will provide a taste of the sort of reasoning and analysis that the use of statistical evidence requires. The tables below do not represent primary sources in the purest sense; they were compiled by the author, James Bonner, in his article on the social history of the white farmers in one slave-holding region (Hancock County, Georgia) before the Civil War.[24] The tables represent, in short, the questions Bonner chose to ask and the categories he used to display the data he had gathered.

The tables show the average ages, occupations, and economic status of the non-slave population of Hancock County in 1860. "Realty" refers to landed property, or "real estate." "Personalty" refers to other forms of personal property.

Table I: Economic Status of Occupational Groups, 1860

Occupational Group	Number	Total in Families	Percent Owning Realty	Percent Owning Slaves	Percent Owning Other Personal Property
Planters and Farmers*					
$10,000 and above	56	267	100.0	100.0	100.0
$9,999 to $1,001	220	1,049	100.0	92.2	100.0
$1,000 and under	85	379	100.0	41.6	91.7
Professional class	48	195	62.4	54.1	77.1
Merchants	29	101	50.0	45.0	75.9
Tradesmen	116	414	13.7	7.7	26.9
Overseers	139	367	1.4	6.4	20.8
Farm laborers	198	610	1.2	0.016	8.4
Factory workers	96	157	0.9	0.0	0.0**
All others	110	276	—	—	—

*While the landowning agricultural subdivision (those whose land was valued at $1,000 and under) is placed third from the top in this table, it is evident that its position would be lower when measured by other criteria. For example, see the values of land and personalty assigned to various groups in Table II.

**The absence of personal property assigned to factory workers is explained by the failure of enumerators to list personal property evaluations of less than $100.

---

[24] James C. Bonner, "Profile of a Late Ante-Bellum Community," *American Historical Review* (July 1944): 663–680. The tables are from pp. 671–672.

Table II: Economic Status of Occupational Groups in 1860

Occupational Group	Average Age of Each Group	Percent Owning Slaves	Average Value of Realty	Average Value of Personalty	Ratio of Personalty to Realty
Planters and Farmers*					
$10,000 and above	49.7	100	$21,786	$45,434	1.99
$9,999 to $1,001	45.8	92.2	4,268	12,904	3.02
$1,000 and under	44.9	41.6	719	2,348	3.26
Professional class	34.85	54.1	2,844	8,025	2.82
Merchants	33.5	45	1,862	5,848	3.14
Tradesmen	38.03	7.7	216	874	4.04
Overseers	28.8	6.4	72	1,524	21.16
Farm laborers	30.0	6.01	15	44	2.87
Factory workers	24.09	0	4	0	0

Using the letters A, B, C, indicate whether each statement below:

A. Can be *proved* using the data in the tables.
B. Can be *neither proved nor contradicted* using the data in the tables.
C. Can be *contradicted* using the data in the tables.

Be prepared to defend your answer orally.

Statements:

Unless stated otherwise, assume all statements refer to Hancock County, Georgia in 1860.

_____ 1. Planters and farmers constituted the majority of the non-slave population of Hancock County.

_____ 2. The largest single occupational group was that of farm laborers.

_____ 3. Generally, the younger people were the less well-off economically than the older people.

_____ 4. The majority of employed whites owned slaves in 1860.

_____ 5. The economic position of farm laborers in Hancock County was the same as the economic position of farm laborers in all of Georgia.

_____ 6. All planters and farmers owned slaves.

_____ 7. The majority of the non-farmers supported the institution of slavery.

_____ 8. Industry was as important to the economy of Hancock County as was agriculture.

_____ 9. The same percentage of people in the North as in the South owned real estate in 1860.

_____ 10. Some merchants and members of the "professional class" were better off economically than were some farmers.

SET B   *Exercise 2*

Using the same numerical tables, write a paragraph in which you try to make some generalizations about class relationships in Hancock County in 1860. Your generalizations should be those statements that are either absolutely true or probably true in light of the evidence. You might also indicate what *additional evidence* you would like to have to improve your essay.

SET B   *Exercise 3 — Oral History (Optional)*

For potential oral history projects, see Set A, Exercise 3.

CHAPTER 11   INTERPRETATION

"The writing of history reflects the interests, predilections, and even prejudices of a given generation."

—John Hope Franklin

"[Y]ou cannot see things till you know roughly what they are."

—C. S. Lewis

One of the most famous episodes in American history is surely the perplexing outbreak of a massive witch-hunt in Salem Village, Massachusetts, in 1692. In the course of about ten months more than one hundred individuals were accused of being in league with the devil, and, before calmer heads intervened, nineteen of the accused were hanged for their "crime" and another was pressed to death with weights in an attempt to force him to enter a plea. Europe endured a massive, decades-long "witch craze" that resulted in the execution of tens of thousands of individuals, most of them women. In North America, however, Salem stands out as a singular example of such a large-scale witch panic.[1]

How do we explain this singular, dramatic outburst of communal bloodletting? Although a veritable mountain of records have survived from the time, coming up with a convincing interpretation (explanation) of these events has not been easy. We can get a sense of this by posing just one of many possible questions: How do we explain the fits and visions of the handful of teenage girls who precipitated the panic? These girls claimed to be tormented by the spirits of those neighbors (witches) who were in league with the devil. According to witnesses, when the devil was assaulting the girls, they displayed physical symptoms that were truly horrifying: "fits so grotesque and so violent that eyewitnesses agreed the girls could not possibly be acting."[2] The Reverend John Hale of Beverly (Massachusetts) wrote, "Their arms, necks, and backs were turned this way and that way, and returned back again, so as it was impossible for them to do of themselves, and beyond the power of any epileptic fits, or natural disease to effect [i.e. to cause]." Other symptoms, according to Salem historian Chadwick Hansen, included loss of hearing, speech and sight along with terrifying hallucinations and physical assaults on their bodies.[3]

So, how can we explain all of this? This is not the place for a full historiographical survey of the literature about the Salem witch hunt. ("Historiography" refers to

---

[1] The story is widely studied in history classes, but many have been introduced to the events via Arthur Miller's fictionalized play *The Crucible* (1953), or perhaps the more recent 1996 film version. For some statistics on accusers and victims, see Set A, Exercise 1 in Chapter 10.

[2] Chadwick Hansen, *Witchcraft at Salem* (New York: George Brazziler, 1969), 1.

[3] Hansen, *Salem*, 1 (including the quotation from Rev. Hale).

Witchcraft at Salem Village, Published in *Pioneers in the Settlement of America,* Vol. 1 Boston: Samuel Walker and Co., 1876, 453.

the study of the writings about—i.e., interpretations of—a given subject. For a fuller definition, see Chapter 13.) But, we can summarize the major schools of thought.

Obviously, seventeenth-century Puritans interpreted the girls' fits as literal assaults from the invisible world of spirits. The age believed in devils, demons, and witches, and that is a primary reason why observers found the girls' behavior so frightening. It didn't take long, however, for skeptics who didn't believe in witchcraft to charge that the girls were frauds and that their "symptoms" were not and had never been real. Charles Upham, a minister who published a study of the episode in 1867 wrote: "There has seldom been better acting in a theatre than displayed in the presence of the astonished and horror-stricken rulers."[4] But modern medicine, specifically psychiatry, provides an equally compelling explanation. Chadwick Hansen wrote a book on the subject because, from his point of view, "The traditional interpretation of what happened at Salem is as much the product of casual journalism and imaginative literature as it is of historical scholarship." According to Hansen, there *were* those in Salem who actually practiced witchcraft and in societies that believe in witchcraft (even today), its effects are produced "through psychogenic [i.e., psychological] rather than occult means, commonly producing hysterical symptoms as a result of the victim's fear." Thus "with minor exceptions the girls' behavior," according to Hansen, "belongs to the history of pathology rather that the history of fraud."[5] Moreover, could it not be the case that the girls' behavior might be explained by a *combination* of psychological trauma and fraud, the exact mix differing from individual to individual?

---

[4] Davidson and Lytle, *After the Fact*, Vol. I, 29–30. Davidson and Lytle's chapter on Salem is one of the best brief introductions to the complexities of the subject. Another excellent introduction is provided by University of Missouri-Kansas City Law Professor Douglas O. Linder's Web site "Famous Trials."
[5] Hansen, *Salem*, x; 2.

Finally, one might ask, why teenage girls and not teenage boys? To answer that we need to know how the lives of young women differed from the lives of young men in late-seventeenth-century Massachusetts. Historian Carol Karlsen does exactly that in her book *The Devil in the Shape of a Woman: Witchcraft in Colonial New England.*[6] Karlsen discusses much more than Salem in her book, but she provides valuable insights into the behavior of the accusers. Her argument is complex and not easily synthesized, but she dramatizes the importance of understanding the broad cultural context of Puritan Massachusetts. Many among the young accusers had lost parents, often from Indian attacks. They had survived as servants in other people's houses, and their prospects for marriage and hence material well-being were dim. And, frankly, life was routine and boring for these women. Any form of rebellion against these constraints would have to have taken place within the religious worldview of the time. "Possessed females did experience profound conflict," says Karlsen, "but their ministers defined this conflict as a theological one—the result of a struggle between God and the Devil for the souls of the possessed."[7] In short, the girls' rebellion was framed (and understood) in ways that conformed to a seventeenth-century Puritan worldview.

This is but a brief example of how challenging a task the historian faces in trying to explain—i.e., interpret—even limited episodes involving a few hundred people. The difficulties are magnified as the chronological and geographic scope of the investigation is expanded. Yet *explaining* the facts (rather than simply recording them) lies at the heart of the historian's enterprise. The primary purpose of this chapter is to underscore why interpretation is the most basic and necessary product of historical study. Its clear-cut presence makes any student paper an intellectual achievement; its absence reduces a paper to an empty recital of facts.

Interpretation is, in its most fundamental sense, *generalization*. It is that mental act in which one rises above the details of a given experience and makes a statement that characterizes the entire experience according to its principal elements. Such a simple statement as "I had a great time last night" can illustrate the essential nature of generalization. What the speaker has done—in an instant—is recall elements of the evening, including the personality and appeal of the person one was with, the food and drink, the atmosphere, the music, the shared conversation. Finding that all of these elements reflect a pattern, the speaker can summarize the whole experience as "a great time." The speaker can then, if asked, supply corroborating detail to support the generalization offered.

So it is with history, though the raw materials you work with are usually historical sources rather than personal experience. A generalization (interpretation) about George Washington's military role in the American Revolution might read: "Washington's military genius manifested itself repeatedly in his avoidance of defeat rather than in a string of victories." Many of us might be inclined to accept that statement. But we should not do so until we are supplied with corroborating details such as Washington's refusal to commit his full army to a frontal battle at Boston, his dilatory campaign around New York, his withdrawal at Monmouth, his patience at Philadelphia, etc. In other words, just as a listener expects to hear certain details

---

[6] Carol Karlsen, *The Devil in the Shape of a Woman* (New York: W. W. Norton, 1998).
[7] Karlsen, *Devil*, 227; 235.

that can justify the "great time" one claims to have had last night, so, too, does a reader expect a historian to provide detailed support for any generalizations he or she makes.

Types of Generalization

"All learning of history," says historian Robert Daniel, "is learning about generalizations—how to form them, how to understand and remember them."[8] A generalization can be treated as belonging at one of three levels: summary, limited interpretive, and broad interpretive.

- A **summary generalization** is essentially a statement that is so obvious and basic that it requires very little proof or argumentation to convince people that it is true: e.g., "The Democratic candidate won the presidential election of 1992." (This statement is a generalization because it summarizes the Electoral College results of the individual state elections.)

- A **limited interpretive generalization** is more sophisticated. It makes a claim that must be supported with evidence and argument in order to convince others that it is true. This type of generalization is also concrete enough to be susceptible to a convincing proof: e.g., "The Democratic party won the presidential election of 1992 *because independent Ross Perot split the opposition votes to Bill Clinton.*" (The clause that begins with "because" makes this a generalization that requires the support of evidence.) These generalizations, the heart and soul of the historical enterprise, are grounded in a historian's intimate knowledge of a specific time, place, and circumstance. Similarly, philosopher William Dray argues that generalizations based on a historian's knowledge of the "established pattern of behavior" of an individual (e.g., the above comments on George Washington) qualify as what he calls "limited law" explanations.[9]

- Finally, **broad interpretive generalizations** are so grand and all encompassing that they are exceedingly difficult to validate with any amount of evidence or argument. Broad generalizations often try to explain so much that even with a massive accumulation of evidence they remain quite speculative. Karl Marx's "all history is the history of class conflict," or Arnold Toynbee's generalizations about the rise and fall of civilizations, or Frederick Jackson Turner's claim that "the primary factor in shaping the American character was the two-hundred-year frontier experience of its people" belong to this category. A more recent example is Francis Fukuyama's controversial essay "The End of History," which argued that as the world in the late twentieth century adopted democracy and capitalism, "history"—i.e., significant change—would come to an end.[10] Generalizations of such magnitude, though often very thought provoking, are best left to philosophers.

Most worthwhile historical interpretations are generalizations at the limited level. They advance claims of a manageable size—modest units of knowledge that can be supported by citing the particulars on which the generalization is based. For example, a carefully written student essay on Franklin Roosevelt's first term in office

---

[8] Robert V. Daniel, *Studying History* (Englewood Cliffs, N.J.: Prentice-Hall, Inc., 1966), 37.
[9] William H. Dray, *Philosophy of History* (Englewood Cliffs, NJ: Prentice Hall, 1993), 23–26.
[10] Francis Fukuyama, "The End of History," *The National Interest* (Summer 1989).

(1933–37) might set forth the generalization: "The emergence of radical political movements in the mid-thirties brought a leftward shift in New Deal policy." The writer could then make such a statement plausible by examining some specific "radical political movements": Huey Long's "Share Our Wealth" crusade; Francis Townsend's over-sixty scheme; Father Charles Coughlin's attack on Roosevelt's monetary policy, followed by a discussion of the new direction signified by the Wagner Labor Act and the Social Security Act. In sum, such limited interpretive generalizations and their supporting elements compel assent, advance understanding, deepen knowledge, and give a signal that the writer knows the subject. Ideally, they also should provide an explanation of how and why something happened as it did: they should explain the causes behind the event.

Developing Interpretations

The reader might ask "Where are we at this stage?"—a good question. To summarize briefly, in order to understand any historical development you must ask the questions described in Chapter 4, consider the context—the cultural and intellectual setting in which events took place (Chapter 5), read what other historians have said about the topic (Chapter 7), and closely study the available evidence (Chapters 9 and 10). Now comes the difficult but rewarding step of trying to interpret the evidence you have found. In essence, you will be trying to answer all of the following questions—What happened? How did it happen? Why did it happen?

We cannot emphasize enough that interpretation is a process, not a singular episode. Usually you begin an investigation with some preliminary and tentative conjectures about why things happened the way they did. As one of C. S. Lewis's characters noted in *Out of the Silent Planet*, "[Y]ou cannot see things till you know roughly what they are."[11] Your initial conjectures may have to be modified or cast aside as you dig deeper into the evidence, and new ideas may be "tried on for size." In essence, you are creating a preliminary hypothesis that will allow you to begin your research with a sense of direction and purpose. At each stage of your project, you will have to refine your interpretation as new evidence comes to light and as your understanding of the material becomes more sophisticated. In the end, your final interpretation, or thesis, must be constructed so that it does justice to *all* the evidence you have discovered.

Of course, all of this is easier said than done. Grappling with the complexities of even a small-scale episode—like the Salem witch panic—is like unraveling a snarled skein of yarn. Perhaps the real source of the difficulty is that the historian is attempting to turn the world, complex and multilayered, into language, which is linear and can express only one idea or relationship at a time. The process is one of mental reconstruction. Eventually the hours of reading, mental shuffling, and reorganizing pay off: there emerges a synthesis, a mental image that combines elements experienced separately. Some would use the term "pattern," others "insight," instead of synthesis. Whatever word is used, the exact processes of the mental experience described here remain a mystery to psychologists. Sometimes the synthesis builds slowly, often

---

[11] Quoted in David Lowenthal, *The Past is a Foreign Country*, 39.

laboriously, occasionally with a sudden flash. Whichever the case, undue haste in trying to "make it come" can be counterproductive, a point perfectly understood by novelist Eudora Welty:

> Connections slowly emerge. Like distant landmarks you are approaching, cause and effect begin to align themselves, draw closer together. Experiences too indefinite of outline in themselves to be recognized for themselves connect and are identified as a larger shape. And suddenly a light is thrown back, as when your train makes a curve, showing that there has been a mountain of meaning rising behind you on the way you've come, is rising there still, proven now through retrospect.[12]

Thus, after studious and extended consideration of the historical situation in which an event is contained, the historian sees (or begins to see) that event as part of a larger whole. The event is like a piece of jigsaw puzzle, which suddenly makes sense when seen in the context of other pieces. It is important to state, however, that the historian should not passively wait for a moment of inspiration. You need to search out a meaningful understanding of the problem you are addressing, using all of your prior experiences and knowledge as guides. Students of history, whatever their experience, will approach historical situations with certain expectations about how human affairs work, and then use these expectations to develop their interpretations. Obviously those with wide experience in human affairs have something of a head start. But however wide one's experience, the rules of the game require that one's expectations serve as a guide (not an inflexible formula) that may (or may not) prove useful in explaining the event under consideration.

Variations in Interpretation

How can we judge the validity of interpretations—our own or those that we encounter? It is best to avoid a counsel of perfection on this matter. For one thing, all historical generalizations are probabilistic rather than certain. Physicists may say with certitude that all physical objects must descend according to a mathematically predictable rate of acceleration. Historians are in no such position, for, as we saw in Chapter 2, their evidence is never complete and they can never be sure that the evidence they do have is representative. The historian is more or less in the situation of a person driving down a street, who, seeing five black cats, is tempted to conclude that all cats on that street are black. Perhaps it is so, but there are likely a number of cats on the block the driver has not seen. As a rule, therefore, most historical generalizations have a tentative quality, since there is always the possibility that new evidence will force us to reconsider our original judgment.

There is, however, another, equally important side to the matter. Any historical occurrence may be interpreted in a variety of ways, and more than one interpretation may be valid, or at least partially valid. This is so because historians themselves are a factor in the equation: each one has different interests, priorities, and points of view. As Patrick Gardiner observes in *The Nature of Historical Explanation*:

---

[12] Eudora Welty, *One Writer's Beginning* (Cambridge, MA.: Harvard University Press, 1984), 90.

"There are no absolute Real Causes waiting to be discovered by historians with sufficiently powerful magnifying-glasses. What do exist are historians writing upon different levels and at different distances, historians writing with different aims and different interests, historians writing in different contexts and from different points of view.[13]

Because historians approach the past with differing points of view and with different interests and goals, they may vary greatly in how they "locate" an event in the broad context of the period they are studying. Thus, the election of Franklin D. Roosevelt in 1932 can legitimately be regarded as part of the public's reaction to economic distress, as the product of a series of political failures by Republicans, as part of an ideological shift by the American people, as a positive reaction to Roosevelt's charismatic personality, or (in a more sophisticated way) as a combination of all these factors. Behind each of these interpretations (patterns) is a particular frame of reference and point of view. And, we might add, each one can be supported with a great deal of evidence. So, like travelers, when historians start from different places, they may travel different roads to reach the same destination.

The simple passage of time can lead to dramatic changes in interpretation. The eminent American historian John Hope Franklin said, "The writing of history reflects the interests, predilections, and even prejudices of a given generation." Compare two American history textbooks on the contributions of women drawn into the workforce on the home front during World War II (U.S. participation, 1941–45). One text was published in 1944, while the war was still going on; the other was published in 1999.

"I've found the job where I fit best!" World War II poster encouraging women to enter the workforce. *Library of Congress, Prints & Photographs Division, FSA/OWI Collection, (LC-USZ62- 99103).*

---

[13] Patrick Gardiner, *The Nature of Historical Explanation* (London: Oxford University Press, 1963), 109.

1944

In these circumstances, especially with so many mothers employed for long hours, by day or by night, outside the home, family life was not only shattered but hordes of young children were turned into the streets to fend for themselves. Older children left school in droves to work in factories for fabulous wages and, refusing to return to schools, took their lives into their own keeping. With children unguided by teachers or parents, juvenile delinquency and crimes increased to an extent that threatened the moral basis of American society. In August 1943, J. Edgar Hoover, head of the federal police force, exclaimed: "The tragedy revealed by our latest survey is found in the fact that the arrests of boys and girls seventeen years of age increased 17.7% [last year]". . . .

While various women's organizations were rejoicing in the equalities of opportunity, honors, and monetary rewards offered to women by the war and were pushing the recruiting of women for war work of all kinds, individual women, and to some extent organized women, began to appreciate the social peril of juvenile delinquency and also the problems of caring for the babies of mothers engaged in war work. [C. A. Beard, and M. R. Beard, *A Basic History of the United States* (Philadelphia: New Home Library, 1944), 474.]

Comment

In 1944 many Americans (especially men) believed that women should and would return to their domestic duties once the war had ended. This passage is remarkable because it argues that the movement of women into the work force was destabilizing society. The authors seem to think that, at best, women workers were a necessary evil. Clearly things would be better if "Rosie the Riveter" (the wartime symbol of the "can-do" woman) returned home once the emergency had passed.

1999

The need for workers opened economic opportunities for women. Now, instead of being dissuaded from taking jobs as they had been during the depression, they were urged to go to work. Six million women joined the 12 million already in the labor force. They took on a wide variety of jobs and surprised the men who said they were too weak and delicate to be lumberjacks, blast furnace operators, stevedores, or blacksmiths. They proved that they could handle all these jobs. . . . Many for the first time could show their talents as doctors, dentists, chemists, and lawyers. "Rosie the Riveter" became an inspiration for all Americans.

Black women benefited too. Before the war a greater percentage of black women worked than white. But they were generally restricted to low-paying jobs as domestic servants or farm laborers. When war came they found more interesting and better-paying jobs. . . .

When World War II ended, it seemed that once again women might be forced to leave their jobs to make places for returning servicemen. But this time a much larger proportion was offered work in peacetime production. Prodded by war, the nation discovered its women and helped women discover themselves. [Daniel J. Boorstin and Brooks Mather Kelley, *A History of the United States* (Upper Saddle River, NJ: Prentice Hall, 1999), 677–78.]

Comment

This passage, written long after the movement for gender equality had
come on the scene, not only praises the contribution of women during
World War II, but it acknowledges that there were 12 million women in
the workforce before the war started. The passage also brings African American women into the narrative. These authors see the war as
a major step in the advancement of opportunities for American women.
[Longer versions of the two excerpts above are also reprinted in Kyle
Ward, *History in the Making*. (New York: The New Press, 2006), 285-286;
288.]

Whose Interpretation?

Increasingly on American campuses, students argue that the test of an "opinion" is
the strength with which it is held, rather than the evidence that supports it. Their
ultimate conclusion, all too often, is that one opinion is as good as another, reasoning that everyone is entitled to his or her own. This is wrong, however, when factual
claims are involved, and it is certainly the enemy of solid historical scholarship. Simply because historical interpretations are tentative and reflect individual points of
view does not mean that any and every interpretation is equally acceptable. Judging
the soundness of a historical interpretation can be a complex and time-consuming
endeavor, but that sober reality should not keep you from trying. From a practical,
day-to-day standpoint, historians ask at least two questions when evaluating an
interpretation.

1. Does the author adequately support the interpretation with evidence? What we as
readers want is an interpretation clearly tied to a *representative sample* of the available evidence. That there is evidence in favor of a claim is important, but it is not
enough. Historians must consider *all* the evidence that has come to light; they can't
cherry-pick only that evidence which fits some prejudged conclusion. We are willing
to recognize that no one can cover everything and that the author is obligated only
to cover the material relevant to the interpretation being developed. But intellectual
honesty demands that historians not stack the deck by ignoring evidence that might
contradict claims they are trying to make.

2. Does the author avoid being overwhelmed by personal biases? All of us are aware that
we have certain biases, be they political, national, racial, class, religious, or moral.
We know that they can decisively shape our viewpoint, leading to a refusal to look
honestly at evidence that does not fit our point of view. Perhaps it is true that history
is "neither made nor written without love or hate," but we must attempt to distance
ourselves from our personal attitudes as much as possible and recognize the inherent dangers in letting them pervade our work. At the very least, we must inform our
readers of our point of view (ideological or otherwise) so that they might consider
our frame of reference as they weigh our historical claims. This is a simple matter
of intellectual honesty. Just as an advertiser can distort the qualities of a product, so
too can a historian distort the reality of the past. In fact, the world's libraries have

many books full of misrepresentations founded on misplaced nationalism, political ideology, or similar preoccupations. (One anonymous cynic said, "All modern wars start in the history classroom.")

EXERCISES

SET A   *Exercise 1 — Classification*

Effective interpretation requires that you put information into manageable units of analysis. This process, *classification*, is fundamental to the study of history, and vital if you intend to write intelligibly about human affairs. The past, as a whole, is so complex and confusing that it is incomprehensible unless broken into small, digestible pieces. The pieces must be *organized* into patterns that make sense to the researcher. Just as books in a huge library are of little use without a clear classification scheme to help you find the one you need, the "facts" of history are useless without similar systems of classification.

Whether classifying books or historical data, the choice of a classification system is often quite arbitrary. Classification systems are trial-and-error undertakings. As we proceed from ignorance to comprehension, most of us find ourselves using tentative categories or names that later prove to be inexact or imprecisely phrased. When this happens, we have to alter our classification scheme. Finally, to classify effectively you have to use a "part-whole" mentality. That is, somewhere along the way you need to establish some major categories (often three or four), along with a number of subcategories appropriate to each.

Since historians choose their own classification schemes, there is the ever-present danger of trying to shoehorn information into configurations that distort more than clarify. The other extreme, approaching historical data with a totally blank mind, is also unsatisfactory (not to mention impossible), as you lack the beginnings of a classification system to make the data manageable. Since you cannot totally eliminate the influence of personal values and biases when creating a classification scheme, at least you can avoid the twin dangers mentioned above if you take to heart the words of Barzun and Graff: "To be successful and right, a selection [i.e., pattern or scheme of classification] must face two ways: it must fairly correspond to the mass of evidence, and it must offer a graspable design to the beholder.[14]

The most basic and obvious of the categories used by historians to classify information are the time periods—decades, reigns, centuries, eras—that constitute the organizational units of history books and college curricula. Period labels, like all classification schemes, are the invention of the historian, a point clearly made by British historian G. J. Renier: "It cannot be stated with sufficient emphasis that the historian's principles of serialization are introduced into history by him, not deduced from it. . . .[15] In Chapter 2 we noted that many historians use the dates 1914–89 to describe the "twentieth century." Balancing this "short" twentieth century, students of British history encounter a very long "eighteenth century" (1688–1815), and Ameri-

---

[14] Barzun and Graff, *The Modern Researcher*, 179.
[15] G. J. Renier, *History: Its Purpose and Method* (New York: Harper and Row, 1965), 176.

can historians talk about the "long nineteenth century" (1787–1914). These spans are convenient fictions based on key events in war and politics. Historians writing on other subjects with other interests might use quite different "eras." There are no absolute openings and closings in history. To think otherwise is fundamentally anti-historical—remember what was said about change and continuity. Historical pots generally boil slowly, so the assigned dates of a historical "period" must be treated with flexibility.

Classification is a natural inclination of the mind, but, like any other human capability, this inclination must be disciplined and thus expanded. Such is the purpose of the exercise that follows. All of the information given below relates to the Confederate States of America, 1861–65. Your task is to classify the information into four categories, using your own headings, except for the first, which we have provided as an example. There should be three items in each category.

a. The Confederate dream of revolutionizing New Mexico and California ended in March 1862, when a rebel force was defeated at Pidgin's Ranch, just east of Glorieta Pass in the territory of New Mexico.

b. The Constitution of the Confederacy provided for a cabinet of six members, who were to serve as administrators of their departments and advisors to the president.

c. The Confederacy sent John Slidell as an envoy to France, but he was unable to secure French recognition of the Confederation as an independent government.

d. A stunning loss for the South occurred in mid-1863 when Vicksburg on the Mississippi fell to General Grant, causing him to telegraph Lincoln that "the Father of Waters again flows unvexed to the sea."

e. In 1861 the seceding southern states formed the Confederated States of America and elected Jefferson Davis as the first president.

f. Though Confederate commissioners were received cordially in London, British dealings with them were minimal because of the strong antislavery feelings of the British common people.

g. In the early stages of the Civil War the Southern government had to refuse the enlistments of tens of thousands of young men because there were no firearms for them.

h. The Southern victory at Chancellorsville in 1863, while decisive, was also extremely costly, as one of the South's greatest field commanders, General "Stonewall" Jackson, lost his life there.

i. Estimates of the total number of men in Confederate uniform during the four years of the war run from 700,000 to 900,000.

j. The first Confederate effort at diplomacy failed when U.S. Secretary of State Seward refused to see the Southern commissioners sent to establish peaceful relations with the United States government.

k. By the mid-point of the war, Southern recruitment of soldiers was bolstered by conscription of able-bodied men between the ages of eighteen and forty-five.

l. Because of the opposition of states' righters, who feared its appellate jurisdiction, the Confederate governmental system had to get along without a supreme court.

Category 1: Basis/Label: *Diplomacy/International Relations*

1. *Envoy Slidell unsuccessful in obtaining French recognition of independence (c).*
2. *Confederates received cordially in London but little accomplished (f).*
3. *U.S. government refuses to see Southern diplomats (j).*

Category 2: Basis/Label: _____

1. _____

2. _____

3. _____

Category 3: Basis/Label: _____

1. _____

2. _____

3. _____

Category 4: Basis/Label: _____

1. _____

2. _____

3. _____

SET A   *Exercise 2 — Generalization*

We are now going to call upon you to interpret an array of facts. For each set of statements below write a carefully worded topic sentence that could serve as a lead-in to the specific pieces of information you are attempting to synthesize.

Note: *At this point we want to remind you of our earlier distinction between "summary" generalizations and "limited interpretive" generalizations. Broadly speaking there are two types of generalization: (1) those that summarize, such as: "It was a very hot day" (based on high temperature readings for several hours) and (2) those that show causal relationships, such as: "High temperatures prevailed today because a lingering high pressure area brought southerly winds." Both of these types of generalization are common in historical discourse. By far the most important of them is the causal, explanatory generalization (type 2).*

A. Using the following statements about the impact of the Model-T automobile in America in the 1920s, write a topic sentence (*summary generalization*) in the spaces provided below the statements.

- The Model-T ended the social isolation of the American farmer.
- By enabling children to get away from their parents, the automobile affected American family life.
- The automobile influenced romantic relationships, as now lovers could have a privacy not possible before.
- One of the factors contributing to the weakening of neighborhood relationships in America was the car, which enabled people to travel easily outside the neighborhood.

_____

_____

B. The following statements relate to German plans to repulse the anticipated Allied invasion of Western Europe in 1944. At that point in World War II, the German leader, Adolf Hitler, knew that the Allied invasion would determine Germany's fate. If the invasion could be repulsed, he thought, Germany might yet win the war. Using the following items, write an *interpretive generalization* that explains why the Germans failed to repulse the invasion that came in June 1944. You should organize the statements chronologically and topically before you decide on the best interpretive sentence.

- Sent from Italy in early 1944 to inspect German defenses against invasion, General Erwin Rommel (the famed "Desert Fox" of the North African campaign) found them uncoordinated and undermanned.
- Shortly after his arrival in Normandy, General Rommel initiated extensive improvement of waterline defenses, including underwater obstacles, concrete dragon's teeth, and offshore mines.
- German western military commander Field Marshal von Rundstedt saw no hope of preventing an Allied landing; however, he believed a German counterattack could throw them back to the beaches.
- German dictator Adolf Hitler, though agreeing with Rommel on where the Allies would strike (in Normandy), thought important diversionary activity would occur in the Calais sector, which was well north of Normandy.
- Rommel believed that once ashore the Allies could not be stopped; therefore, they must be stopped at the water's edge.
- Rommel was convinced that the main Allied invasion effort would be mounted in Normandy, which, as distinct from Calais, had not been mined by the Allies.
- Von Rundstedt, no admirer of Hitler, thought the main invasion strike would be in the Calais area.
- During the invasion itself, Allied air supremacy, destroying German transportation and communication facilities, immobilized German forces.

- Hitler compromised between the von Rundstedt view and the Rommel view; though believing Rommel to be correct, he allowed large army groups to remain committed to the Calais area.

_____

_____

C. In the mid-1950s a new music widely known as "rock and roll" (rhythm and blues in the African American community where it originated) began to displace in popularity older musical forms, such as crooning and the big band style. Write an *interpretive generalization* about that development based on the following statements.[16]

- One of the attractions of rock is that it makes few if any intellectual demands on the listener.
- Earlier popular black performers, such as Nat King Cole and Duke Ellington, adjusted their performances to white norms, as contrasted with black rock and rollers, who cared little for white gentility in clothing, dance, and language.
- Sam Phillips, a Memphis recording executive, was heard to say (in 1953), "If I could find a white man who had the Negro sound and the Negro feel, I could make a million dollars."
- As a group, teenagers of the 1950s had more money, more freedom, and less family orientation than any of their predecessors.
- As contrasted with earlier "white" popular music, rock featured hard-driving rhythm, shouted, repetitive lyrics, heavy dependence on guitar and drums, all this with ear-popping amplification.
- Pat Boone, a clean-cut college educated white, also did a few rock songs, thus giving the music a respectability to those who did not care for the ribald antics of Elvis Presley and various black performers.
- Widely popular in the 1930s, "swing" music had lost its momentum by the late 1940s, and had also lost much of its earlier audience to newly emerging television and to the movies.
- The white popularizer of rock, Elvis Presley "created a definitely 'antiparent' outlook. . . . His music and he, himself—appeared somewhat insolent, slightly hoodlum."
- Regarded as the "first" rock and roll song, "Rock a Beaten Boogie" was written by Bill Haley, a white band leader who with his "Comets" performed it for white audiences thus breaking the color line for this new music.
- Expressing the view of older Americans, popular crooner Frank Sinatra described rock music as "phony and false, and sung, written and played for the most part by cretinous goons."

_____

_____

_____

[16]These statements, some quoted and some paraphrased, were drawn from Daniel P. Szatmary, *Rockin' In Time* (Englewood Cliffs, NJ: Prentice-Hall, Inc. 1987); and James L. Baughman, *The Republic of Mass Culture* (Baltimore: The Johns Hopkins University Press, 1997).

SET A   *Exercise 3* [Optional: Consult your instructor.]

On a separate sheet of paper, write a full paragraph that synthesizes the information found in either Item B (German plans to repulse an Allied invasion) or Item C (the rise of rock and roll) from Exercise 2 above. Begin with your topic sentence (which should be a "limited interpretive"—explanatory—generalization) and support it with evidence drawn from the informational statements provided in Exercise 2. You need not use all of the statements in your paragraph, but it is important that you take account of them.

SET A   *Exercise 4 — Bias and Historians' Frames of Reference*

The French writer, François Fénelon, once said, "The good historian belongs to no time or country: though he loves his own, he never flatters it in any respect. The French historian must remain neutral between France and England. . . ." Difficult counsel indeed. What Fénelon was talking about is bias.

Earlier in this chapter we discussed the matter of the historian's "intellectual preoccupations"—the biases that might be national (despite the above advice), political, racial, class, religious, or moral. Remember, all interpretations reflect, to some extent, the historian's frame of reference. But bias is more than an acceptable intrusion of the historian's point of view; bias is, in the words of Barzun and Graff, *"an uncontrolled form of interest"* (italics ours). The presence of bias does not automatically mean a piece of history is worthless, but it is important that you develop the ability to identify obvious intrusions of bias so that you are better able to weigh the credibility of what you read.

Below are some examples of history writing that reflect the biases of their authors. Your task with the following excerpts is to identify in each passage any kind of bias you detect. Pay attention to each author's choice of words, emphasis, tone, and the like. Under each passage record the type(s) of bias you detect (political, racial or ethnic, class, national, religious, moral) along with your reasons perceiving them. *In choosing your labels decide what particular religion, class, ideology, etc. the historian is biased for or against.*

> 1. Cuba, our land, emerged from the condition of being a Spanish colony at the close of the past century, only to become a protectorate and semi-colony of the United States.
>
> The efforts of the Cuban people to gain full independence and sovereignty—the heroic sacrifices of the Ten Years' War, the little Way, the War of [18]95, the aspirations expressed . . . above all by Antonio Maceo and by José Marti—were frustrated and flouted by North American intervention in the Cuban-Spanish War at a time when the Cubans had practically defeated Spanish colonialism and were on the verge of gaining full independence.
>
> In 1902 it was said that Cuba was a free and sovereign republic. It had an anthem and a flag. But above these symbols of sovereignty . . . we had the Platt Amendment, an instrument of oppression and of foreign domination over the country. . . .
>
> The United States imperialists had militarily occupied the island. They maintained here their army of occupation; by trickery they had disarmed the Army of Liberation and had organized a rural militia and a police force under their command. . . .

_____

_____

_____

2. Eisenhower and his administration have lived off the accumulated wisdom, the accumu-lated prestige, and the accumulated military strength of his predecessors who conducted more daring and more creative regimes. If our margin for error is as great as it has tradi-tionally been, these quiet Eisenhower years will have been only a pleasant idyll, an inex-pensive interlude in a grim century. If our margin for error is much thinner than formerly, Eisenhower may join the ranks of history's fatal good men, the Stanley Baldwins and the James Buchanans. Their intentions were good and their example is pious, but they be-queathed to their successors a black heritage of time lost and opportunities wasted.

_____

_____

_____

3. The first element in the negro problem is the presence in America of two alien races, both practically servants. The Indians were savages, and helped to keep alive savage traits in the souls of white settlers; but there was no considerable number of mixed bloods, and the Indians faded away as the white people advanced. The original slaves were also sav-ages, just out of the jungle, who required to be watched and handled like savages, but they steadily increased in numbers, and from the beginning there was a serious race admixture. Their descendants in the second and third generation were milder in character, and were much affected by at least a surface Christianity; but their standards of character were much lower than those of the dominant white community, and tended to pull the superior race down. To the present day the low conditions of great numbers of negroes has a bad effect on the white race.

_____

_____

_____

4. In pride and vanity, he [Henry VIII] was perhaps without a parallel. He despised the judgment of others; acted as if he deemed himself infallible in matters of policy and religion; and seemed to look upon dissent from his opinion as equivalent to a breach of allegiance. He steeled his breast against remorse for the blood which he shed, and trampled with out scruple on the liberties of the nation. When he ascended the throne, there still existed a spirit of freedom, which on more than one occasion defeated the arbitrary mea-

sures of the court; but in the lapse of a few years that spirit had fled, and before the death of Henry, the king of England had grown into a despot, the people had shrunk into a nation of slaves.

_____

_____

_____

5. During the last century the [New England] manufacturer imported the Irish and Fr[ench] Canadians . . . thus the American sold his birthright in a continent to solve a labor problem. Instead of retaining political control and making citizenship an honorable and valued privilege, he intrusted the government of his country and the maintenance of his ideals to races who have never yet succeeded in governing themselves, much less anyone else.

   Associated with this advance of democracy and the transfer of power from the higher to the lower races, from the intellectual to the plebian class, we find the spread of socialism and the recrudescence of obsolete religious forms.

_____

_____

_____

Sources
   1. Donald Robinson, ed., *As Others See Us* (Boston: Houghton Mifflin, 1969), 108–109.
   2. William V. Shannon, "Eisenhower as President," in *Perspectives on 20th Century America,* Otis L. Graham, Jr., ed. (New York: Dodd, Mead, 1973), 323.
   3. Albert B. Hart, "Negro Problem," *Cyclopedia on American Government* (Chicago: Appleton, 1914), 513.
   4. John Lingard, *History of England,* Vol. IV (Paris: W. Galignani, 1840), 215.
   5. Madison Grant, "The Passing of the Great Race," in *Antidemocratic Trends in Twentieth-Century America,* Roland L. DeLorme and Raymond G. McInnes, eds. (Reading, MA.: Addison-Wesley, 1969), 45.

SET B   *Exercise 1 — Classification*

See discussion under Set A, Exercise 1 (pp. 190–191).

All the information given below relates to Adolf Hitler's Germany (1933–45) and World War II (1939–45). Your task is to classify the information into four categories, using your own headings, except for the first, which we have provided as an example. There should be three items in each category.

   a. Though he lacked the qualities of a statesman, Hitler shaped events by the force of his personality. He exuded personal magnetism.

b. In September 1939 the world saw a new form of military power, as the German *blitzkrieg* (lightning war) smashed through Poland in a matter of days.

c. At Munich, in September 1938, the leaders of Germany, France, Italy, and Great Britain "solved" the Czechoslovakian problem with an international agreement that gave the Sudetenland to Germany.

d. By the Nuremberg decree of 1935, German Gentiles were forbidden not only to marry Jews but even to touch them.

e. The Austrian *Anschluss* (union with Germany) in 1938 had been signaled earlier by German-Austrian diplomatic negotiations concerning trade relations.

f. One of the most brilliant achievements of the German *Wehrmacht* (army) was its "end run" around the fortified French Maginot Line, leading to the destruction of the French army as a fighting force.

g. Because he thought in black-and-white terms, Hitler had no difficulty in perceiving those who opposed him as wholly evil.

h. Extensive German demands on Poland in 1939 led to a flurry of diplomatic negotiation between Germany and Russia, culminating in the Nazi-Soviet Pact of that year.

i. Exercising the power given him in the Enabling Act, Hitler decreed that all political parties but his own Nazi party were to be abolished.

j. The German *Füehrer* (Hitler) was an opportunist, a man who knew clearly what he wanted and patiently waited for a chance to strike.

k. In 1933 Hitler maneuvered the German Reichstag into passing the Enabling Act, which gave him the power to pass laws without consent of the Reichstag, thus making him a dictator.

l. After a highly successful campaign in North Africa, General Erwin Rommel's *Afrika Korps* was repulsed and thrown back at El Alamein, the first major defeat of a German army in World War II.

Category 1: Basis/Label: *Aspects of Hitler's personality*

1. *Influenced events by blunt force of personality rather than statesmanship (a)*
2. *Not a subtle thinker—thought in categorical terms (g)*
3. *Had clear goals and patiently awaited opportunities (j)*

Category 2: Basis/Label: _____

1. _____

2. _____

3. _____

Category 3: Basis/Label: _____

1. _____

2. _____

3. _____
Category 4: Basis/Label: _____

1. _____

2. _____

3. _____

SET B   *Exercise 2 — Generalization*

For each set of statements below write a carefully worded topic sentence (generalization) that could serve as a lead-in to the specific pieces of information you are attempting to synthesize. Before beginning, review the note on summary and limited interpretive generalizations in the directions of Set A, Exercise 2 (pg. 192).

A. Using the following statements concerning the technological development of the United States in the late nineteenth and early twentieth centuries, write a *summary generalization* in the space provided.

- In 1879, Thomas Edison perfected the light bulb and three years later, in 1882, developed the first power transmitting station, thus bringing a major new form of power to U.S. industry.
- In the late nineteenth century the "open hearth" process of steelmaking was developed, marking a notable advance in machine tool production.
- By the early years of the twentieth century, American industrial production vastly exceeded that of her nearest rival.
- Development of the internal combustion engine in the late 1800s greatly increased the market for industrial products.
- The continuing development of petroleum products in the years after 1870 significantly influenced American industrial markets.

_____

_____

B. The following statements relate to the rejection of the Versailles treaty by the U.S. Senate in 1919–20. President Woodrow Wilson had gone to Versailles and personally negotiated this treaty ending World War I. The treaty he brought home called for American acceptance of League of Nations participation. Write an *interpretive generalization* in the space provided.

- Though temporarily sidetracked in 1917–18 by anti-German feeling, traditional American isolationism remained strong.
- In 1918, Americans elected a Republican Senate, an ominous sign for the Democratic administration of President Woodrow Wilson.
- Americans of German and of Irish ethnic background opposed the League of Nations, although for different reasons.
- The wrangling of European diplomats at the Versailles Peace Conference of 1919 confirmed many Americans' view of European countries as narrow and self-serving.
- To get the League of Nations principle accepted in the peace treaty, President Wilson had to compromise several of his ideals.
- The chairman of the Senate Foreign Affairs Committee was Republican Henry Cabot Lodge, a major political enemy of President Wilson.
- Wilson's peace treaty incorporating the League of Nations principle, which had to be approved by the Senate, was eventually decisively rejected.
- Wilson's refusal to take any Republican with him to the Versailles Peace Conference eventually proved costly to his hopes of Congressional acceptance of the treaty.

C. During the 1960s rock and roll music became something of a national passion. Using the following statements as the base, write an *interpretive generalization* in the space provided.[17]

- Emerging as rivals to the Beatles were the Rolling Stones, who cultivated a rebel image and whose songs represented more overt sexuality through pornographic lyrics.
- Acid rock as played by such drug-influenced groups as the "Jefferson Airplane" and the "Grateful Dead" had taken over much of American airwaves by 1968.
- Even Bob Dylan, whose protest songs infused with a folk style had gained a wide following among better-educated teens, saw the Beatles as the wave of the future.
- During the early sixties the [Elvis] Presley fan following was diluted when the musical tastes of rural and blue-collar youth shifted to country music.
- The Beatles' popularity was partly traceable to their somewhat more moderate image: their tailored suits, their mod haircuts, and their self-mocking style.
- As measured by record sales, rock and roll appeared to be on the way out in the early 1960s.

---

[17]These statements, some quoted and some paraphrased, were drawn from Daniel P. Szatmary, *Rockin' In Time* and James L. Baughman, *The Republic of Mass Culture.*

- By 1969 the "rock revolution" had become the staging area for drug addiction, indiscriminate sex, and full-scale rejection of traditional American values.
- In 1964 the Beatles, already popular in England, became an American sensation when they appeared on the Ed Sullivan show, followed by two concerts at Carnegie Hall.

_____

_____

SET B   *Exercise 3* [Optional: Consult your instructor.]

On a separate sheet of paper, write a full paragraph that synthesizes the information found in either Item B (U.S. rejection of the Versailles Treaty) or Item C (rock and roll music) from Exercise 2 above. Begin with your topic sentence (which should be a "limited interpretive"—explanatory—generalization) and support it with evidence drawn from the informational statements provided in Exercise 2. You need not use all of the statements in your paragraph, but it is important that you take account of them.

SET B   *Exercise 4 — Bias and Historians' Frames of Reference*

See comments introducing Exercise 4 of Set A (pg. 195).

Below are some examples of history writing that reflect the biases of their authors. Your task with the following excerpts is to identify in each passage any kind of bias you detect. Pay attention to each author's choice of words, emphasis, tone, and the like. Under each passage record the type(s) of bias you detect (political, racial or ethnic, class, national, religious, moral) along with your reasons for perceiving them. *In choosing your labels decide what particular religion, class, ideology, etc., the historian is biased for or against.*

> 1. We love to indulge in thoughts of the future extent and power of this [American] Republic—because with its increase is the increase of human happiness and liberty. . . . What has miserable, inefficient Mexico—with her superstition, her burlesque upon freedom, her actual tyranny by the few over the many—what has she to do with the great mission of . . . the New World. . . .

_____

_____

_____

2. God has not been preparing the English-speaking and Teutonic [Germanic] peoples for a thousand years for nothing but vain and idle self-contemplation and self-admiration. No, He has made us master organizers of the world to establish system where chaos reigns. [Hint: "Religious Bias" is not the answer!]

_____

_____

_____

3. The Romanism [Catholicism] of the present day [late nineteenth century] is a harmless opinion, no more productive of evil than any other superstition, and without tendency, or shadow of tendency, to impair the allegiance of those who profess it. But we must not confound a phantom with a substance; or gather from modern experience the temper of a time when words implied realities, when Catholics really believed that they owed no allegiance to an heretical sovereign, and that the first duty of their lives was to a foreign potentate. This perilous doctrine was waning, indeed, but it was not dead. By many it was actively professed.

_____

_____

_____

4. An underlying weakness of his [F. D. Roosevelt's] leadership lay in his acceptance of the pragmatic approach to the solution of both domestic and foreign problems. In essence, it was a refusal to take the stand for a distinctively American approach to the basic problems of capitalism. No political program that emerged in the Roosevelt administration was distinctly the expression of the American tradition. In the course of twelve years, at home and abroad, the President stood with the radicals, using the political party parlance of the "middle way" in both instances.

_____

_____

_____

5. In fighting the War for Independence in North America, the bourgeoisie led the popular masses of the colonies against the English landed aristocracy and against the colonial yoke of England. This war of the colonies for independence was a bourgeois [middle-class]

revolution which overthrew the landed aristocracy and brought to power the American bourgeoisie in union with the slaveholders. The American bourgeoisie used the struggle of the popular masses against the English as a means of achieving power; then, having come to power, like the English bourgeoisie of the seventeenth century, they oppressed the popular masses. In North America under the title "sovereignty of the people," (democracy), a so-called bourgeois democracy (in actual fact, the power of the bourgeoisie), was established.

_____

_____

_____

Sources
1. Walt Whitman, editorial, *Brooklyn Daily Eagle* (July 7, 1846), in *The Mexican War*, Ramon Ruiz, ed. (New York: Holt, Rinehart and Winston, 1963), 8.
2. Albert J. Beveridge, *The Meaning of the Times and Other Speeches* (Indianapolis: Bobbs-Merill, 1908), 84–85.
3. James A. Froude, *History of England*, Vol. II (New York: Charles Scribner, 1872), 321.
4. Edgar E. Robinson, *The Roosevelt Leadership, 1933–45* (New York: Lippincott, 1955), 404.
5. Donald Robinson, ed., *As Others See Us* (Boston: Houghton Mifflin, 1969), 321.

CHAPTER 12 WRITING: THE HISTORY PAPER

"Writing is easy. All you do is stare at a blank sheet of paper until drops of blood form on your forehead."

—Gene Fowler

"As works of the imagination, the historian's work and the novelist's do not differ. Where they do differ is that the historian's picture is meant to be true."

—R. G. Collingwood[1]

Many students spend their college days going from class to class, often without appreciating the close relationships between the different subjects they are studying. These relationships are especially pronounced when the courses are in literature, journalism, and history. As British historian R. G. Collingwood has argued above, the overlap between novelists and historians is especially close, a truism illustrated by the career of American author Truman Capote.

Capote emerged as a writer of some importance on the New York scene in the late 1940s. Over the next thirty-six years he produced several novels and many short stories, but it was as a journalist that he achieved his greatest fame. In 1965 he published what would prove to be his best-known work, *In Cold Blood*, a six-year project that was the hit of that year's literary scene.[2] *In Cold Blood* was a 343-page account of the murder of four members of the Clutter family in Holcomb, Kansas, an account distinctive because it was presented as a "non-fiction novel." To some observers the term "non-fiction novel" is self-contradictory, but many others credit Capote with having created a new art form. Essentially what Capote did was to use the conventions of the novel to tell a true story. What resulted was a book that read like engrossing fiction but was actually a work of history. According to one literary critic, it is "quite possibly the best piece of artistic journalism ever written."[3]

Although Truman Capote died in 1984, he was re-introduced to younger generations in the award-winning film *Capote* (2005) starring Philip Seymour Hoffman.[4] The film was nominated for five Academy Awards and Hoffman won the Oscar for best actor. The focus of the film is the period in which Capote researched and wrote *In Cold Blood*—a process that offers many lessons for historians who desire to write elegant, effective prose. Capote's work on *In Cold Blood* clearly illustrates the ele-

---

[1] R. G. Collingwood, *The Idea of History*, 246.
[2] Truman Capote, *In Cold Blood* (New York: Random House, 1965). A film based on the book was released in 1967.
[3] William L. Nance, *The Worlds of Truman Capote* (New York: Stein and Day Publishers, 1970), 178.
[4] A similar film, *Infamous*, came out in 2006, with Toby Jones getting rave reviews for his portrayal of Truman Capote.

Author Truman Capote reading in 1966. *Library of Congress, Prints & Photographs Division,* New York World-Telegram *and the* Sun *Newspaper Collection (LC-USZ62-119326).*

ments of good historical writing: choosing a topic, research, analysis, organization, and composition.

Topic Selection

Choosing a topic is, in many ways, the most difficult part of any writing project. In Capote's case, he said he was looking for "a subject that would have sufficient proportions." When he read about the Clutter murders in *The New York Times* he thought he might have a worthy topic since it was "a total mystery . . . how it could have been, and what happened." Here, in a nutshell, we have the two essentials of a good topic: it must interest the writer, and it must present a question in need of an answer. To quote R. G. Collingwood again: "Every actual inquiry starts from a certain problem, and the purpose of the inquiry is to solve that problem."[5] When choosing a topic, then, make sure you have a clear question that you want your paper to answer. Rather than saying, for example, "I want to write about the Salem witch trials" (which is much too general), ask something like "Why were the Salem courts so willing to accept the accusations of adolescent girls?" The latter is much more specific and limited; it is a doable topic.

---

[5] Collingwood, *Idea,* 312. "A sensible question," he states, "is a question which you think you have or are going to have evidence for answering." (p. 281).

Research

Capote could not have been more thorough in his exploration of the facts of the Clutter case. He was interested not only in the physical setting of Holcomb, Kansas, but also in the mentality of the local citizenry. Further, since in the first stages of his research the prevailing town opinion was that the murderer was likely a local person, he found it necessary to interview everyone with even the remotest connection to the victims. His passion for accuracy was shown in his avoidance of using a tape recorder in his interviews. Finding that such equipment made interviewees nervous and un-communicative, he trained himself in total recall, becoming "his own tape recorder" as he put it.[6] Within three hours of the interview he would write out in longhand the interview contents, label its various points, cross index the material with earlier interviews, and next morning type up the previous day's material.

The search for the Clutter family killer soon widened beyond the town of Holcomb. After six weeks of work by the Kansas Bureau of Investigation, two transients in a Las Vegas, Nevada, jail cell were charged with the murders, and within a few days they had confessed to them. Now Capote entered a new phase of research: lengthy, repeated interviews with the killers in an attempt to understand their motivations and outlook. These interviews continued through the trial (both men were convicted and sentenced to hang) and for five years afterward during the long appeal process. Over this period Capote conducted more than two hundred intensive interviews with the killers, and he carried on a weekly correspondence with them as well. He came to know them "as well as I know myself," and when the time came for their execution, they asked for their new "best friend" to be present. He was there. He said he threw up a "whole two days before the execution" and "cried for two and a half days afterward." Yet, despite this emotional involvement, Capote continued writing his story.[7]

This account of Capote's work is intended to illustrate two aspects of the research process. (1) Research is frequently an arduous undertaking: It requires an understanding of the context of the event under study; it calls for thoroughness in the search for evidence, and (sometimes) a resourcefulness in adapting to the medium in which the evidence is found (in this case, interviewing); it often takes time for the researcher to achieve a strong focus on what really is vital to the undertaking; it benefits from a more-or-less continuous effort to relate a new piece of evidence to what is already known. (2) Research and writing frequently require an ability to distance oneself from emotional leanings and sentimental attachments—which, by the way, Capote often failed to do.

Analysis

By the time Capote neared the end of his project, he had accumulated about six thousand pages of typewritten notes in addition to boxes upon boxes of pertinent documents. You can bet that he did not at that point say to himself, "Well, now I've

---

[6] To develop this ability he would have a friend read to him for a certain length of time—without Capote's taking notes—and tape record the reading at the same time. Then, when the friend finished, Capote would write down his recall of what had been said, after which he would compare what he said with the tape recording. At last, Capote said, he was able to achieve nearly 100 percent accuracy.

[7] Nance, *Worlds*, 175, 176, 169.

got to sit down and begin to analyze this stuff." This stage of writing doesn't work that way. Analysis begins early and is an ongoing process throughout a project. In Capote's case it perhaps began with his second interview, during which he realized he was heading down a blind alley with this particular interviewee. Analysis is like that. Even the negatives often help in focusing the inquiry, letting the researcher know what is not involved. Capote's undertaking achieved an enhanced definition when interview subject Susan Kidwell, best friend of the murdered Nancy Clutter, described in detail the habits of the Clutters, their recent experiences as a family, and the identity of their closest associates in town. Slowly the pieces began to fit together—remember the counsel of the last chapter: "Connections emerge slowly."

Capote's investigation took a big step forward with the arrest and confessions of the killers. Still, much remained unanswered, chiefly: What could possibly have motivated the two men to slaughter an entire family? The months and years of personal contact with the killers eventually brought Capote to conclude the reason for the murders was that Perry Smith, the trigger man, saw the middle-class Clutters as symbols for the many ways in which American society had wronged him. This essentially was Capote's final piece in his structure of analysis—his interpretation.

All of this took Capote a long time. "I worked for a year on the notes before I ever wrote a line," he said.[8] Writers of papers and essays in university classes obviously won't have that sort of time, but it is good to remember that analysis is a gradual, often frustrating process. With patience, however, you will arrive at a clear sense of how the many pieces fit together into a coherent whole.

Organization

Organization, as we are using the term here, refers to the development of an overall plan for the composition to follow. The importance of such a plan can be seen in Capote's remarks about *In Cold Blood*: "[W]hen I wrote the first word, I had done the entire book in outline, down to the last detail."[9] Historians proceed in much the same way. A piece of writing should have a determinable beginning (Introduction), a developmental middle (Body), and an identifiable end (Conclusion).

1. The Introduction

The introduction is a critically important part of every paper. It is usually a paragraph that provides a gradual lead-in, something of a broad, stage-setting orientation to the subject of the paper. Remember that having done your research you are now quite familiar with that certain segment of the past, but your reader probably is not. You must describe, at least in broad terms, the context of the event you are exploring.

Next, either as a part of such a paragraph or in a paragraph immediately following it, you should unequivocally state the basic interpretive generalization (thesis) you intend to support in the pages to follow. This interpretation, which, as we have seen, is developed during the analysis process, is the cornerstone of any effective history paper. A major misconception of many students is that history papers merely present

---

[8] Nance, *Worlds*, 180.
[9] Nance *Worlds*, 180.

"facts." Not so. The historian, more than simply reciting facts, tries to explain them with a thoughtful generalization. As historian G. R. Elton said: "What distinguishes history from the collection of historical facts is generalization."[10] Facts have no meaning apart from the generalization (interpretation) the historian supplies. So it makes sense to make sure you have a clearly expressed, carefully stated generalization that you intend to support with evidence through the course of your paper. Unless this generalization is in the forefront of a writer's mind, there will be no clear basis for deciding what goes where in the body of the paper, and the result is, inevitably, chaos. If you can articulate your central thesis in a sentence or two, you are on the right track. If you can't, there may be trouble ahead.

2. The Body

The body (middle) of the paper is where you set down the main supporting points, along with necessary corroborative detail, that make your thesis believable. Some writing coaches speak of the body of the paper as its proof structure wherein you make the paper's main point convincing. Our late colleague Harry James Cargas, a much-published writer, says this about the developmental section of the paper:

> Here is where you present powerful arguments to support your thesis. Here is where you prove you are right. As in all parts of your paper, write clearly and simply and be sure that you follow this guide: overprove rather than underprove your point. So often students will try to buttress an argument with a quotation or two on the topic in question when in fact, ten or fifteen references or examples would be better.[11]

3. The Conclusion

The conclusion (end) presents, briefly, a restatement or reemphasis of the thesis along with a summary of the paper's major points. A paragraph or two is usually sufficient. This overall structure of beginning, middle, and end may seem simplistic, but it remains the organizational plan that experienced historians follow, principally because it is the most logical form and the one that most readers expect.

----

[10] Quoted in E. H. Carr, *What is History* (New York: Alfred A. Knopf, 1967), 82.
[11] Harry James Cargas, "The Term Paper: An Overview."

The Formal Outline

If you do choose to use a formal outline, keep the following in mind:[12]

1. Put the thesis (your unifying generalization) at the top.
2. Use parallel grammatical structure for parallel ideas.
3. Use sentences or fairly complete phrases in the outline. (This helps you keep the logical structure of the paper clear.)
4. Use the conventional outline format, which allows you to subordinate less-general concepts to more general ones—e.g.,

I. National government
      A. State government
            1. County government
                  a. Local government, etc.

The traditional outline format is as follows.

I. First major point/unit
      A.
      B.
           1.
           2.
                a.
                b.
                      (1)
                      (2)
                          (a)
                          (b)
II. Second major point/unit
      A.
      B.

Note, each level—I, A., 1., etc.—should have at least two subordinate points under it.

Composition

One of our favorite comments about writing is that its success is determined by "the length of time one can keep the seat of one's pants in contact with the seat of the chair." Pretty good counsel, that, but not enough to insure quality work. Therefore, we offer a few items of more specific advice.

1. Writing Coherent Paragraphs

The paragraph is the basic unit of all effective writing, since it constitutes the *thought-unit* that enables the reader to follow the writer's train of thought. Strong paragraph-

---

[12] Based on Diana Hacker, *A Writer's Reference,* 5th ed. (Boston: St. Martin's Press, 2003), 12.

ing can be achieved *only* through the creation of meaningful topic sentences. To put it more precisely, each paragraph must have a topic sentence, which, in most cases, should initiate it. The topic sentence is followed by several sentences that elaborate and develop its meaning. Whether phrased in a narrative mode (this happened, then that happened) or an analytical mode (describing effects, structures, and segments) the topic sentence points to a cluster of related elements. It is something like a master chord that resonates and reverberates throughout a paragraph. It is the most vital factor in the readability of a passage, an essay, or a research paper.

Just as an essay or paper must be clearly organized, so too the paragraph. Organization involves putting ideas and elements in proper relationship to one another, i.e., putting smaller details where they belong—under larger ideas. Readers have a right to expect this basic arrangement and get understandably irritated when they do not find it. Consider this simple illustration:

> We've been having trouble with the family car during the past few weeks. In learning to drive my most difficult task was shifting gears smoothly. My parents didn't allow me to take driving lessons until I was seventeen. Our car seems to vibrate when its speed gets over thirty-five. My driving instructor told our class that we should learn on stick-shift automobiles because it would mean a saving when we get our own cars.

This is an almost ridiculous example of a paragraph that combines several elements that don't clearly relate to each other. Truman Capote said it best: "That's not writing, that's typing!" Yet such arrangements of ideas are common in history papers and account for much of the red ink that stains work returned to student writers.

To summarize, ordering your ideas is a basic task. When you write a paper begin by putting down your basic generalization in an explicit statement, followed by 2–4 supporting points that make the generalization plausible. When writing paragraphs on each supporting point, add the detail necessary for that point to make sense. This is the fundamental principle of organization.

2. Transitions

Well-organized paragraphs are the essential building blocks writers use to develop supporting points for their interpretation. But just as building blocks have to fit together, so too do paragraphs. In other words, a careful writer must give attention to the flow between paragraphs. Quite often a new paragraph shifts to a different facet of the subject—turns a corner, so to speak. It is exactly at such points that readers might get lost unless the writer gracefully steers them into the turn. Many experienced writers do this by making the final sentence "lean" in the direction of the forthcoming shift. Sample transitions are phrases such as: "But a different factor soon made its appearance" or "As important as this development was, it was not the only influence involved." Other writers prefer to use very short two- or three-sentence transitional paragraphs (distinct from the developmental paragraph described above). This type of paragraph first summarizes then redirects the reader's attention by announcing that a new aspect of the subject is about to be discussed. Such transitional paragraphs can add greatly to the continuity of a narrative. Writers of history should use them whenever there is a danger that the reader will get lost. (Review "Writing Capsule 3" in Chapter 3, page 34.)

3. Story Shifts

A major challenge for writers of history is expressing in linear fashion (one sentence after another) the complex multi-layered reality of the past. In real life many events happen simultaneously. Therefore, sometimes the writer must interpret the historical situation in order to give the reader a more nuanced grasp of it.

- **Managing Historical Time:** A historian is something like a wilderness guide who takes a tenderfoot through the woods to a view a backwoods stream—the stream of time. The reader is invited to step into the stream to meet some of the people there, and then, stepping back on the bank, to look upstream and downstream to see a broader panorama.

  Here we are speaking of the importance of managing historical time. The reader is free to stay in the stream for awhile and follow the struggle going on there, get back on the bank, or to look up or downstream—provided the narrator gives the proper signals. Suspension of the story for political analysis, sociological commentary, psychological insights, or geographical fact are all tolerable interruptions provided the writer gives signals of the shift in attention. It is perfectly acceptable for a writer to break the flow of action, as long as it is done with careful concern about the reader's switch in mental orientation, and as long as the writer remembers to return gracefully to the main story line.

- **Shift in perspective:** Given the fact that one person's path often crosses another's, a story of the past is often a story of conflicting individuals and groups. But the dramatic values evident in conflict will remain dormant unless clearly developed by the narrator. That is, the narrator (you) must shift at critical points in the story from a description of the viewpoint or perspective of one historical figure (or group) to that of another with whom there is conflict. Thus, after discussing, say, the initiatives of U.S. military leaders at a given point in the Vietnam War, a historian might immediately switch focus and discuss the same events from the perspective of their counterparts in the North Vietnamese and South Vietnamese militaries.

4. How Much Detail is Enough?

When writers adhere to the foregoing principles, their readers begin to relax a little, knowing that a considerate hand is guiding them. Yet something more is necessary. An effective writer must not overburden the account with excessive detail, lest readers get to the point where they fail to see the larger picture. Experienced historians make this point over and over: Too much detail can obscure any argument and ultimately confuse the reader. Barbara Tuchman, a superb historian and a fine writer, expresses the same idea in this way:

> The writer of history, I believe, has a number of duties vis-à-vis the reader, if he wants him to keep reading. The first is to distill. He must do the preliminary work for the reader, assemble the information, make sense of it, select the essential, discard the irrelevant—above all, discard the irrelevant. . . . To offer a mass of undigested facts, of names not identified and places not located, is of no use to the reader and is simple laziness on the part of the author, or pedantry to show how much he has read. To discard the unnecessary requires courage and also extra work. . . .[13]

---

[13] Tuchman, *Practicing History*, 17–18.

Thus, too much information is the enemy of form. In the next breath, however, we must also warn against overcorrecting in the opposite direction.[14] As we stated earlier in this chapter, it is important to "overprove rather than underprove your point." The key principle must be that of selectivity, which, as a famous ballerina once said, is "the soul of art."

Documentation: Footnotes, Endnotes and Bibliographies

The quirks and eccentricities of English kings, aristocrats, and politicians have long intrigued the history-reading public. In the period during and after World War I there was an especially interesting collection of British public figures who loved to ridicule each other's weaknesses with witty barbs. Lord Kitchener, for instance, said: "My colleagues tell military secrets to their wives, except X who tells them to other peoples wives." X, it has been suggested, was Prime Minister H. H. Asquith. And Asquith, as historian A. J. P. Taylor notes, "was the first prime minister since the younger Pitt who is said to have been manifestly the worse for drink when on the Treasury Bench."

This type of detail makes history come to life. What is curious about the above stories is that they were drawn from footnotes in the first chapter of A. J. P. Taylor's, *English History, 1914–1945.*[15] Taylor was an eminent historian and a master of the informational footnote. Reading some of Taylor's works, which are uniformly provocative and well written, can be slow going since the reader doesn't want to miss the interesting tidbits that Taylor imbeds in his footnotes. Where else might we learn that King George V creased his trousers at the sides, not front and back? Or that General Haig said of the Earl of Derby: "like the feather pillow he bears the mark of the last person who sat on him"?[16]

In light of this we might be tempted to say: "Footnotes can be fun." We hardly think you would believe it, but such a thought shouldn't be rejected out of hand. What is indisputable is that the use of footnotes is not an affectation or a sign of snobbish pedantry. In history writing, footnoting is essential. (A footnote, by the way, is placed at the "foot" of the page. If the notes are all collected at the end of the paper they are called "endnotes." We use the term "footnote" to refer to both variations.)

There are two types of footnotes (or endnotes). The first, the *informational footnote,* you are already familiar with from the examples above. Often you have information that could clarify or expand remarks in the text but would interrupt the flow of the narrative if actually put in the body of the paper. Such footnotes provide a sort of running commentary on the material that forms the central core of your work. Very few students, in our experience, take advantage of the opportunities presented by the informational note. Give them a try, since the use of explanatory footnotes will allow you to include a good deal of important information that you otherwise might have to leave out.

---

[14] As was the case with a nineteenth-century railroad supervisor named Finnegan, who, after having been cautioned against excessive wordiness, sent railroad headquarters the following message after one in a series of derailments: "Off again, on again, gone again, Finnegan."

[15] A. J. P. Taylor, *English History,* 1914–1945 (Oxford: Clarendon Press, 1965), 3, 15.

[16] Taylor, *English History,* 2, 53.

The informational footnote is optional; the second type, the *source reference foot-note*, is not. Source references record the origin of, or authority for, material used in the text of the paper. The credibility of a piece of historical writing depends on the integrity of the historian. It is through source references (footnotes or endnotes) that we can hold writers accountable and verify the accuracy and legitimacy of their facts and generalizations. Documentation of this sort allows the reader to follow more easily the reasoning processes of an author; it allows the reader to test the links between fact and conclusion. From the author's standpoint, footnotes acknowledge the intellectual debt every writer owes to those who have gone before. Finally, in an academic setting, proper citations may shield one from the suspicion of plagiarism.

All direct quotations, of course, need be footnoted—remember the verse: Every quote, requires a note! But there is more. You also need to cite the sources of paraphrases (indirect quotations) and unique pieces of information. If you owe a debt to a specific author, whether you quote directly or not, you should provide a source reference.

How do you know if you have too many or too few citations? There is no universal standard on this matter. Footnoting, like much else in the world of scholarship, is as much art as it is science. Gradually, through practice, you will get a "feel" for what is appropriate. You will want to avoid littering your writing with an avalanche of references, or leaving the reader with the feeling that key references have been left out. Three to four references per typed page should suffice. Less or more than that and you flirt with doing your reader an injustice. Ultimately, though, the number of citations depends on the type of paper you are writing, the nature of the sources, and the expectations of your reader. Just remember, as Harry Cargas put it, "your paper is your whole presentation. You will not be there to amplify or to clarify when your reader is looking it over. Cite as many sources as necessary to leave no doubt in the reader's mind that what you say is absolutely true."[17]

Every paper should also include a bibliography or "works cited" page. A bibliography (list of the sources you consulted) serves a different function than footnotes or endnotes. A source reference tells the reader the specific location (author, title, date and place of publication, and page number) of a quotation or piece of information used in the text of a paper or book. A note has a one-to-one relationship with a particular segment of the text. A bibliography, on the other hand, gives the reader, in one place, a complete list of all the sources that were used by the author, whether they were cited in the notes or not. In some large works, authors list only the most valuable sources. This is called a "selective bibliography." A "Works Cited" page lists only those works actually mentioned in the source references (footnotes or endnotes) themselves. Whatever the case, the works listed in bibliographies or works-cited pages are alphabetized according to the first letter of the authors' last names. It is common, in larger bibliographies, to divide the sources according to type: books, articles, manuscripts, government documents, etc., or according to whether they are primary or secondary sources. In such cases, each section is alphabetized accordingly.

Although there is no substitute for owning your own style manual (along with a good dictionary), Appendix B covers some of the basics regarding the formatting

---

[17] Cargas, "The Term Paper."

of source notes and bibliographic entries. Keep in mind that source-reference styles differ among academic disciplines, and the appendix shows the style preferable in history.

The Elements of Style

The points made above are those most essential to success in writing a history paper. But what often separates the merely good paper from the memorable one is something less concrete: style. Author Truman Capote brought a novelist's perspective to his account of the Clutter murders. What this meant in practice was a richness of expression that enlivened the pages of *In Cold Blood*. His description of Holcomb, Kansas, the setting of the murders, evoked a sense of prairie loneliness: "Holcomb, too, can be seen from great distances. Not that there is much to see—simply an aimless congregation of buildings divided in the center by the main-line tracks of the Santa Fe Railroad, a haphazard hamlet bounded on the South by a brown stretch of the Arkansas [River]. . . ." His physical characterization of the murderer foreshadowed the doom that awaited the Clutters: "It was a changeling's face, and mirror-guided experiments had taught him how to ring the changes, how to look now ominous, now impish, now soulful; a tilt of the head, a twist of the lips, and the corrupt gypsy became the gentle romantic."[18]

Though history and fiction (novels) are quite distinct in their aims, as noted earlier, written history does have a good deal in common with fiction. Both historical narratives and novels deal with the gradual unfolding of a causally connected series of incidents (i.e., they both have a "plot"); both must make human acts meaningful

History as Story-telling

Narrative techniques shared by historians and novelists include:

Character Development: Obviously, many historical situations are crucially influenced by the strengths, weaknesses, and peculiarities of individuals. Consequently, the novelist's habit of putting individuals at the center of the story is one well worth imitating. There's nothing "forced" about this technique; given our ambitions, hates, and loves, all of us are continually being carried decisively across the paths of others, often with fateful consequences. This means that in a narrative the writer must present us with more than a character's actions. The central subject must also be seen remembering, reflecting, fearing, worrying, predicting, and yearning. In other words, a historical figure is both a doer and a thinker, and a comment upon his or her thinking and perceptions will much clarify the basis on which action was, or was not, taken. Of course a historian cannot "invent" motivations as can a novelist. But provided there is a basis in evidence, the historian can legitimately infer motivations, states of mind,

(Continued)

---

[18] Capote, *In Cold Blood*, 3, 15–16.

and character qualities. To do so adds much to the story being told—and much to the reader's enjoyment.

Plot Development: The term *plot* refers to a causally connected series of events. Telling the "best true story" almost always involves explaining why something happened as it did. That often means you must consider the motivations and interactions of individuals, groups, institutions, etc., and describe the web-like connections among them. Good plots also involve conflict between differently motivated individuals and groups, the give and take of compromise, and the action and reaction that led to an issue's resolution. We are bored by an account that simply tells us "The king died and then the queen died." Change this to "after the king died, the queen, all but consumed by her grief, died as well," and you have a story of inherent promise. We learn not only what happened but why.

Description of Setting: Since readers need mental pictures to facilitate their understanding, novelists are masters at describing the physical setting in which actions take place. Historians are well advised to describe not only the physical setting but the social, ideological, and cultural environment as well—the *context*. It seems enough to reiterate that cultural conditions really are the "scenery" necessary to appreciate the action. And, of course, it goes almost without saying that when writers shift the focus of the action to a totally new setting, they must reorient the reader, describing the different cultural and ideological conditions.

within the context of the central values of the society in which the acts take place; both must blend description and background with action in order to make their accounts understandable. Many students (and, also professional historians) do not fully appreciate these parallels, and, as a result, they write accounts that dull the intellect as well as the imagination. Not surprisingly, both teachers and students find such writing boring and put it aside with relief when they have a chance.

EXERCISES

SET A   *Exercise 1 — Sorting*

A hallmark of an effective writer is the ability to subordinate less important facts and generalizations to those that are more important. This first exercise asks you to list a number of items in descending order from the most general or comprehensive category to the most specific. ("War," for example, is a more comprehensive, or general, category than "riot.") In the spaces provided, number the items in sequence, using "1" for the most general item and so on. In some cases you may have to assign the same number to two or more items.

a. _____ Gen. Robert E. Lee
_____ nineteenth-century America
_____ southern military capability
_____ the Civil War
_____ southern generalship

b. _____ a regional coal strike
_____ a family fight
_____ industrial turmoil
_____ local race riot
_____ world war
_____ national strife (i.e., within a nation)

Note: In the next two sets you should consider *logical progression* as well as ordering from general to specific.

c. _____ Irish monks became well known for their missionary zeal and their learning.
_____ Irish Christianity, isolated from the rest of Europe by pagan England and Scotland, developed distinctive customs of its own.
_____ The monks converted certain areas of Scotland and later extended their activities to the European mainland.
_____ Organized around the monastery rather than the diocese, its leaders were the abbots, not the bishops.
_____ St. Patrick had converted Ireland to Christianity in the fifth century.

d. _____ Imprisonment in a concentration camp was an occasional alternative to the death penalty.
_____ The definition of "treason" was expanded to include such minor offenses as circulation of banned newspapers.
_____ Hitler made major changes in the German legal system.
_____ The death penalty, without the right of appeal, could be invoked upon conviction for treason.
_____ The root principle of Hitler's new "justice" was subordination of the individual to the state.

SET A *Exercise 2 — Sequencing*

This exercise extends further the principle of organizing from the general to the specific. Here the task is to find the most general point (the most comprehensive sentence) and label it "1." Then, find the most logical sequence in which the other sentences should follow, using "2," "3," "4," etc.

_____ Nebraska farmers stopped trains and took off carloads of cattle.
_____ Wisconsin farmers dumped milk on the roadsides and fought with deputy sheriffs.

_____   Especially in the Midwest were extreme actions taken by farmers.

_____   In the depression summer of 1932, American farmers organized and prevented products from reaching the market, the movement moving gradually westward as the summer wore on.

_____   In eastern Iowa many farmers drowned pig litters because it was unprofitable to raise them.

_____   Near Spragueville in eastern Iowa, some farmers reverted to subsistence farming, refusing to send anything to market.

_____   In the states further west, such as Colorado and Wyoming, the movement lacked force because of the low productivity of these areas.

SET A   *Exercise 3 — Organizing a Paragraph*

This exercise is a somewhat different version of the one just completed. You should do two things: (1) work out the relations between the general and the specific, and (2) organize the pieces so they are logically related. Use number "1" for the first sentence, "2" for the second, etc., to indicate the proper sentence order.

_____   His [John F. Kennedy's] backing of the Cuban invasion in April 1961 further fanned the Cold War.

_____   (It may be said that "needlessly" is too strong a word; perhaps Kennedy thought he needed to arouse the country to obtain a more balanced military program. . . .)

_____   At a Vienna conference with Khrushchev in June he [Kennedy] over-reacted to Khrushchev's ultimatum, for in recent years Khrushchev's repeated deadlines and backdowns over West Berlin had become a kind of pattern.

_____   His [Kennedy's] inaugural was alarmist, already historically off key, more suited to the Stalinist era than to 1961.

_____   His statement to newspaper publishers and editors gathered at the White House in May—that the United States was in the most critical period of its history—increased the popular anxieties.

_____   His late January State of the Union message was even more alarmist, as Kennedy told the nation that it was drawing near the maximum danger.

_____   On his return from Vienna he appealed to Americans to build do-it-yourself bomb shelters, an appeal that produced a war psychology in the country and all manner of frenetic behavior.

_____   During his first two years in office, beginning in January, 1961, President John F. Kennedy seemed needlessly to have fanned the tensions of the dying Cold War.

SET A   *Exercise 4 — Outlining*

In the following exercise there are ten "pieces" that, when put together correctly, represent a simplified sentence outline for a short essay. Though much is missing, specifically included are a main thematic statement (topic sentence), three supporting points, five subpoints belonging somewhere under the supporting points, and a summary statement. Put all the pieces in their proper place (by number) in the form provided below.

1. The strong, jungle-like beat of early 1960s music brought another: the twist.
2. This four-person group powerfully affected American youth in clothing, in hair fashion, and in drug usage.
3. He dressed shabbily and had wild long hair.
4. Beatlemania began in England in 1963 and crossed the ocean to America in 1964.
5. Taken together these developments formed the foundation of an alternative American lifestyle.
6. He exploited the generation gap and soon developed a large cult following.
7. Three major developments in the world of music were influential in shaping the counterculture of the 1960s.
8. No group was as influential as the Beatles, who were perhaps artistically superior to most other musical quartets.
9. The twist was a highly individualistic dance form completely divorced from the romantic foxtrot of earlier years.
10. Of foremost importance was Bob Dylan [who was not a Beatle], whose hard-driving version of folk music brought sympathy to "down and outers."

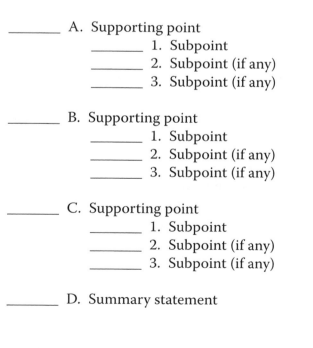

_____ Main thematic statement

        _____ A. Supporting point
                _____ 1. Subpoint
                _____ 2. Subpoint (if any)
                _____ 3. Subpoint (if any)

        _____ B. Supporting point
                _____ 1. Subpoint
                _____ 2. Subpoint (if any)
                _____ 3. Subpoint (if any)

        _____ C. Supporting point
                _____ 1. Subpoint
                _____ 2. Subpoint (if any)
                _____ 3. Subpoint (if any)

        _____ D. Summary statement

SET A   *Exercise 5 — The History Paper*

If you did not take the opportunity to write a short paper based on the documents in Appendix A dealing with American trade on the upper Missouri River, now is the time to do so.

Read the documents and the introductory comments in Appendix A (pp. 257–64) and write a 3–4 page history of the Ashley expedition. Do not just recount events, however. Use your paper to develop a distinctive theme that you can support with evidence from the documents. Remember, the documents (and the introductory remarks) are all you have to utilize.

Make sure your paper has an introduction that provides necessary background information and states a clear claim (thesis) about the expedition that you want to convince a reader is true. In the 2–4 paragraphs that follow, support that claim with concrete evidence, including direct quotations drawn from the documents. Finish with a brief conclusion that summarizes your central point(s). Give your paper a title that reflects the central theme. The introduction to the documents in Appendix A suggests possible themes you might want to develop.

SET B   *Exercise 1 — Sorting*

A hallmark of an effective writer is the ability to subordinate less important facts and generalizations to those that are more important. This first exercise asks you to list a number of items in descending order from general to specific. ("War," for example, is a more comprehensive, or general, category than "riot.") In the spaces provided, number the items in sequence, using "1" for the most general item and so on. In some cases you may have to assign the same number to two or more items.

a. _____ city government
    _____ national government
    _____ an organized neighborhood
    _____ state government
    _____ county government

b. _____ a history of North America
    _____ a history of the world
    _____ a history of the United States
    _____ a history of the western hemisphere
    _____ a history of General Washington as a military leader
    _____ a history of the American Revolution
    _____ a military history of the Revolution

Note: In the next two sets you should consider *logical progression* as well as ordering from general to specific.

c. _____ One of Vallee's favorite songs was the "Stein Song."
    _____ Though some parts of the country could get no radio signal, urban areas were quite well served by 1925.

_____ Radio broadcasting began in 1920 and quickly spread across the land.

_____ In the 1920s the electronic media changed American entertainment habits.

_____ Radio listeners soon warmed to the baritone voice of Rudy Vallee.

d. _____ During the 1930s depression the WPA built 881 new parks and 1,500 new athletic fields.

_____ In the 1920s and 1930s organized recreation experienced a great surge in popularity.

_____ The head of the WPA was [Franklin] Roosevelt's closest advisor, Harry Hopkins.

_____ The twentieth century has seen enormous expansion of sports activity of all kinds.

_____ Local governments in the 1920s spent large amounts in building new city playgrounds and golf courses.

SET B *Exercise 2 — Sequencing*

This is another form of exercise aimed at enhancing the ability to subordinate specific ideas to more general ones. What follows is a scrambled paragraph; unscramble it, using numbers ("1" for the first sentence, "2" for the second, etc.) to indicate proper sentence order. Keep in mind that the first sentence or two must provide the framework for the entire paragraph.

_____ The administration quickly disposed of most of its war plants, usually by turning them over to private interests on very generous terms.

_____ Under such pressure, the politicians of both parties simply collapsed.

_____ Business was permitted to move ahead quickly into civilian production.

_____ The pressures for a return to civilian life were overwhelming by mid-1945.

_____ In November 1945, Congress approved a $6 billion tax cut, even though it would obviously contribute to inflation.

_____ Business interests demanded lower taxes, immediate demobilization, and the end of lend-lease and other measures assisting other foreign competitors in international markets.

_____ The armed forces, 12 million strong in 1945, had only 3 million by mid-1946, and 1.6 million by mid-1947.

_____ Lend-lease shipments were cut.

_____ And—feeling secure with an atomic monopoly—it brought the boys home.

_____ Soldiers insisted on being allowed to come home, and officeholders were swamped with postcards from Asia labeled, "No boats, no votes."

SET B   *Exercise 3 — Organizing a Paragraph*

This exercise is a somewhat more complex version of the one you just completed. You should do two things: (1) work out the relations between the general and the specific and (2) organize the pieces so they are logically related. Use number "1" for the first sentence, "2" for the second, etc., to indicate the proper sentence order. Again, remember that the first sentence provides the framework for the entire paragraph.

_____   Surface raiders, such as the pocket battleships *Graf Spee* and *Deutschland* caused much concern.

_____   But the enduring enemy was the U-boat [submarine].

_____   But later in the war U-boats found it very difficult to operate, as the British used a version of sonar, and American hunter-killer groups sent many submarines to the bottom.

_____   The Germans successfully planted magnetic mines that did much damage to British shipping in coastal waters.

_____   If, in 1940 the defeat of France had been offset by the British success in the Battle of Britain, in 1941 the defeat of Great Britain became once more a possibility to be reckoned with.

_____   In 1940, however, the U-boat fleet, reinforced by a production drive, began to score abundantly.

_____   One British convoy lost thirty-two ships in a U-boat attack that continued through four consecutive nights.

_____   In the first year of the war, 1939, the German U-boat fleet had been small and was not particularly successful.

_____   Because Britain was an island nation she was especially vulnerable to German sea warfare, which included mines, surface raiders, and U-boats.

SET B   *Exercise 4 — Outlining*

The following exercise presents ten "pieces" that, when put together correctly, represent a simplified sentence outline for a short essay. Though much is missing, we specifically include a main thematic statement (topic sentence), three main points, five subpoints belonging somewhere under the main points, and a summary statement. Put all the pieces in their proper places (by number) in the form provided below.

1. A powerful new military bureaucracy developed during the war, with increasingly strong links to major industrial firms.
2. During the war more than a million blacks moved out of the South to northern cities seeking a better life than they had known on southern farms.
3. The deficit mentality lingered on after the war, and contributed to the acceptance of new governmental programs in later years.
4. Indeed these three changes brought by the war affected American society permanently.
5. The war also deepened public willingness to accept enormous government deficits as the national debt doubled and redoubled from 1941 to 1945.

6. Huge numbers of civilians migrated to ship and aircraft production facilities, seeking the high wages paid there.

7. World War II brought deeper changes in American life than any other development since the Civil War.

8. In fact much later, President Dwight Eisenhower, himself a military man, was to warn the nation of the dangers of this combination of interests, often called the "military-industrial complex."

9. First and foremost it caused a vast uprooting of Americans from their traditional homes.

10. Millions of men and women became temporary citizens of military camps all cross America

_____ Main thematic statement

   _____ A. Supporting point
       _____ 1. Subpoint
       _____ 2. Subpoint (if any)
       _____ 3. Subpoint (if any)

   _____ B. Supporting point
       _____ 1. Subpoint
       _____ 2. Subpoint (if any)
       _____ 3. Subpoint (if any)

   _____ C. Supporting point
       _____ 1. Subpoint
       _____ 2. Subpoint (if any)
       _____ 3. Subpoint (if any)

   _____ D. Summary statement

SET B *Exercise 5 — The History Paper*

See instructions under Set A, Exercise 5 (p. 220).

PART IV: HISTORIOGRAPHY

CHAPTER 13 THE HISTORY OF HISTORY

"History does not repeat itself. The historians repeat one another."

—MAX BEERBOHM

"History has to be rewritten because history is the selection of those threads of causes or antecedents that we are interested in."

—OLIVER WENDELL HOLMES, JR.

A university professor once berated a young graduate student for what he termed "stale historiography." A fellow student later said this sounded something akin to bad breath. What the professor meant, of course, was that the student was not familiar with the most recent scholarly interpretations in a particular subfield of history.

"Historiography" is not a word normally found in everyday reading, but you probably already know the concept even if the word itself is unfamiliar. Literally the word means "the writing of history." In modern usage, however, the word refers to the study of the way history has been and is written—the history of historical writing, if you will. When you study "historiography" you are studying how individual historians have interpreted and presented specific subjects, such as the collapse of the Roman Empire, the causes of the industrial revolution, or the end of the Cold War. For example, to learn about the variety of ways historians have tried to explain the coming of the American Civil War is to become familiar with the "historiography" of that subject.[1]

Our purpose in this chapter is to provide a thumbnail sketch of the history of historical writing in the West in order to acquaint you with some of the defining moments in the evolution of the discipline. Keep in mind, however, that such a brief survey can only trace the faint outlines of a subject so rich in both variety and complexity. In addition, be warned that you should view with suspicion any secondhand summary—including ours—of another historian's work. If you want to know what a historian says about a subject, you should read that historian's work yourself. As a final caution, remember that we discuss historiography in terms of broad trends and patterns, and that individual works will never fit the pattern exactly.

The Western tradition of historical writing began with the ancient Hebrews (Jews) and Greeks. The Jews, in their long struggle for freedom and autonomy, developed the belief that they were special in the eyes of God and that their historical experi-

---

[1] Some historians see that war as a conflict between an agrarian economy (the South) and an industrializing economy (the North); others emphasize slavery as the primary cause; still others see states' rights versus federal sovereignty as the issue at stake. And, this is only the tip of the iceberg.

227

ences reflected God's will. Conscious of their role as God's "chosen people," the Jews wrote history as a chronicle of their continuing and evolving relationship with the Creator. Essentially the books of the Old Testament of the Bible (some elements of which may date as far back as 1000 B.C.E.) constitute a written history of the Jewish people and Hebrew nation. This God-centered historical perspective of the Old Testament was destined to have a long and influential run in Western intellectual history, as we shall see.

If Jewish historical writing was "God-centered," it was the ancient Greeks who first wrote history in self-consciously human terms. At first the Greeks saw both their own past and the workings of the physical universe as the products of supernatural forces and the intervention of the gods. Later, in the sixth century B.C.E., a number of Greek philosophers began to reject supernatural explanations in favor of natural ones. They saw nature as functioning according to concrete "natural" laws that could be comprehended through human reason. Likewise, in the realm of human affairs, the Greeks increasingly saw history as the product of human actions and decisions, and believed that accounts of the past should be based on solid evidence, not legend or myth.

Herodotus (ca. 484–ca. 425 B.C.E.), often called the "Father of History," wrote the first systematic historical work based on personal observations and the examination of witnesses and surviving records. In his account of the Greek wars against the Persians he admittedly included many fanciful myths and unsubstantiated legends, but essentially his was a history of human actions told in human terms. Thucydides (ca. 460–400 B.C.E.), who, a generation later, wrote a justly famous history of the Peloponnesian Wars (431–404 B.C.E.), was even more careful in his use and analysis of evidence. He insisted that his history include only relevant, verifiable facts, and that it explain events only in ways that could be substantiated by the evidence. (The English word "history" comes from the Greek word for "research.") In Thucydides' work we first see what moderns would call a true historical spirit.

There was little change in the nature of written history after Greece succumbed to the power of Rome in the second century B.C.E. However, during the European Middle Ages (ca. 500–1400 C.E.) a change of some magnitude took place. With the triumph of Christianity, history writing again became more concerned with the relationship between humanity and Christian perceptions of God's eternal plan. Christian historiography mirrored that of the Jews, not that of the Greeks and Romans, although Greek and Roman influences persisted. To Christian writers in the Medieval period, human experiences on earth were but a minor part of a larger drama—the unfolding of God's divine plan for humanity. It was the job of written history, therefore, to find and reveal the transcendent design of God hidden in the chaos of day-to-day events. That is why many histories written in the Middle Ages began with the biblical story of creation and incorporated that part of the Jewish Old Testament tradition that fit the redemptive message of Christianity. The proper subject of written history, in the eyes of the Christian monks who wrote it, was not the earthly fate of a particular state or people, but the universal drama of humanity's quest for salvation.[2]

---

[2] We might note in passing that those very monks were also the inventors of the conventional western calendar that distinguishes between the events that occurred before the birth of Christ (B.C. or, now, B.C.E.—"Before the Common Era") and those that came after (A.D. Anno Domini, "in the year of the lord"—now C.E.—"the Common Era").

Only in the Renaissance (the 1400s and 1500s) did historians return to the more secular, humanistic style of the Greeks. Especially important were a number of Italian historians, Niccolò Machiavelli (1469–1540) and Francesco Guicciardini (1483–1527) being the best known. Although the Renaissance historians were Christians, they believed that the function of history was to narrate the experiences of particular states and individuals, not to reveal God's designs in the earthly affairs of humanity. The Renaissance also saw the gradual emergence of new critical standards for collecting, reading, and interpreting evidence. History was not yet recognized as an independent field of study (like theology or law), but the path was now clearly marked.

In spite of the long tradition of history writing in the West, history emerged as a formal academic study only in the early nineteenth century. Of course, there were many pre-nineteenth-century historians who produced works of great power and sophistication, as any reader of Edward Gibbon (*The Decline and Fall of the Roman Empire*) or Thucydides can attest. On the whole, though, such works were few and far between, for history still lacked a coherent and workable critical methodology. Much history was written, but seldom did the historians actively consider the criteria for writing good history. Many pre–nineteenth-century historians handled evidence with a cavalier disregard for critical standards. Often they cited no sources whatever; on other occasions they accepted myth, legend, and gossip as established fact; on yet others, they read or interpreted records with too much credulity and too little skepticism.

In another way, the pre–nineteenth-century historians had a blind spot. They did not fully understand that past ages differed from their own; they had difficulty realizing that styles, habits, and values changed over time. For instance, even though a number of Renaissance scholars became increasingly conscious that the classical past that they studied was radically different from their own time, this insight was never fully internalized. There are many Renaissance paintings, for example, that portray biblical scenes in which individuals from the time of Christ are dressed as fifteenth-century Florentines and surrounded by buildings constructed in the architectural styles of the Italian Renaissance. The equivalent today would be a painting of George Washington crossing the Delaware River in a car ferry while dressed in a double-breasted pinstriped suit.

Conversely, when many of the early historians did perceive differences between their age and another, their response was not to try to understand that which was different, but to denounce it. Thus did Voltaire, in the eighteenth century, dismiss the Middle Ages as unworthy of study because medieval men and women were not "enlightened," as he thought himself to be. Such an attitude, as we have seen, is a historical. (See Chapter 5, "Context.")

Leopold Von Ranke and the Rise of Modern History

Historical studies came into their own following the immense political and social upheavals associated with the French Revolution (1789–1815). The French Revolution represented a massive break with the past and, paradoxically, made people much more "history-conscious" than ever before. Thus, it was in the nineteenth century that history became the "Queen of the Sciences" and earned a permanent place in the academy.

The man most responsible for elevating the study of history to a new plateau was the German historian Leopold von Ranke (1795–1886). Ranke's contributions were threefold: (1) he played a leading role in establishing history as a respected discipline in the universities, (2) he firmly established the notion that all sound history must be based on primary sources and a rigorous methodology, and (3) he reflected the broader nineteenth-century attempt to define the concept of "historical-mindedness." Of these, the latter two points require further elaboration.

Ranke and Historical Method

Previously, as we mentioned above, much history was written, but "there was no systematic use of sources and no accepted methodological principles."[3] Many pre-Rankean historians relied heavily on the work of other authors (secondary sources) rather than going to the original documents, or primary sources. Ranke (pronounced "Ron-kuh"), on the other hand, stressed the importance of basing any historical narrative firmly on the reading of primary sources. Furthermore, he insisted that the historian constantly inform the reader of the specific sources upon which a given point was based. Hence the central importance, after Ranke, of thorough footnotes (or endnotes) and bibliographies. (Now you know whom to blame.) In a word, Ranke popularized the idea that history could be "scientific"—not in the sense that history could discover general laws of behavior, but in that historical writing should be based on rigorous critical standards.

Ranke and Historical Thinking

Ranke also contributed to the rise of the conviction that one should not study a past age in terms of one's own values and culture but in terms of the values and realities of the age itself. According to Ranke, one should not make moral judgments on past individuals and past cultures but try to understand them on their own terms. To Ranke, every age was "immediate to God" (had its own inherent worth) and worthy of our sympathy and understanding. Ranke appreciated the fact that things do change over time, and this basic insight is central to the whole process of thinking historically.

Ranke, then, and many other eminent scholars, established the study of history on a firm methodological foundation. But what sorts of things did these pioneers write about? Space forbids a detailed treatment of history and historians in the nineteenth century, but two general points can be made:

1. Most nineteenth-century history was political, legal, or diplomatic in emphasis, as historians began to get access to government archives that had hitherto been closed to researchers. Their work, which reflected the character of the documents, naturally focused on the actions of kings, parliaments, law courts, armies, navies, and diplomats—"drum and trumpet" history as it came to be called. The nineteenth-century historians also studied and wrote about the history of ideas, especially the political and legal ideas that had played a role in the evolution of nations and legal systems—usually their *own* nation and legal system, as discussed below.

---

[3] Arthur Marwick, *What History Is and Why It Is Important* (Bletchley, England: Open University Press, 1970), 42.

2. Nineteenth-century history, especially in Europe, tended to have a national focus—more in the sense of "nationality" than "nation-state." During that era a number of "new" nations, or ethnic groups, perceiving their cultural and historical uniqueness, began to explore their own historical roots with great vigor. Even history coming out of the more established nations, such as England and France, reflected this compulsion to probe the depths of their national experience. Much the same could be said of the histories produced in nineteenth-century America. Across the board, historiography during this period tended to be ethnocentric and nationalistic.

Karl Marx and History

If Ranke and his contemporaries saw only politics and diplomacy as worthy of the historian's attention, it was the German economist and revolutionary philosopher Karl Marx who opened historians' eyes to the importance of social and economic forces in human affairs. Marx (1818–1883) is widely recognized as one of the most influential thinkers of the last two centuries. Much modern scholarship in history, economics, political theory, sociology, and philosophy cannot be fully appreciated without some understanding of Karl Marx's ideas. This is not the place to discuss Marx's system in detail, but a few words concerning his impact on the discipline of history are in order. It should be noted from the start, however, that a consideration of Marx the historian can be effectively divorced from consideration of Marx the prophet of socialism. In the latter guise Marx, and his collaborator Friedrich Engels, postulated a broadly "progressive" theory of history, which held that human societies would evolve through a number of stages culminating in the establishment (through revolution) of a "dictatorship of the proletariat" and, eventually, a classless society. This was a secular version of the medieval Christian conviction that the human race was moving toward a "preordained goal."

More important for our purposes is the fact that Marx opened new intellectual vistas by breaking out of the political-diplomatic straitjacket that had bound most historical investigations before his time. Marx, says one American historian, "became the first to formulate, in explicit fashion, the economic interpretation of history."[4] Marx (and Engels) argued that, at any given point in time, the mode of economic production determined, to a great extent, the character of the entire society—its ideas, values, political structure, and social relations. To some of Marx's more dogmatic followers, this insight was converted into a thoroughgoing economic determinism. That is, economic forces were seen to determine totally the nature of society, and changes in the economic structure were considered the sole engine of historical change. Marx himself never went so far; late in life he even commented: "I am not a Marxist." Marx and Engels did not deny that noneconomic factors could be contributing causes of events. They simply asserted that economic factors were of primary importance.

Within this general framework, the history of economic and social classes was more relevant than the history of great men or ruling elites. "The history of all hitherto existing society," wrote Marx and Engels in *The Communist Manifesto,* "is the history of class struggle." This, of course, is a debatable conclusion. Of significance

---

[4] Nevins, *Gateway to History*, 268.

though is the fact that Marx and Engels saw class interests as a vital element in any historical equation.

Marx's impact on politics and political thought has been immense and requires no further comment. But what of Marx's impact on the writing of history? Naturally communist countries, where Marxism in some form or another was (and, in a few cases, still is) an official ideology, historical writing has been "Marxist" in the extreme. And, quite frankly, much of it is not good history. Evidence was chosen, organized, analyzed, and interpreted more with an eye to validating the ideology and the policies of the state than establishing the best true account of the past. Much official communist history written before 1989 in Russia and Eastern Europe, and elsewhere even today, suffers from this defect.[5] In fairness, we should also note that noncommunist history is not immune from this failing, and any time scholarship is subordinated to the dictates of an ideology—Marxism or any other—it is truth that suffers.

In the noncommunist West the influence of Marx, while great, has been less direct. In the broadest sense Marx is significant because, by emphasizing the importance of economic factors in history, he opened the door to a new approach to the past. Few historians today, whatever their political orientation, would deny the validity of exploring the role of social classes, economic interests, and modes of production in the historical process. Economic interpretations have, in fact, become a staple of American historiography. A famous (and controversial) example is Charles A. Beard's *An Economic Interpretation of the Constitution of the United States* published in 1913. In that work Beard examined the economic interests of the framers of the Constitution and concluded that the Constitution was designed more to protect property rights than political rights. Whatever the accuracy of this interpretation (and it has been vigorously challenged), the important thing to note is the explicitly economic focus of the work. Beard was no Marxist, but he acknowledged a debt to Marx just the same. Few historians have gone as far as Beard in emphasizing economic factors so single-mindedly, but even fewer would deny that the economic "question" is one that must be asked in order to understand any given segment of the past.

For some Western scholars the influence of Marx has been more direct. There have been many scholars, historians among them, who consciously called themselves "Marxists," and they adopted an explicitly Marxist (i.e., class-based economic) approach to the study of history and society. In England, for example, the popularity of social history (see further discussion that follows) owed much to a group of Marxist scholars like Christopher Hill, Eric Hobsbawm and E. P. Thompson who wrote classic works that focused on the conflict between social and economic classes. Even the emergence of the folk music movement in that country in the 1950s and 1960s owed "its inspiration and much of its historical scholarship" to Marxist scholars.[6] Such scholars are a distinct minority within the profession, yet they have published solid

---

[5] David Remnick says of the Soviet Union and its distaste for open inquiry: "The regime created an empire that was a vast room, its doors locked, its windows shuttered. All books and newspapers allowed in the room carried the Official Version of Events, and the radio and television blared the general line day and night." It was Mikhail Gorbachev who finally decreed that the time had come to fill in the "blank spots" of history and, in so doing, precipitated the collapse of the USSR (see Chapter 1). *Lenin's Tomb: The Last Days of the Soviet Empire*, 4.

[6] Raphael Samuel, "People's History," quoted in Tosh, ed., *Historians on History*, 114.

scholarly works that have greatly enriched our understanding of the past. Remember, the test of good history is not the author's ideology, but the thoroughness, accuracy, and soundness of the research and the argument.

The Twentieth Century and Beyond

Since the turn of the twentieth century, especially since 1945, we have witnessed a knowledge explosion. Books, articles, reviews, and reports have been pouring off the presses in ever-increasing numbers. This "explosion" has been most dramatic in the sciences, but the generalization is applicable to history as well. Moreover, recent historical writing has displayed such kaleidoscopic diversity in subject matter and methodology that history is a more exciting field than ever before. Unfortunately, the mass and diversity of recent historical scholarship also makes it impossible to summarize neatly even the most prominent trends in twentieth- and twenty-first-century historiography. What follows, therefore, is a very selective sampling of what we see to be some of the defining characteristics of recent historiography—especially American historiography.

The New Social History

There is nothing especially "new" about social history. Social history, simply put, is the history of life in the broadest sense: the history of the everyday experiences of "average" men and women. It is the history of social and economic classes, occupations, lifestyles, leisure activities, family structures, eating habits, sexual practices, reading preferences, beliefs, and values; it is "grass roots" history; it is, in the memorable words of G. M. Trevelyan, history "with the politics left out"—or, to the irreverent, "rum and strumpet history." Historians have been writing social history for some time. Even today, a frequently cited example of brilliant social history is the famous third chapter of Thomas Babington Macaulay's *History of England* (5 vols., 1849–61), in which he draws a fascinating portrait of English society during the 1680s.

Although social history has long been with us, it was only in the 1960s and 1970s that it became a thriving cottage industry in the historical profession. In Macaulay's day, social history was strictly subordinated to what historians considered the more important priority of writing about political, constitutional, and military affairs. Social history was used to "set the scene" or provide a pleasant interlude in the narrative. Today, however, social history is taught and studied as a field of inherent interest and importance. Only to this extent is social history "new."

Social history is new in another sense—it is much more "scientific" and less anecdotal than most previous history. Social history is one area in which the application of statistical methods and computer analysis has been especially productive. Much social history today is, in effect, historical demography (demography is the statistical study of populations), by which historians systematically analyze large-scale population trends and calculate such things as average family sizes, death and birth rates, marriage ages, and average incomes. The more literary tradition of social history has by no means been abandoned, but statistical methods have given the social historian a potent analytical weapon.

The most fruitful contribution of the social historians has been to focus the spotlight on groups that have typically been ignored in traditional history—women, racial and ethnic minorities, blue-collar and migrant workers, farmers, peasants, children, the aged, criminals, outcasts, and groups otherwise marginalized by society.[7] The popularity and vitality of social history is in part a reflection of the increasing sense of identity among various ethnic subcultures. It is also a product of the democratization of the history profession as women, members of minority groups, and the sons and daughters of recent immigrants increasingly have entered the field. Witness the proliferation of books, just in the United States, on women's history, African American history, Chicano history, Native American history, and the history of various immigrant groups. In sum, the "new" social history has brought to life the experiences of countless groups previously bypassed in historical studies traditionally focused on the experiences of political and economic elites.

Finally, in spite of G. M. Trevelyan's comment that social history is history with the politics left out, much social history is indeed quite political. Writers of social history often have a conscious or unconscious political agenda. As one historian puts it: "People's history, whatever its particular subject matter, is shaped in the crucible of politics, and penetrated by the influence of ideology on all sides."[8] Those English Marxist historians mentioned earlier were self-consciously writing to expose the political and economic oppression of workers, peasants, and ethnic minorities in the past. "The right-wing version of people's history," on the other hand, does conform to Trevelyan's dictum that social history is "history with the politics left out . . . a history devoid of struggle, devoid of ideas, but with a very strong sense of religion and of values."[9] Historians on the political left, in other words, often emphasize the injustices of the past (e.g., E. P. Thompson's *Making of the English Working Class*, 1963), while those on the right are nostalgic for parts of the past we seem to have lost (e.g., Peter Laslett's *The World We Have Lost*, 1965).

Women's History

One category of social history, women's history, deserves special comment. In light of the fact that women constitute more than half of the human race, it is sobering to discover that only after World War II did historians begin to pay systematic attention to the role of women in history. Of course, larger-than-life figures such as Queen Elizabeth I of England or Catherine the Great of Russia always had their fair share of attention from historians. But women as a group? For decades the male-dominated history profession systematically ignored them.

Today the situation is dramatically different. Modern feminists and a growing number of historians have generated interest in both women's history and, more broadly, gender studies (the study of the roles played in society by gender relations

---

[7] In the area of Renaissance studies alone we find the following titles: Samuel Cohn, Jr., *The Laboring Classes in Renaissance Florence* (1980); Judith Brown, *Immodest Acts: The Life of a Lesbian Nun in Renaissance Italy* (1986); Edward Muir, *Mad Blood Stirring: Vendetta and Factions in Fruili during the Renaissance* (1993); Michael Rocke, *Forbidden Friendships: Homosexuality and Male Culture in Renaissance Florence* (1996); Carlo Ginzburg, *The Night Battles: Witchcraft and Agrarian Cults in the Sixteenth and Seventeenth Centuries* (1992).

[8] Samuel, "People's History," Tosh, ed., *Historians on History*, 111.

[9] Samuel in Tosh, *Historians on History*, 112.

and concepts of gender—i.e., the relationships of men *and* women in society). The result has been an avalanche of new scholarship not only on the history of women, but also on the history of gender relationships, histories of children and families, and gay and lesbian history.

In writing the history of women, many practitioners not only wanted to recover an overlooked past but they wanted to use their scholarship to advance the cause of women's equality. An underlying assumption was that women everywhere, past and present, were more alike than different, and that writing the history of women would advance their quest for equal political and economic equality.[10] But what women's historians discovered was that there is no such thing as a universal "women's history" relevant to all women everywhere. Research revealed that there was often a great gulf separating the experiences of middle-class and working-class women, black and white women, Western and non-Western women, sixteenth-century and twentieth-century women, etc. And, to make matters even more complex, there were many differences within each category. As Joan Wallach Scott argues, "not all black women or Islamic women or Jewish women share the same conceptions of femininity, or social role or politics."[11]

In sum, the same fragmentation and diversity that has characterized recent history writing in general also characterizes women's history and many of the other subcategories we mention. The result has been both the immense enrichment of the discipline and the frustration inherent in knowing that a single individual will never become familiar with even a small portion of the fascinating histories being written about the myriad aspects of the past.[12]

----

[10] See Joan Wallach Scott, ed., *Feminism and History* (Oxford: Oxford University Press, 1996), "Introduction," 1–13.

[11] Scott, *Feminism*, 7.

[12] A sampling of titles on only the American experience dramatizes the point. On the subject of **women in America** books published in the 1990s and 2000s include: Susan Ware, *Still Missing: Amelia Earhart and the Search for Modern Feminism* (1993); Susan Faludi, *Backlash: The Undeclared War Against American Women* (1991); Susan K. Cahn, *Coming on Strong: Gender and Sexuality in Twentieth-Century Women's Sport* (1994); Susan J. Douglas, *Where the Girls Are: Growing Up Female with the Mass Media* (1994); Sharon Thompson, *Going All the Way: Teenage Girls' Tales of Sex, Romance, and Pregnancy* (1995); Matthew Avery Sutton, *Aimee Semple McPherson and the Resurrection of Christian America* (2007); and Mary C. Brennan, *Wives, Mothers, and the Red Menace: Conservative Women and the Crusade against Communism* (2008).

In **African American history** we find the following recent works, focusing either on a distinctive theme or locale: Patricia A. Turner, *I Heard It Through the Grapevine: Rumor in African-American Culture* (1993); John Egerton, *Speak Now Against the Day: The Generation before the Civil Rights Movement in the South* (1994); John Dittmer, *Local People: The Struggle for Civil Rights in Mississippi* (1994); Michael Eric Dyson, *Making Malcolm: The Myth and Meaning of Malcolm X* (1995); Charles M. Payne, *I've Got the Light of Freedom: The Organization Tradition and the Mississippi Freedom Struggle* (1995); Brenda Gayle Plummer, *Rising Wind: Black Americans and U.S. Foreign Policy, 1935–1960* (1996); Curtis J. Austin, *Up Against the Wall: Violence in the Making and Unmaking of the Black Panther Party* (2006); Jane Rhodes, *Framing the Black Panthers: The Spectacular Rise of a Black Power Icon* (2006); Elizabeth Jacoway, *Turn Away Thy Son: Little Rock, the Crisis That Shocked the Nation* (2008); and Jason Chambers, *Madison Avenue and the Color Line: African Americans in the Advertising Industry* (2008).

Studies that consider both **African American and Women's history** include: Angela Davis, *Blues Legacies and Black Feminism: Gertrude "Ma" Rainey, Bessie Smith, and Billie Holiday* (1998); Nikki Brown, *Private Politics and Public Voices: Black Women's Activism from World War I to the New Deal* (2007); Susannah Walker, *Style and Status: Selling Beauty to African American Women, 1920–1975* (2007); and Anne M. Valk, *Radical Sisters: Second-Wave Feminism and Black Liberation in Washington, D.C.* (2008).

Many thanks to our colleague John Chappell for suggesting these titles.

Sigmund Freud (1856–1939), whose psychoanalytic theories imspired the emergence of "Psychohistory." *Library of Congress, (LC-USZ62-72266).*

Computers and Quantification

A phenomenon that first emerged in the twentieth century is the growing use of computers and statistical methods in history. Quantitative techniques have been especially productive (as we saw in Chapter 10) in the realms of economic and social history. Historical studies of voting behavior have also benefited from the application of well-thought-out computer programs to historical evidence. There are, of course, problems with this type of history. The most obvious is that computers, however sophisticated their software, cannot answer many of the most important historical questions. Quantification, therefore, has an important place in historical studies, but the limitations of "mere numeration" must be kept firmly in mind. For a fuller discussion of this topic see Chapter 10.

Psychohistory

Psychohistory is another twentieth-century innovation in historical scholarship. Although psychohistory has never been fully accepted or widely practiced by most historians, you should be aware of some of its central characteristics and claims. Psychohistory is essentially an outgrowth of the work of Sigmund Freud (1856–1939), who drew attention to the importance of the unconscious mind and irrational impulses in human behavior. Just as Marx had emphasized the importance of economic forces in human affairs, Freud underscored the role played by hidden psychological drives that originated in the traumas and experiences of infancy and early childhood. It was Freud and his followers who pioneered the practice of psychoanalysis as a method for discovering the "unconscious" roots of human behavior by probing for the suppressed and repressed experiences of childhood. Psychoanalysis, Freud argued, could help those whose early, even unremembered, childhood traumas had made them dysfunctional as adults. Freud also claimed—and here we get to the crux of psychohistory—that psychoanalysis could also be applied to historical figures long dead.

Freud's message was reinforced in his lifetime by the senseless slaughter of World War I (1914–18), which dramatized for a complacent Europe how easily irrationality and animal brutality could triumph over intellect and reason. In the years after that war, psychiatry and psychoanalysis came into their own; in the years after World War II (1939–45), psychohistory itself made its debut. One of the pioneers in the field was Erik Erikson, whose masterful study *Young Man Luther* (1958) seemed to put psychohistory on a firm intellectual footing.

Though many psychohistorical studies have been written, in recent years the enthusiasm over the approach has dimmed. Since the publication of Erikson's book, many historians have challenged the legitimacy of psychohistory on methodological grounds. Psychoanalysis involves the recovery of repressed childhood memories, but direct evidence for the early experiences of most historical figures is sketchy or nonexistent. More significant, even if we can find out something about the earliest experiences of an individual, the explanatory value of that information is questionable. Martin Luther, for example, had some rough experiences when he was growing up, but those experiences were not atypical of his time and place. Yet it was only Luther who ended up as the standard-bearer of the Reformation. Factors other than Luther's childhood development must have been more important. Even though psychohistory is not in history's mainstream, it has made its mark. Whatever the merits or defects of Freud's theory of personality, his work opened historians' eyes to the importance of psychological dimensions of the individuals (and groups) they study. Today the writing of historical biography is still a thriving enterprise, and it is the rare biographer who would totally ignore questions of psychological motivation and the psychological roots of character. To that extent psychohistory has permanently changed the way historians do business.[13]

History in the Information Age

A glaring modern paradox is that even as many critics bemoan America's increasing historical illiteracy, history has never clamored so insistently for our attention. The last fifty years have seen a tremendous growth in the amount of history targeted for mass audiences. Originally, cheap paperback books and then television and film (see Chapter 8) brought popularized history into the marketplace. More recently, cable and satellite television networks (e.g. the History Channel, the Learning Channel) and the Internet (e.g., H-Net [Humanities and Social Sciences Online], HNN [History, News Network], and countless blogs), have greatly increased the options for those interested in some aspect of the past.

Ultimately this is a good thing, for unless historians communicate their findings to a larger audience, they are serving no useful function in a society. On the other

---

[13] For a much more detailed overview of the diverse insights and models that constitute psychohistory see Part 3, "Psychosocial History," in Richard E. Beringer, *Historical Analysis: Contemporary Approaches to Clio's Craft* (New York: John Wiley and Sons, 1978), 69–191.

hand, popular history (whether presented in books, on television, on the big screen, or on the Internet) can also be a dangerous thing. All too frequently good entertainment is bad history, for to emphasize the dramatic and sensational is often to distort a more mundane reality. Moreover, whatever the advantages of historical essays and sources on the Internet (and there are many advantages—see Chapter 6), literally anyone with an ax to grind or an overactive fantasy life can create a Web page accessible by computers around the world. As a result, there is a staggering amount of nonsense and misinformation on the Internet, making it increasingly difficult for the average citizen to discriminate between accurate and inaccurate information, between good and bad history.

Moreover, so insatiable is the public appetite for the inside story of recent dramatic events that "instant" histories have become commonplace. Whether the subject is world conflict, a sensational murder case, the death of a rock star or popular idol, or the latest terrorist outrage, hastily written paperback "histories" and TV documentaries and miniseries are sometimes published and aired only days, or weeks, after the event.[14] The potential limitations of such productions should be apparent. They are often put together in haste, their evidence is even more incomplete than normally would be the case, and public passions may still be fully aroused. The authors, in many cases, are not trained historians or even trained journalists. Obviously, one should read and view such instant histories with a very critical eye.

Conclusion

If one can perceive a trend over time, it is this: historical writing in the West has become broader in geographic scope, casting its attention on civilizations and cultures hitherto ignored; it has become more eclectic and diverse, with few aspects of life escaping critical attention; it has discovered (at last) the histories of groups hitherto ignored in traditional narratives; and it has become ever more rigorous and imaginative in its use of evidence, our comments on "instant history" notwithstanding. History as a discipline is alive and growing, telling its story of change, but telling also of how tenaciously the past survives in the present. Nevertheless, we cannot end without a note of caution.

As positive as all these trends are, the writing of history from many and diverse perspectives is not without its costs. As one historian noted recently, "History no longer sets forth common stories that presumably speak for the identity and experience of all readers. . . . We no longer possess a past commonly agreed upon."[15] To the extent that shining history's lamp on all peoples, and not just on male elites, has helped Americans find a history that is personally relevant and meaningful, we say bravo! To the extent that groups of Americans no longer think they share either a common past or a common destiny, this trend is unhealthy.

Another indirect consequence of the recent proliferation of historical subcategories and subdisciplines has been an unsettling relativism. It is a small leap from saying that it is important to study the history of African Americans, women, or Native

---

[14] A search for books on 9/11, when terrorists flew planes into the World Trade Center and the Pentagon, will provide literally hundreds of titles published since 2001.

[15] Mark T. Gilderhus, *History and Historians*, 3rd ed. (Englewood Cliffs, NJ: Prentice Hall, 1996), 134.

Americans to saying that history is simply what each of the myriad groups says it is from their own perspective. And, from that point, it is but a short step to argue that there is no objective truth at all, only what different groups perceive it to be. This sort of relativism has been reinforced by an array of trendy theories coming out of literary criticism and the social sciences, including postmodernism, deconstruction, semiotics, and structuralism and poststructuralism. The complexity of these various "isms" precludes a detailed discussion here, but one historian who laments their impact summarizes the situation:

> In the 1990s, the newly dominant theorists within the humanities and social sciences assert that it is impossible to tell the truth about the past or to use history to produce knowledge in any objective sense at all. They claim we can only see the past through the perspective of our own culture and, hence, what we see in history are our own interests and concerns reflected back at us. The central point upon which history was founded no longer holds: there is no fundamental distinction any more between history and myth.[16]

Personally, we would argue against the most extreme forms of relativism implicit in many of the fashionable "isms" mentioned above. But we would also acknowledge, as much of this book has argued, that of necessity history reflects the values and interests of the historians and societies that produce it. And the multiplication of perspectives that has characterized our time is much more a cause for celebration than a cause for despair. As three representatives of the "new" history have so pointedly argued, "truths about the past are possible, even if they are not absolute."[17] What the future will bring no one can say, but if the last century is any guide, the intellectual journey should be an exciting one.

---

[16] Keith Windschuttle, *The Killing of History: How Literary Critics and Social Theorists are Murdering Our Past* (New York: The Free Press, 1996), 2. This book provides an excellent, understandable overview of the various theories mentioned in this paragraph, as well as a detailed critique of those theories. For a more sympathetic treatment of some of the newer theories and methodologies, see Norman J. Wilson, *History in Crisis? Recent Directions in Historiography,* 2nd ed. (Upper Saddle River, NJ: Pearson Education, 2005).

[17] Joyce Appleby, Lynn Hunt, and Margaret Jacob, *Telling the Truth About History* (New York: W. W. Norton & Co., 1994), 7.

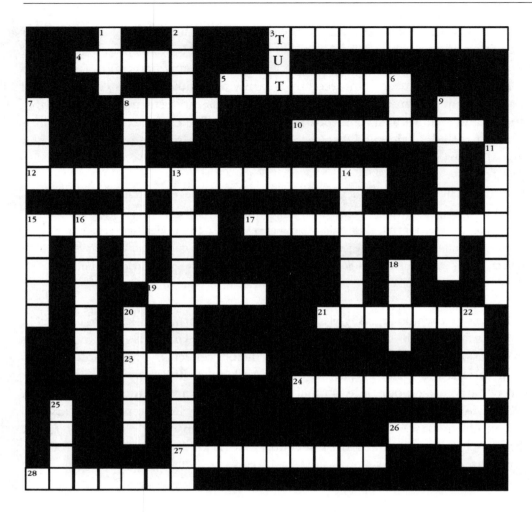

EXERCISE

The answers to the crossword puzzle above are, with a couple of minor exceptions, based on the information in this chapter. Remember, when authors or titles are mentioned, a footnote can be your friend. One word, not in the chapter, has been completed for you. Enjoy.

Across

3. Wrote history of the Peloponnesian War.
4. Proponent of critical history based on primary sources.
5. 19th-century histories tended to have a_____ focus.
8. Believed economic forces were key to historical change.
10. Period of God-centered history.
12. Types of studies (pl.) with politics left out.
15. Susan Faludi's _____.
17. Renaissance historian.
19. Created psychoanalysis.
21. Macaulay's History of _____.
23. Partner of Marx.

24. Contemporary history writing is characterized by fragmentation and ___.
26. Increased attention is paid to this group in new social history.
27. The "Father" of history.
28. English word derived from Greek word for "research."

Down

1. Erikson's *Young _____ Luther.*
2. Units of time commonly used to date events.
3. Egyptian pharaoh with famous tomb.
6. Historians should tell the truth; they should never _____.
7. Wrote history as story of the relationship with Yahweh.
8. Wrote early example of social history.
9. Subject of M. E. Dyson's book.
11. Historians usually divide the past into large blocks of time called _____.
13. The history of history.
14. Psychohistorian.
15. Wrote economic history of the Constitution.
16. Thinking historically means considering _____ over time.
18. Many people now get much of their history from _____.
20. First to write history in human terms.
22. Author of a local study of the Civil Rights Movement.
25. Psychohistory came into its own after _____. (Abbr.)

HISTORY AND THE DISCIPLINES

"[H]istory offers living proof of the complementary nature of art and of science."
—H. Stuart Hughes[1]

"All sciences are devoted to the quest for truth; truth can neither be apprehended nor communicated without art. History therefore is an art, like all other sciences."
—C. V. Wedgwood[2]

There is an old joke about two historians who meet at one of the annual history conventions. One historian asks the other if she knows what happened to their mutual friend, Smedley, who seems not to be in attendance. "Haven't you heard the sad news," responds the first historian. "Smedley has abandoned history to become a political scientist." "My goodness," exclaims the first, "next thing you know we'll hear that Smedley's become a sociologist!"

We didn't say it was a good joke. But the intellectual snobbery implicit in the story reveals an important truth: Even if the general public is indifferent to the labels that intellectuals give themselves, the professors themselves take the labels quite seriously. Academics derive a good part of their identity from the disciplines they study and teach. Further, since colleges and universities are usually divided into departments and schools based on those disciplinary labels, students should be minimally aware of what the labels represent.

History, clearly, is something of an intellectual chameleon. In its attempt to establish solid "truths" (or at least viable hypotheses) about humans and their world, history shares a good deal with the sciences; as a discipline concerned primarily with women and men as social beings, it shares much with the social sciences; and as a discipline that so often emphasizes telling a story about the past in a literate and engaging fashion, it aspires to the status of an art. Yet the differences between history and its sister disciplines are equally striking.

History and Science

In the nineteenth century some of the pioneers of modern historical studies were convinced that history could attain the status of an experimental science like chemistry or physics. N. D. Fustel de Coulanges, a nineteenth-century French historian, was typical when he claimed: "History is and should be a science." A moment's reflection will show that such optimism was misplaced.

---

[1] H. Stuart Hughes, *History As Art and As Science* (New York: Harper and Row, 1964), 3.
[2] Ferenc M. Szasz, *The History Teacher*, "The Many Meanings of History," Part IV of the series, 9 (February 1976), 224.

The aim of many sciences is to discover regularities in nature—"laws" that can be used to generalize (i.e., predict) future occurrences. Precise measurement, careful observation, and laboratory experiments are the basic methods used for establishing such scientific "laws." For instance, repeated experiments at sea level will show that water boils at 100 degrees Celsius (212 degrees Fahrenheit). On the basis of such experiments the scientist (and the rest of us) can be reasonably sure that under similar circumstances water will always boil at that temperature.

Historians, obviously, can never discuss the past with such precision, since past events are unique and unrepeatable. Historians cannot "experiment" on the past. They can't, for instance, run the French Revolution over and over again to discover which variables were the critical ones, nor can they, except in the case of relatively recent events, interview the participants. Historians can never establish the revolutionary boiling point of a human community with anything like the precision with which the scientist can establish the boiling point of a liquid. The historian, then, does not aim (at least does not primarily aim) to establish universally convincing generalizations on the scientific model. Given the nature of the subject matter (unique, concrete, unrepeatable events) the historian is more interested in reconstructing specific episodes in all their diversity and particularity. The historian aims at truth, but not universal, timeless truth.

In spite of these differences, history shares more with science than first meets the eye. Originally "science" simply meant "knowledge," and if we think of a science as any search for knowledge based on a rigorous and objective examination of the evidence (whether the evidence is a beaker of boiling water or a diplomatic dispatch), then clearly history has some claim to being "scientific," if not a science per se. Second, not all sciences are totally experimental in approach. Such fields as astronomy, geology, ecology, climatology, evolutionary biology, and paleontology are much akin to history in their methodology, and may even be labeled "historical sciences."[3] Like history, all of them rely heavily on systematic observation and classification of data and must make their claims by studying the "records" of past events, whether the fossils that record the existence of past species, the rock formations that betoken upheavals thousands of years ago, or the light and radio waves of stars that originated eons in the past.

The elusive line between "history" and "science" is well illustrated by a spate of recent books. In *Guns, Germs, and Steel: The Fates of Human Societies*, biologist Jared Diamond writes: "The book's subject matter is history, but the approach is that of science—in particular, that of historical sciences such as evolutionary biology and geology."[4] Another scientist, geologist Richard Fortey, has written a "history" of life

---

[3] Physiologist and evolutionary biologist Jared Diamond writes: "Thus the difficulties historians face in establishing cause-and-effect relations in the history of human societies are broadly similar to the difficulties facing astronomers, climatologists, ecologists, evolutionary biologists, geologists and paleontologists. To varying degrees, each of these fields is plagued by the impossibility of performing replicated, controlled experimental interventions, the complexity arising from enormous numbers of variables, the resulting uniqueness of each system, the consequent impossibility of formulating universal laws, and the difficulties of predicting emergent properties and future behavior." *Guns, Germs, and Steel: The Fates of Human Societies* (New York: W. W. Norton & Co., 1997), 424.
[4] Diamond, *Guns, Germs, and Steel*, 26.

What Science Can Tell Us about Human History

Discoveries in science have long added to our understanding of the human past. One of the most revolutionary developments in recent years has been the decoding of the human genome. In his book, *Before the Dawn,* Nicholas Wade reminds us that the human story goes back literally millions of years, but written records appeared only 5,000 years ago. How can we unlock the secrets of the far-distant human past? Wade writes:

> No deep understanding, it might seem, could ever be gained of these two vanished periods, the 5 million years of human evolution and the 45,000 years of prehistory. But in the past few years an extraordinary new archive has become available to those who study human evolution, human nature and history. It is the record encoded in the DNA of the human genome and in the versions of it carried by the world's population. Geneticists have long contributed to the study of the human past but are doing so with particular success since the full sequence of DNA units in the genome was determined in 2003.

> Why should the human genome . . . have so much to say about the past? As the repository of hereditary information that is in constant flux, the genome is like a document under ceaseless revision. Its mechanism of change is such that it retains evidence about its previous drafts and these, though not easy to interpret, provide a record that stretches deep into the past.

Wade goes on to show how study of the human genome can help us answer myriad questions about the pre-literate human past: When did humans gain the power of speech and how did various language families evolve? When did humans start wearing clothes? How large was the ancestral population that ultimately left Africa to populate the earth? And, much, much more.

Nicholas Wade, *Before the Dawn: Recovering the Lost History of Our Ancestors* (New York: Penguin Books, 2006).

on planet earth. He tells a story that covers a period of more than four billion years, the overwhelming majority of which predated human life.[5]

Even though history can never hope to achieve the level of certainty attainable in the pure experimental sciences, it can, through the application of rigorous canons of research, strive to attain increasingly closer approximations of the past it seeks to recover. Remember, as difficult as it is to reconstruct the events of the past, those events did happen, and historical study can be used to understand and illuminate those events.

---

[5] Richard Fortey, *Life: A Natural History of the First Four Billion Years of Life on Earth* (New York: Alfred A. Knopf, 1998). Also consider British writer and photojournalist John Reader's *Africa: A Biography of the Continent* (New York: Alfred A. Knopf, 1998), which devotes more than half its chapters to the millions of years of geology and prehistory that most traditional histories would pass over with scarcely a mention. Finally, University of Reading Professor Steven Mithen has written *After the Ice: A Global Human History, 20,000–5,000 BC* (Harvard Univ. Press, 2006).

History and the Social Sciences

History is related even more closely to the social and behavioral sciences (e.g., anthropology, sociology, political science, economics, and psychology). Indeed, many would include history among the social sciences. Whether history is a bedfellow or simply a close relative of the social sciences need not, for the moment, concern us. What is clear is that historians and social scientists share much in common. On the simplest level it is fair to claim that history provides much raw material for the social sciences. It would even be arguable (rightly we think) that history is in many ways the mother of the social sciences. Historians Jacques Barzun and Henry Graff have noted that the social sciences "are in fact daughter disciplines [to history], for they arose, each of them, out of historical investigation, having long formed part of avowed historical writing."[6]

Both history and the social sciences are bodies of knowledge that deal with women and men in society. Indeed it is often difficult to tell where one discipline leaves off and another begins, but, in general, the social sciences tend to be more "present-focused" than history. Still, in recent years more and more works of "history" have incorporated theories and methods of the social sciences, for example the works of psychohistory discussed in the previous chapter. It is best, therefore, to think of history and the social sciences not as distinct categories, but as colors in an intellectual spectrum, with one hue shading imperceptibly into another. The degree of overlap notwithstanding, each discipline approaches the study of the individual and society in a slightly different way.

- **Anthropology** literally means the "study of humanity." Physical anthropologists study the centuries-long physical evolution of human beings, whereas cultural anthropologists attempt to describe similarities and differences among the world's peoples and cultures (often concentrating on primitive cultures) and to explain the evolution of human social patterns. Anthropologists are historians of a sort, and history has been defined as "retrospective cultural anthropology." In general, though, anthropologists have traditionally concentrated on preliterate peoples whom they can observe directly, whereas historians have concentrated on the study of past societies for which we have written records. Practically speaking, this limits historians to the last five or six thousand years of the human experience, and to the study of those societies that could write.

- **Sociology**, a close relative of anthropology, studies the characteristics and behavior of social aggregates and groups, especially their institutions and modes of social organization. Whereas anthropologists have focused attention on primitive societies, sociologists have concentrated on more advanced, technologically sophisticated societies. To the extent that anthropology and sociology might study the same cultural groups and institutions, they are almost indistinguishable as disciplines. Again, the overlaps with history are many. Much sociology is based on historical evidence, and many historians (for instance, social historians) have adopted a sociological approach in their historical studies of social classes, occupational groups, and institutions.

- **Political Science**, like sociology, attempts to unlock the secrets of institutional and group behavior but, as the name implies, concentrates especially on political

---

[6] Barzun and Graff, *Modern Researcher*, 218.

behavior and governmental and legal institutions. The evolution and nature of political and legal ideas (political theory) has also been a longtime interest of the political scientist. The shared interests of the political scientist and historian are many, since law, politics, war, and diplomacy are among the most traditional objects of historical study. Many scholarly works on government, international relations, and politics are impossible to categorize as history or political science with any degree of certainty.

• **Economics** is the discipline that attempts to lay bare the mechanisms through which a society produces, trades, and distributes material goods. That the historian is also vitally interested in the economic side of human affairs goes without saying (recall the comments on the influence of Marx). Economic history is a thriving subspecialty within the discipline of history.

• **Psychology** is the study of "mental, emotional, and behavioral processes." The psychologist is interested in the unseen forces within the individual and within the social environment that make people behave the way they do. More than the other social and behavioral sciences, psychology emphasizes the mental processes and behavior patterns of the individual, although some branches of psychology (e.g., social psychology) deal with group behavior. Recently, as we have seen, historians have shown a growing interest in the psychological dimension of human behavior, and a growing number of studies have attempted to apply the insights of psychology to historical individuals and groups.

Clearly, there are many parallels between history and the various social sciences. But how do they differ? First, and this verges on massive oversimplification, a major preoccupation of the social sciences is to explain how societies, economies, governments, and other groups behave *today*. History, on the other hand, is more interested in explaining how societies functioned and developed in the past—that is, how they changed through time. Of course, the political scientist or economist does not ignore history (i.e., the past); nor does the historian ignore the lessons of the present. But generally the social sciences are much more "present oriented" than is history. The social scientist (often using historical evidence) tries to account for present behavior; the historian (often using current insights) tries to account for past behavior.

History and the social sciences diverge in yet another way. The social sciences, like the physical sciences, often emphasize the precise quantification (measurement) of data, experimentation (when appropriate), and the development of generalizations that permit prediction (and even control) of future behavior. While the historian attempts to reconstruct individual events in all their uniqueness, social scientists attempt to discover general principles that can be used to understand many events. To oversimplify, the historian examines the uniqueness of past events; the social scientist searches for the commonalities. For instance, a historian may desire to know all there is to know about the presidential election of 2008 in order to write a thorough history of that event. A political scientist, however, might want to compare voter behavior in 2008 with that in other presidential elections in order to discover voting patterns that might help predict the outcomes of future elections.

Of course, the historian will be more than happy to utilize whatever information the political scientist discovers (intellectual parasitism has a long and noble history), but it is not the historian's primary purpose to establish such regularities. Nor is the historian especially interested in prediction, as it is difficult enough to find out what has already happened. "It is the historian's aim," claims one writer, "to portray the bewildering, unsystematic variety of historical forms—people, nations, cultures, customs, institutions, songs, myths, and thoughts—in their unique, living expressions and in the process of continuous growth and transformation."[7]

Whether history is a bona fide social science or just a close relative is a matter best left unresolved at this time. Whatever your view of the matter, it is clear that the lines separating history from the various social sciences discussed in this section will never be easy to draw with absolute clarity.

History and Art

If, at times, history seems to "belong" to the social sciences, at other times it seems more reasonable to count it among the literary arts (classified in most universities as part of the "humanities"). After all, in its most basic form, written history is, as the name suggests, a "story." To tell a story well, as we have seen, the good historian must utilize the literary skills and conventions of the novelist or poet. Arnold Toynbee, the famous British historian, said "no historian can be 'great' if he is not also a great artist," and it is true that some of the "greatest" (at least most widely read) historians have been superb literary stylists. The war histories of Winston Churchill, Edward Gibbon's *Decline and Fall of the Roman Empire*, T. B. Macaulay's *History of England*, Bruce Catton's Civil War histories, and the works of American historians Barbara Tuchman and David McCullough are as much worth reading for their literary qualities as for what they say about the past. And what they say about the past, we might add, is very much worth our attention.

The historian must be an "artist" in another sense. To make the past come alive for current readers, a historian must be able to re-create on paper the passions, beliefs, and feelings of people long dead. This requires more than literary grace. The historian, as we have noted more than once in this book, must be able to empathize and sympathize with individuals, institutions, customs, and ideas that may seem foreign or strange. Like poets or novelists, historians must be able to "feel" themselves into the periods and cultures they are studying. Dispassionate objectivity is, of course, essential to good history; but so too is the imaginative insight and vision of the creative artist.[8] The basic difference between a great historian and a great novelist is that the historian's story must conform to known facts. The plausibility of the historian's narrative is determined by its adherence to the evidence. Good fiction, on the other hand, must be internally consistent and it must correspond to commonsense notions of how human beings behave, but it need not conform to any external body of source materials.

---

[7] Meyerhoff (ed.), *The Philosophy of History in Our Time*, 10.

[8] John Clive, until his recent death a Professor of History and Literature at Harvard University, made a career of studying the works and ideas of the great historians. What makes these historians (Macaulay, Jules Michelet, Alexis de Tocqueville, etc.) worth reading, Clive argues, is that their writing is a product of "the encounter between personal commitment and scholarly curiosity which lies at the heart of all great history." Clive says: "the quality of their writing, which turns out to exert the greatest power over us . . . is intimately related to each historian's chief intellectual and personal concerns." Quoted in Windschuttle, *Killing of History*, 244.

A Summary: The Main Features of History

If you are still somewhat confused about exactly where history fits into the jigsaw puzzle of intellectual life, don't despair. The lines that separate one branch of knowledge from another have never been precise. In simplest terms, the basic characteristics of history are three:

1. History is concerned with human beings operating in society. The historian is not primarily concerned with the origins of the earth (the task of the geologist), or with the organic processes of life (the task of the chemist and biologist), or with when and how humanoid creatures emerged on the land (the task of the anthropologist and paleontologist). The historian's work only begins in the presence of reliable records—especially written records—that indicate that a specific human group shared a specific set of experiences in a specific time and place.

2. History is concerned with change through time. Quite obviously, human society is also a central concern of many disciplines other than history. As distinct from these other disciplines, however, history traces and explains a society's experiences through time. It is important to note that history—good history—does not merely list events like a chronicle or a diary; history attempts to explain how and why things happened as they did.

3. History is concerned with the concrete and the particular. This is not always true, of course, because many historians do try to make generalizations that apply beyond a single situation. But, in the final analysis, a basic defining characteristic of history is its continuing preoccupation with the unique circumstance, and with the particulars that give substance to generalizations and distinctiveness to a given point in time. In other words, broad generalizations, however important, are secondary to those insights that provide knowledge of a particular, unique past.

EXERCISES

The distinctions you are asked to make in the exercises below are, to some extent, artificial and overly simplistic. In reality the line separating one discipline or approach from another is quite ambiguous; each discipline tends to shade imperceptibly into the next. However, there are differences between history and the other disciplines, and even an overly simplified set of contrasts can help you more effectively perceive those differences.

Exercise 1

This chapter is devoted to outlining some of the major similarities and differences between the study of history and the other disciplines. In the selections below, see if you can distinguish the examples of historical writing from those drawn from a variety of other disciplines. Before doing so, however, recall the central characteristics of history: (1) a concern with humans in society, (2) a preoccupation with change through time, and (3) a preference for explaining the interrelationship of concrete, particular events rather than elaborating comprehensive generalizations or hypotheses. Also, historians generally (with exceptions, of course) limit themselves to the study of societies for which there are written records.

Mark the passages drawn from history with an "**H**." Mark the passages drawn from other disciplines with an "**O**"—for "other." You need not identify the other disciplines specifically. Do, however, show your reasons for choosing as you do by indicating the absence or presence of the characteristics of history (1, 2, and 3) listed previously under "The Main Features of History" (page 249). See the example below.

Example:

___O___ A. We have now got so close to our present that we have to count in tens of thousands of years rather than in millions. Beginning at some undefined point in time, perhaps 70,000 years ago, Neanderthal Man appeared on the scene. As we shall see in Chapter IX, he represents the beginning of civilized man in the sense that he went in for religious observances, which suggests an intellectual capacity for abstract concepts. It also suggests that he must have had the kind of spoken language we have, if less refined and subtle. Indeed, his brain was as large as ours, although presumably rather different, for his skull was low-browed and bun-shaped rather than domed. . . . They inhabited Europe, the Middle East, and central Asia until roughly 35,000 b.p. [before the present], when they disappeared, perhaps because they were unable to compete with or defend themselves against men of our own kind, who were replacing them.

Comment

This passage is challenging to categorize. If you labeled it history, we would not object too strenuously. The passage does deal with humans in society (note the reference to religious observances), and it attempts to describe and explain change through time. Yet we would label this passage with an "O" because the author is describing a period long before the invention of writing and hence written records—a period sometimes referred to as "prehistoric." The subject matter belongs more properly in the domain of the anthropologist.

_____ B. Naturally, the larger and more massive a star, the more tremendous a red giant it will balloon into. The red giant into which our Sun will someday bloat will not be a particularly impressive specimen of the class. Red giants such as Betelgeuse and Antares developed out of main sequence stars considerably more massive than the Sun.

Reasons: _____

_____

_____ C. Leadership of Europe moved north to France, England, and Holland in the seventeenth century. In France, Henry IV (1589–1610) restored the monarchy to authority after a long bout of civil and religious wars. The state remained officially Catholic; but French national interests were kept carefully distinct from the cause of the papacy or of international Catholicism. Effective royal control of the Church in

France dated back to the fourteenth century and was vigorously and successfully maintained against the revivified papacy in the sixteenth and seventeenth centuries.

Reasons: _____

_____

_____ D. The day after his landslide defeat in 1984, Walter Mondale observed, "Modern politics requires a mastery of television. . . . The thing that scares me about that," he added, "is American politics is losing its substance. It's losing the depth." Since the presidential campaign season of 1980, candidates of both parties have tended to treat voters less like citizens of the polity than like consumers considering the purchase of a major product. High-tech mass marketing of particular candidates does not always work, but all candidates must have copious access to the media, and for this access to be used effectively, they must surround themselves with media advisers who can package the candidate effectively.

Reasons: _____

_____

_____ E. The Administration that came to power in January 1961 under President John F. Kennedy presented an attitude towards American responsibilities for "leadership" of the free world that one could call either "vigorous" or "frenzied," depending on how one felt about it. Our NATO allies were quickly apprised of the fact that the Americans had many new ideas for the defense of Europe, and that the Europeans would have to make some endeavor to understand and implement them. These ideas were themselves significant for what was to happen in the Far East, because they involved a complete dismantling of the "massive retaliation" concept in favor of a whole new complex of ideas stressing the use of conventional forces in limited wars. The man who as a true believer presided intimately over this change was the new Secretary of Defense, Robert S. McNamara.

Reasons: _____

_____

_____ F. **410** In this year Rome was destroyed by the Goths, eleven hundred and ten years after it was built. Then after that the kings of the Romans no longer reigned in Britain. Altogether they had reigned there 470 years since Gaius Julius first came to the land.
596 In this year Pope Gregory sent Augustine to Britain with a good number of monks, who preached God's word to the English people.
671 In this year there was the great mortality of birds.
715 In this year Ine and Ceolred fought at "Woden's barrow."
733 In this year Aethelbald occupied Somerton, and there was an eclipse of the sun.

Reasons: _____

_____

_____ G. We have already seen the two major models of economic organization: the market mechanism and the command economy. . . . Today, neither of these polar extremes represents the reality of the American economic system. Rather ours is a "mixed economy," in which both private and public institutions exercise economic control: the private system through the invisible direction of the market mechanism, the public institutions through regulatory commands and fiscal incentives.

Reasons: _____

_____

Sources

   A. Louis J. Halle, *Out of Chaos* (Boston: Houghton Mifflin, 1977), 241.
   B. Isaac Asimov, *The Universe* (New York: Avon, 1966), 162–63.
   C. William H. McNeill, *The Rise of the West* (New York: Mentor, 1965), 635.
   D. Daniel Hellinger and Dennis Judd, *The Democratic Facade,* 2nd ed. (Belmont, CA.: Wadsworth Publishing Co., 1994), 87.
   E. Bernard Brodie, *War and Politics* (New York: Macmillan, 1963), 124–25.
   F. "The Anglo-Saxon Chronicle" from B. L. Blakeley and J. Collins (eds.), *Documents in English History* (New York: John Wiley & Sons, 1975), 18.
   G. Paul Samuelson and William Nordhaus, *Economics,* 12th ed. (New York: McGraw-Hill, 1985), 41–42.

Exercise 2

As noted earlier, many historians have applied some of the categories, insights, and methods of the various social sciences to historical problems. In the *history passages* below—all dealing with witch beliefs and witchcraft persecutions—see if you can determine which of the social science approaches (i.e., anthropology, sociology, political science, economics, psychology) the historians have tried to utilize. If more than one answer seems appropriate, please so indicate. Also, identify those passages that simply narrate "what happened" in a more traditional manner. Use the word "traditional" for such passages. You might want to review the brief definitions of the various social sciences on pages 246–247.

A. Among the Navaho, witches are active primarily at night. This is also so among the Tale, the Azande and the Amba, but there is little trace of night meetings in Essex, [England]. Navaho witches are believed to meet most frequently in a cave, and there is general agreement that all types of witch activity must be carried on away from home. Likewise, witches among the Kaguru meet in unfrequented places. . . .

Answer: _____

B. Early in the year 1692 several girls of Salem Village (now Danvers), Massachusetts, began to sicken and display alarming symptoms [interpreted later as manifestations of witchcraft]. . . . These symptoms are readily recognizable. The most cursory examination of the classic studies of hysteria—of Charcot, of Janet, of Breuer, and Freud—will demonstrate that the afflicted girls in Salem were hysterical in the scientific sense of that term.

Answer: _____

C. The preliminary hearings began on Tuesday, March 1 [1692]. The magistrates arrived via the road from Salem town, gathering into formation around them the local constabulary and other prominent personages in a solemn yet impressive entourage. With 'pennants flying and drums athrob,' as one writer has described it, they arrived at Ingersoll's ordinary, where the court was to meet. Finding the space too small to accommodate the crowd that had gathered, the magistrates moved the hearing to the nearby meetinghouse.

Answer: _____

D. [In Salem, Massachusetts] almost every indicator by which the two Village factions may be distinguished, in fact, also neatly separates the supporters and opponents of the witchcraft trials. . . . The connection is clear: that part of Salem Village which was an anti-Parris stronghold in 1695 (the nearest part of Salem Town) had also been a center of resistance to the witchcraft trials, while the more distant western part of the Village, where pro-Parris sentiment was dominant, contained an extremely high concentration of accusers in 1692 . . . . Similarly with wealth: . . . the average 1695–96 tax of the Villagers who publicly opposed the trials was 67 percent higher than that of those who pushed the trials forward. . . .

Answer: _____

E. The association of witchcraft with "weak points in the social structure" suggests two research questions of large importance. First, what was the predominant pattern of relationship between the parties chiefly involved? Second, what situations most frequently yielded witchcraft suspicions—and accusations?

Answer: _____

F. As Lyndal Roper states, 'witchcraft confessions and accusations are not products of realism, and they cannot be analyzed with the methods of historical realism.' She draws out how individuals borrowed the language and stereotypical images of witchcraft to express their own psychic conflicts, which centered on the earliest stages of the mother-child relationship. Although this approach is particularly effective for the Augsburg material, with its exceptional focus on the care of infants in the strictly feminine space, it can be extended more widely.

Answer: _____

Sources
  A. A. D. J. Macfarlane, *Witchcraft in Tudor and Stuart England* (New York: Harper & Row, 1970), 211.
  B. Chadwick Hansen, *Witchcraft at Salem* (New York: Mentor, 1970), 21–22.
  C. Bryan F. Le Beau, *The Story of the Salem Witch Trials* (Upper Saddle River, NJ: Prentice Hall, 1998), 68.
  D. Paul Coyer and Stephen Nissenbaum, *Salem Possessed* (Cambridge, MA.: Harvard University Press, 1974), 185.
  E. John Putnam Demos, *Entertaining Satan: Witchcraft and the Culture of Early New England* (New York: Oxford University Press, 1982), 278.
  F. Robin Briggs, *Witches and Neighbors: The Social and Cultural Context of European Witchcraft* (New York: Viking, 1996), 282.

Exercise 3

Among historians there is disagreement whether history is more a social science (like political science or sociology) or a humanity/art (like literature). As we have seen, history shares characteristics with both camps. Usually historians do not state explicitly where they stand on this issue, but often their attitudes are implicit in the books and articles they write. In the passages below indicate whether you think the historian in question seems to view history as a discipline more in the social sciences or the humanities.

One clue to look for is the emphasis given to literary evidence (written records) versus statistical and quantifiable evidence. A preference for the latter would indicate a more social-scientific approach. Another clue would be the relative weight given to description and analysis of *particular* events versus analysis and generalization about a range of *similar* events or situations. Again, the latter emphasis may indicate a more social-scientific approach to the study of the past.

Mark the more social-science-oriented passages with an "**S**" and the more humanities-oriented (or "literary") passages with an "**H**." **Be prepared to defend your answer.**

_____ A. [In the Middle Ages] one sound rose ceaselessly above the noises of busy life and lifted all things unto a sphere of order and serenity: the sound of bells. The bells were in daily life like good spirits, which by their familiar voices, now called upon the citizens to mourn and now to rejoice, now warned them of danger, now exhorted them to piety. They were known by their names: big Jacqueline, or the bell Roland. Every one knew the difference in meaning of the various ways of ringing. However continuous the ringing of the bells, people would seem not to have become blunted to the effect of their sound.

_____ B. At whatever level one conducts research, roll-call votes offer versatile data that can be used to explore a variety of questions. Along with collections of session-laws and statutes, they comprise the most systematic body of data extant on the legislative process in the states. Roll calls offer data with which to discriminate systematically between contested and consensus issues and to compare the levels of voting conflict evoked by particular policy areas among various states.

_____ C. The extravagant conversations recorded by Hermann Rauschning for the period 1932–34, and by Dr. Henry Picker at the Fuehrer's H. Q. for the period 1941–42, reveal Hitler in another favorite role, that of visionary and prophet . . . . The fabulous dreams of a vast empire embracing all Europe and half Asia; the geopolitical fantasies of inter-continental wars and alliances; the plans for breeding an elite, biologically pre-selected, and founding a new Order to guard the Holy Grail of pure blood; the designs for reducing whole nations to slavery—all these are fruits of a crude, disordered, but fertile imagination soaked in the German romanticism of the late nineteenth century. . . .

_____ D. To be more precise, only one of the manifestations of sexual change will occupy us here: a rapid increase in the incidence of illegitimate births between the mid-eighteenth and mid-nineteenth centuries . . . . We may bring to bear other kinds of evidence as well upon sexual history, such as the observations of contemporaries, various 'medical' surveys of the population conducted by the camera list governments of western and central Europe, court records on sexual crimes and aberrancies, or the study of pornography . . . . Yet in this paper, I wish to present the evidence of illegitimacy alone.

First we examine potential objections to illegitimacy data as a measure of real sexual attitudes and practices; second, we briefly discuss the dimensions of the increase in illegitimacy between mid-eighteenth and mid-nineteenth centuries; third, a review of some current theories about sexual behavior and illegitimacy is in order; fourth, a general model linking modernizing forces to sexual change and illegitimacy will be proposed; finally I shall present empirical data confirming some of the linkages in this model from a region of central Europe which participated in the illegitimacy explosion—the Kingdom of Bavaria.

_____ E. In 1941 Frederick Williams introduced Frederick Mosteller to the problem which we shall consider in detail in this paper, namely the problem of the authorship of the disputed Federalist papers. Williams and Mosteller, influenced by the work of Yule and of C. B. Williams (1939), studied the undisputed Federalist works of Hamilton and Madison but found that sentence length did not discriminate between the two authors. They then computed for each known paper the percentages of nouns, of adjectives, of one- and two-letter words, and of the's. On the basis of these data they constructed a statistic that was intended to separate Hamilton's writings from Madison's. This statistic, however, was not sensitive enough to assign the disputed papers with any degree of confidence, although it pointed to Madison for most of them.

_____ F. Joan [of Arc (1412–31)] was born in that atmosphere of legend, of folklike dreamings. But the countryside offered another and very different kind of poetry, fierce, atrocious, and, alas! all too real: the poetry of war . . .War! That single word sums up all the emotions; not every day was marked by assault and pillage; but rather by the anguished expectancy, the tolling of the alarm bell, the sudden awakening, and, far in the plain, the sullen glare of fire . . . . A horrible condition: yet with an aura of poetry: even the most down-to-earth of men, the Lowland Scots, turned into poets amid the perils of the Border; from that blasted heath, which still seems under a curse, the ballads blossomed forth like wild and vigorous flowers.

_____ G. It all seems clear and consistent enough. The women in Shakespeare's plays, and so presumably the Englishwomen of Shakespeare's day, might marry in their early teens, or even before, and very often did.

Yet this is not true. We have examined every record we can find to test it and they all declare that, in Elizabethan and Jacobean England, marriage was rare at these early ages and not as common in the late teens as it is now. At twelve marriage as we understand it was virtually unknown . . . .

It is indeed hazardous to infer an institution or a habit characteristic of a whole society or a whole era from the central character of a literary work and its story. . . . The outcome may be to make people believe that what was the entirely exceptional, was in fact the perfectly normal. . . . This is a cogent argument in favour of statistical awareness, and of the sociological imagination, in studies of this sort.

_____ H. For Churchill it [the Japanese attack on Pearl Harbor and U.S. entry into World War II] was a moment of pure joy. So he had won, after all, he exulted. Yes, after Dunkirk, the fall of France, the threat of invasion, the U-boat struggle—after seventeen months of lonely fighting and nineteen months of his own hard responsibility—the war was won. England would live; the Commonwealth and the Empire would live. The war would be long, but all the rest would be merely the proper application of overwhelming force. People had said the Americans were soft, divided, talkative, affluent, distant, averse to bloodshed. But he knew better; he had studied the Civil War, fought out to the last desperate inch; American blood flowed in his veins. . . . Churchill set his office to work calling Speaker and whips to summon Parliament to meet next day. Then saturated with emotion, he turned in and slept the sleep of the saved and thankful.

For Discussion

In what ways might the books/articles represented by the passages you labeled "S" (social-science approach) be superior (or inferior) as history to those books and articles represented by passages labeled "H"? Is one approach better than the other or do both approaches have potential benefits and liabilities?

Sources
   A. J. Huizinga, *The Waning of the Middle Ages* (New York: Anchor, 1954), 10.
   B. Ballard Campbell, "The State Legislature in American History: A Review Essay," *Historical Methods Newsletter*, September 1976, 193.
   C. Alan Bullock, *Hitler*, rev. ed. (New York: Bantam, 1969), 325–26.
   D. Edward Shorter, "Sexual Change and Illegitimacy: The European Experience," *Modern European Social History*, ed. Robert Bezucha (Lexington, MA.: D.C. Heath, 1972), 231–32.
   E. Ivor S. Francis, "An Exposition of a Statistical Approach to the Federalist Dispute," *Quantification in American History*, ed. Robert P. Swierenga (New York: Atheneum, 1970), 98.
   F. Jules Michelet, *Joan of Arc* (Ann Arbor, MI: University of Michigan Press, 1967), 10.
   G. Peter Laslett, *The World We Have Lost*, 2nd ed. (New York: Scribner, 1971), 84, 90–91.
   H. James M. Burns, *Roosevelt: Soldier of Freedom* (New York: Harcourt Brace Jovanovich, 1970), 163.

FUR TRADE ON THE UPPER MISSOURI RIVER: DOCUMENTS

The documents that follow regard the beginnings of American fur trade on the upper Missouri River—i.e., present day North Dakota and South Dakota. This trade had great potential economic value, since animal furs and hides were regarded as the major resource of the developing West. The events described in the documents took place within what was legally American territory (as part of the Louisiana Purchase in 1803). One must remember, however, that for more than a hundred years British fur traders had operated successfully throughout the forest and mountain areas of North America, with little regard to who owned them. These documents refer to the expedition of General William H. Ashley and Major Andrew Henry in the summer of 1823, and their ill-fated encounter with the Arikara Indians (also "Rickaree," and other spellings).

The central question here is: Why did the expedition end so violently when the original intention was to trade peacefully with the Native American groups along the Missouri River? There are many possible themes you might choose to develop, e.g., the role of the British in the failure of the Ashley expedition, leadership deficiencies of Gen. Ashley, the cowardice of Ashley's men, blunders of the federal government, Rickaree grievances, the attitudes and outlooks of the men on the expedition, or some combination thereof. There may be yet other possibilities.

Documents

These documents are taken from *The West of William H. Ashley,* edited by Dale L. Morgan (Denver: Old West Publishing Co., 1964), 17, 20, 22, 29–31, 33-34, 36–38. Published with permission. The original spelling and punctuation has been retained.

John C. Calhoun, Secretary of War, to William Clark, Superintendent of Indian Affairs at St. Louis, Washington, July 1, 1822

Sir,

. . . I have received a letter from Major O'Fallon, in which he states that he understands a licence has been granted to Gen. Ashley and Major Henry, to trade, trap, & hunt, on the upper Missouri, and expresses a hope that limits have been prescribed to their trapping and hunting on Indian lands, as, he says, nothing is better calculated to alarm and disturb the harmony so happily existing between us and the Indians in the vicinity of the Council Bluffs.

The license which has been granted by this Department by order of the President to Gen. Ashley & Major Henry confers the privilege of trading with the Indians only, as the laws regulating trade and intercourse with the Indian tribes do not contain any authority to

Map of the Lousiana Territory, 1903. *U.S. National Archives, Record Group 49, ARC Identifier 594889. filename: ARC594889. LAPurchMap.jpg*

issue licenses for any other purpose. The privilege thus granted to them they are to exercise conformably to the laws and regulations that are or shall be made for the government of trade and intercourse with the Indians, for the true and faithful observance of which they have given bonds with sufficient security; consequently, it is presumed, they will do no act not authorized by such laws and regulations, which would disturb the peace and harmony existing between the government and the Indians on the Missouri, but rather endeavor, by their regular and conciliatory conduct, to strengthen and confirm them.

William Clark, Superintendent of Indian Affairs at St. Louis, to John C. Calhoun, Secretary of War, St. Louis, January 16, 1823.

Sir,
. . . The British North West Traders [i.e., Hudson's Bay Company] have lately established a trading house at no great distance from the Missouri, much nearer the Mandans [North Dakota] than their former Trading establishments, and within the bounds of the United States. I beg leave mearly to observe that it is to be lamented that our military posts could not have been extended to the Yellow Stone river indeed it has been decidedly my opinion that a show of troops in that upper country, would have a very good effect in securing, our friendly relations with the Indians, and producing favourable checks on British Traders in that quarter . . . .

Missouri Republican, *St. Louis, March 12, 1823*

Two keel-boats belonging to general Ashley, left this place on Monday [March 10] for the Yellow Stone [River], having on board about 100 men. They have started to join the establishment commenced by that gentleman last year, above the mouth of the Yellow Stone, for the purposes of hunting and trapping. If enterprise could command success, it would certainly await upon the exertions of the head of these expeditions.

We understand a man fell overboard from one of the boats, on Monday morning, and was drowned.

William H. Ashley to a Gentleman in Franklin, Missouri

On board the keel boat *Rocky Mountains,* opposite the mouth of the Shegan River [a tributary of the Missouri River], June 7, 1823.

As I ascended the river I was informed by some gentlemen of the Missouri Fur Company, that in a recent affray [quarrel or brawl] which they had had with a war party of the Rickaree Indians, two of the Indians were killed, and that their conduct during the last winter, had shewn a hostile disposition towards the Americans. I therefore used all the precaution in my power for some days before I reached their towns; not one of them, however, did I see until my arrival there on the 30th of May, when my boats were anchored about the middle of the river. I took with me two men & went on shore, where I was met by some of the principal chiefs, who professed to be very friendly disposed, and requested me to land some goods for the purpose of trading with them. I had just received an express from Maj. Henry, desiring me to purchase all the horses I could get; consequently I proposed to exchange goods for horses, intending to send a party of forty men by land to the Yellow Stone River. I requested that the principal chiefs of the two towns would first meet me on the sand beach, where there should be a perfect understanding relative to the principles of our barter. After some consultation, the chiefs made their appearance at the place proposed. I then stated to them what I had heard below relative to their conduct, and the impropriety of repeating it. They said they much regretted the affray between some of their nation and the Americans, and confessed that they had been much displeased with us, but that all those angry feelings had left them; that then they considered the Americans their friends, and intended to treat them as such.

The next morning I commenced the purchase of horses, and on the evening of the 1st inst [of the present month, hence June] was ready to proceed on my voyage, intending to set out early the next morning. Late in the afternoon an Indian came down with a message to me from the principal chief (the Bear) of one of the towns, requesting that I would come and see him. After some hesitation (as I did not wish to let them know that I apprehended the least danger from them) I went to the lodge of the chief, where I was treated with every appearance of friendship.—The next morning, about half past 3 o'clock, I was informed that Aaron Stephens, one of my men, had been killed by the Indians, and that in all probability the boats would be attacked in a few minutes. The boats were anchored in the stream, about 90 feet from the shore. My party consisted of ninety men, forty of whom had been selected to go by land, and were encamped on the sand beach, to whose charge the horses were entrusted. The men on the beach were placed as near as possible between the two boats.

At sunrise the Indians commenced a heavy and well directed fire from a line extending along the picketing of one of their towns, and some broken land adjoining, about six hundred yards in length. Their aim was principally at the men on shore. The fire was returned by us, but, from their advantageous situation, I presume we did but little execution. Discovering the fire to be destructive to the men on shore, the steersmen of both boats were ordered to weigh their anchors and lay their boats to shore; but, notwithstanding every exertion on my part to enforce the execution of the order, I could not effect it—the principal part of the boatmen were so panic struck, that they would not expose themselves in the least. Two skiffs, one sufficient to carry twenty men, were taken ashore for the embarcation of the men, but, from a predetermination on their part not to give way to the Indians as long as it was possible to do otherwise, the most of them refused to make use of that opportunity of embarking, the large skiff returned with four, two of them wounded, and was immediately started back, but unfortunately one of the oarsmen was shot down, and by some means the skiff set adrift. The other was taken to the opposite side of the river by two men, one mortally wounded; some swam to the boats, others were shot down in the edge of the water and immediately sunk, and others who appeared to be badly wounded sunk in attempting to swim. To describe my feelings at seeing these men destroyed, is out of my power. I feel confident that if my orders had been obeyed I should not have lost five men.

If our government do not send troops on this river, as high as the mouth of the Yellow Stone, or above that place, the Americans must abandon the trade in this country—The Indians are becoming more formidable every year. The Rickarees are about six hundred warriors, three fourths of whom, I think, are armed with London fusils, which carry a ball with considerable accuracy and force—others have bows and arrows, war axes, &c. [etc.]. They are situated in two towns about three hundred yards apart.—Immediately in front of them is a large sand bar, nearly in the shape of a horse-shoe. On the opposite side of the river the ground is very high and commanding, and at the upper end of the bar they have a breast-work made of dry wood. The river there is narrow, and the channel near the south side.

From the situation of my men and boats, when the men had embarked, I concluded to fall back to the first timber, and place them in a better state of defence, then to proceed on my voyage; but to my great mortification and surprise, I was informed, after my men had been made acquainted with my intentions, that they positively refused to make another attempt to pass the towns, without a considerable reinforcement. I had them paraded, and made known to them the manner in which I proposed fixing the boats and passing the Indian villages. After saying all that I conceived necessary to satisfy them, and having good reason to believe that I should be, with but very few exceptions, deserted in a short time by all my men, as some of them had already formed a resolution to desert, I called on those disposed to remain with me under any circumstances, until I should hear from Maj. Henry, to whom I would send an express immediately, and request that he would descend with all the aid he could spare from his fort at the mouth of the Yellow Stone.—Thirty only have volunteered, among whom are but few boatmen; consequently I am compelled to send one boat back, having secured [some of] her cargo here [opposite the mouth of the Cheyenne]. I am determined to descend no lower until I pass the Rickarees, should it be in my power so to do.

Hugh Glass to the Parents of John S. Gardner

[June, 1823]

Dr Sir,

My painfull duty it is to tell you of the deth of yr Son wh befell at the hands of the indians 2nd June in the early morning. He lived a little while after he was shot and asked me to inform you of his sad fate We brought him to the ship where he soon died. Mr Smith a young man of our company made a powerful prayr wh moved us all greatly and I am persuaded John died in peace. His body we buried with others near this camp and marked the grave with a log. His things we will send to you. The savages are greatly treacherous. we traded with them as friends but after a great storm of rain and thunder they came at us before light and many were hurt. I myself was hit in the leg. Master Ashley is bound to stay in these parts till the traitors are rightly punished.

Yr Obt Svt
Hugh Glass

Letter by One of Ashley's Men to a Friend in the District of Columbia

Fort Kiawa, ten miles below the Big Bend of the Missouri, June 17th, 1823.
. . . We retreated down the river about 20 miles, intending to fortify ourselves until we could get assistance from the Bluffs [a military post]; the French boatmen were so panic-struck they would listen to no terms—they would return and forfeit their wages sooner than remain. Ashley paraded his men, told them his situation, and called for volunteers; one third, being twenty-five, only remained, and of these one half are boatmen, who intend returning when Henry's boat comes down. Out of one hundred men, the number he left St.

Arikara villages as seen by George Catlin in 1832. Smithsonian American Art Museum, Gift of Mrs. Joseph Harrison, Jr. 1985.66.386.

Louis with, I question much whether he will arrive at the Yellow Stone with more than ten, (and of this number I hope to be one;) finding he could not obtain men enough to remain with sufficient to man both boats, he determined to fortify his own [the Rocky Mountains]—take all those on board who were willing to stay, and those goods only that might be wanted—send the balance of the goods to this place and the large boat to St. Louis. With the goods, I was left in charge, and shall remain here until I hear from him or Henry. . . .

Council Bluffs is 600 miles below this, a very injudicious place for a military post. Here, and above this, is the spot where the Indians have always been most troublesome. You will hardly believe it, but I assure you it is a fact, our Indian Agent has never been above the Bluffs. He has never made himself known to the Indians in this quarter. They have been told of troops, &c. &c. at the Bluffs, but they do not believe it; they have never seen more of the white people than the few traders that come among them; and each tribe thinks we are less numerous than they—they have reason to think so, having never been punished for the numerous robberies and murders committed by them. The hostility of the Indians may be very easily accounted for. It is but six or seven days journey from this place, but five from the Ricarees . . . to the English posts on the Red river.

I have been told, though I cannot vouch for its authenticity, although I think it highly probable, from their determined hostility, that they [the British] have erected trading establishments within our territories. One thing is certain, they are not willing we should rival them in this valuable trade. All the injury they can do us they will do. The hostility of the Ricarees, Black-feet, Snake, Chiaus [Cheyennes], and Assiniboines, is entirely owing to the influence of the Northwest or Hudson Bay Company [a British Company]. The late act [of May 6, 1822] prohibiting the sale of spirituous liquors to the Indians has not that good effect which the framers of it had in view. It was passed without mature deliberation and a knowledge of the circumstances. No act that Congress could have passed could have such a tendency to aggrandize the North-West Company. In consequence of this, most of those tribes that formerly frequented the river have now left it, and more contemplate doing so, should that act not be repealed or amended. From the English they can get what liquor they want, and the distance is nothing to an Indian, when he has in view the gratification of his passions. Among the Ricarees I saw several English medals, and some of British manufacture.

The government must remedy these abuses; she must divest herself of that appalling slowness that attends all her operations. She must show more energy than she has done, if she wishes to preserve the fur trade; otherwise, our traders may as well abandon the business. The risque is too great for individual enterprise when unaided and unassisted by the government. Adieu. For myself I am determined to have revenge for the loss of two young men to whom I became very much attached, and I never will descend this river until I assist in shedding the blood of some of the Ricarees. It would give me pleasure beyond the power of language to express, could I personally extend my hand and greet you, &c.

Benjamin O'Fallon, U.S. Indian Agent, Upper Missouri Agency, to Ashley's Deserters, Fort Atkinson, June 19, 1823

To

Forty three men who deserted Gen. Ashley . . .

Your unexpected return with those wounded men announces to me a circumstance which not only mortifies my national pride, but distresses my heart greatly . . . . I feel most deeply the necessity of recounting your shame, your shame in leaving, in thus abandoning your employer, and as Missourians your General—in thus abandoning him in the savage wilderness, far from home . . . .

[In the rest of the letter, O'Fallon urges the deserters to join a relief expedition to rescue the survivors and "revenge the death, and bury the bones (of) your more than brave Comrads."]

Benjamin O'Fallon, U.S. Indian Agent, Upper Missouri Agency, to William Clark, Superintendent of Indian Affairs at St. Louis, Fort Atkinson, June 24, 1823

Dear Sir,

I arrived at this place [from St. Louis] on the 6th instant after a long and disagreeable trip of more than twenty days and have been anxiously waiting an opportunity to write you a long letter on many subjects, but more particularly on the subject of Indian affairs—But I now take up my pen to announce to you a circumstance, which not only wounds my national pride, but grieves my heart greatly—it is the defeat of Gen. Ashleys Expedition by the Aricharars [i.e., Rickarees]—One of his boats arrived here on the 18th instant with forty three men including five wounded, who are now in the Hospital, bringing me a letter from the General which I herewith enclose, giving a more detailed account of the affair, than I without reference to it would be enabled to do—From his hurried account and that of the most intelligent of his men with whom I have conversed it appears to have been the most shocking outrage to the feelings of humanity ever witnessed by Civilized men—unexampled in the annals of the world—

As those inhuman monsters will most probably be made to atone for what they have done by a great effusion of their blood, I shall (however painful it may be) endeavour to restrain my feelings, and defer (untill a later period) giving you a gloomy picture of a scene, which if justly portrayed would from a man of your sensibility extract tears of blood—Although young in years, and without a polished or even a common education, I have for a long time been endeavouring to Arouse the better feelings, and excite the Sympathy of my Country in favour of the most daring, the most energetic, and enterprising portion of the community. I mean those of our fellow Citizens, who from our forbearance are dayly exposed, and falling victims to the tomihauk and sculping knife of the Indians

On being apprised of this unfortunate circumstance, which has not only put in Jeopardy upwards of two hundred of our Citizens, who are legally engaged in the fur trade above this, but threatens to arrest for a long time the individual enterprise of the fairest portion of the western country Co. Levenworth and myself consulted, and considering the best interests of our Country, was not slow to determine what steps should be taken, consequently, he lost no time in organizing and fitting out an Expedition of upwards of two hundred regular troops, exclusive of Officers, which set out on the 22nd inst. accompan[i]ed by Mr.

Pilcher, several other Partners of the Missouri fur Company and about fifty of their men . . . This expedition, when it reaches the A'richarar Village, will including trading [traders?] and trading men, consist of upwards of three hundred effective white men, and about five hundred Souix Indians I expect will join them at or near the grand Bend—enough to look down all opposition-no Indian force can posibly resist them—

This unprovoked and dreadful massacre of white men, by the A'rickarar nation of Indians (men, women and Children Concerned) has awakened the peaceful natives of the land It has directed the attention of all the neighboring tribes, who are suspending their opinion of us untill they hear the result of this expedition—Now, say the Indians "all will see what the white people intend to do—We will see the extent of their forbearance—We will also see (if they have any) the extent of their spirit of resentment—" For a long time we have been presuming upon the forbearance of the whites, slowly bleeding their veins, and they have born it patiently, for we have heard but the murmer of a single man—"But now the A'richarars have by sticking and sticking made a deep incision—They have made a dreadful wound, in which even their men, women, and children have stained their hands with blood—"

This expedition (as your experience of the Indian character will tell you) is big with great events The peace, and tranquility of this Country depends upon its success, which, with great anxiety I calculate on surely—The Indian nations about here continue as friendly as usual—The Ottoes & Missouris are here and now assembling to council with me.

Missouri Intelligencer, *Franklin, July 1, 1823*

INDIAN OUTRAGE!

We learn from one of our citizens . . . that the boat, commanded by Gen. Ashley in person, was visited about a hundred and fifty miles above Council-Bluffs by a large body of the Rickaree Indians, who demanded of Gen. Ashley some remuneration for the lives of two or their warriors who were killed in a skirmish with a party of men belonging to the Missouri Fur Company some time last winter. Gen. Ashley gave them powder and twenty five muskets, which appeared at first to content them; they became dissatisfied however in a short time, and returning to the boat demanded more presents, with a threat that if refused they would attack and kill the crew.

APPENDIX B

SOURCE REFERENCES AND BIBLIOGRAPHIES

In Chapter 12 we discussed the importance of documenting university-level papers with source references and a bibliography. You will find that instructors in different disciplines—English, Psychology, the sciences, etc.—require different formats for citing sources and preparing bibliographies. This may be irritating, but it is a fact of life. In history the standard is to use footnotes or endnotes according to the so-called "Chicago Style" based on the *Chicago Manual of Style,* 15th ed. Chicago: University of Chicago Press, 2003.

What we include here is but a beginning primer that only scratches the surface. You really need to own a formal style guide. The two best options are Kate Turabian's long-time classic *A Manual for Writers of Research Papers, Theses and Dissertations,* 7th ed., Chicago University Press, 2007, or (our favorite) Diana Hacker's, *A Writer's Reference,* 6th ed., Bedford St. Martins, 2006. We prefer Hacker because it comes with an easy-to-use plastic comb binding and it provides information on all the common citation formats students are likely to encounter in their university or college careers (Chicago Style, APA, MLA).

Regardless of the guide you choose, always use the most recent edition. Much of this material is also accessible online, but it helps to have an actual book that you can refer to while using your computer to write your assignments.

Footnotes and Endnotes

Footnotes (or endnotes) tell the reader the exact source of quotations, paraphrases, and key pieces of information used in your paper. When using endnotes or footnotes (remember, the format is identical), insert numbers, preferably superscript numbers, to mark the passages that require a source citation—like this.[1] Then, under that footnote number (at the bottom of the page) or endnote number (at the end of the paper) include a full source reference **including the page number(s)**. There is a basic format, but that format changes subtly depending on the type of source you are using—book, journal article, newspaper, Web site, etc. You will need to pay close attention to word order and punctuation. Note that in source citations authors are listed first name first. The most common types of source references are shown below. If you use sources that don't fit these models (e.g., primary documents, separately authored chapters in a single volume, book reviews, etc.), you will need to consult a style manual. Single-space the notes.

---

[1] To review comments on footnotes see Conal Furay and Michael Salevouris, *The Methods and Skills of History,* 3rd ed. (Wheeling, IL.: Harlan Davidson, Inc., 2010, 213–214. To see how notes are sequenced, look at the footnoting in any chapter of this book.

A. Book with a Single Author:

1. Carl Abbott, *Urban America in the Modern Age: 1920 to the Present*, 2nd ed. (Wheeling, IL.: Harlan Davidson, Inc. 2007), 49–50.

   - Insert edition numbers only for editions after the first.
   - For online books (e-books) simply add the URL—i.e., Internet address.

B. Book with Two or Three Authors:

2. George Brown Tindall and David E. Shi, *America: A Narrative History*, Brief 2nd ed. (New York: W. W. Norton & Co., 1989), 431.

   - If there are more than three authors, list the name of the first author and then write "and others" or "et al." which means the same thing.

C. Edited Work Without an Author:

3. John Tosh, ed., *Historians on History* (Harlow, England: Pearson Education, 2000), 65.

D. Article in a Scholarly Journal:

4. Francine Hirsch, "The Soviets at Nuremberg: International Law, Propaganda and the Making of the Postwar Order," *American Historical Review* 113, No. 3 (June 2008): 722.

   - The "113" is the volume number. Articles, or sections of a book, are set off by quotation marks.

E. Article in a Magazine:

5. Evan Thomas, "The Mythology of Munich," *Newsweek*, June 23, 2008, 24.

F. Article in a newspaper:

6. James Glanz and T. Christian Miller, "Official History Spotlights Iraq Rebuilding Blunders." *The New York Times*, December 14, 2008, sec. 1.

   - For newspaper articles—print or online—page numbers are not necessary. Include a section number, if one is available.

G. Electronic Database:

7. Jack Santino, "Public Protest and Popular Style: Resistance from the Right in Northern Ireland and South Boston," *American Anthropologist*, New Series, 101, No. 3 (Sept. 1999): 520–21. JSTOR.

H. World Wide Web Site:

8. Douglas O. Linder, "Famous Trials," University of Missouri-Kansas City, 2009, <http://www.law.umkc.edu/faculty/projects/ftrials/ftrials.htm> (26 January 2009). Internet.

I. Short-form citations for previously cited works:

If you cite a source a second time or more, there is no need to repeat the full citation. The short form provides an easy short cut—simply list the author's surname and a page number.

9. Abbott, 112.

10. Tosh, 66.

If you use more than one book by a single author, or more than one author has the same last name, include a short version of the title.

11. Abbott, *Urban America,* 112.

Bibliographies

A bibliography, or works-cited page, provides in one place a comprehensive list of all the sources you used in your paper. The main differences in the citation format are: (1) works are listed alphabetically according to authors' last names (the author's last name is listed first in the citation), (2) there are no internal parentheses, and (3) the punctuation differs—note the use of periods instead of commas. For articles include the entire page range. For lengthy bibliographies it is common to list primary sources and secondary sources in separate sections.

Entries should be single-spaced and indented after the first line. This is called a "hanging indent." Double-space between entries. Compare the following with the footnotes shown above.

Abbott, Carl. *Urban America in the Modern Age: 1920 to the Present.* 2nd ed. Wheeling, IL.: Harlan Davidson, Inc., 2007.

Glanz, James and T. Christian Miller. "Official History Spotlights Iraq Rebuilding Blunders. *The New York Times,* December 14, 2008, sec. 1.

Hirsch, Francine. "The Soviets at Nuremberg: International Law, Propaganda and the Making of the Postwar Order." *American Historical Review* 113, No. 3 (June 2008): 701–730.

Linder, Douglas O. "Famous Trials." University of Missouri-Kansas City. 2009. <http://www.law.umkc.edu/faculty/projects/ftrials/ftrials.htm> (26 January 2009). Internet.

Santino, Jack. "Public Protest and Popular Style: Resistance from the Right in Northern Ireland and South Boston." *American Anthropologist,* New Series, 101, No. 3 (Sept. 1999): 515–28. JSTOR.

Thomas, Evan. "The Mythology of Munich." *Newsweek,* June 23, 2008, 23–26.

Tindall, George Brown and David E. Shi. *America: A Narrative History.* Brief 2nd ed. New York: W. W. Norton & Co., 1989.

Tosh, John, ed. *Historians on History.* Harlow, England: Pearson Education, 2000.

———, *The Pursuit of History.* London: Longman, 1984. (Another book by the same author.)

Tri-County Historical Society

For and in consideration of the participation by *Tri-County Historical Society* in any programs involving the dissemination of tape-recorded memoirs and oral history material for publication, copyright, and other uses, I hereby release all right, title, or interest in and to all of my tape-recorded memoirs to *Tri-County Historical Society* and declare that they may be used without any restriction whatsoever and may be copyrighted and published by the said *Society* which may also assign said copyright and publication rights to serious research scholars.

In addition to the rights and authority given to you under the preceding paragraph, I hereby authorize you to edit, publish, sell and/or license the use of my oral history memoir in any other manner which the *Society* considers to be desirable and I waive any claim to any payments which may be received as a consequence thereof by the *Society*.

PLACE *Indianapolis, Indiana*

DATE *July 14, 1975*

Harold S. Johnson
(Interviewee)

Jane Rogers
for *Tri-County Historical Society*

Source: From Collum Davis, Kathryn Back, and Kay MacLean, *Oral History: From Tape to Type* (Chicago: American Library Assn., © 1977), 14. Reprinted with permission from the American Library Association.

SUGGESTIONS FOR FURTHER READING

The Nature of History—The Philosophy of History

Ankersmit, Frank, and Hans Kellner, eds. *A New Philosophy of History.* Chicago: The University of Chicago Press, 1995.

Becker, Carl. *Everyman His Own Historian.* New York: Appleton-Century-Crofts, 1935.

Beringer, Richard E. *Historical Analysis: Contemporary Approaches to Clio's Craft.* New York: John Wiley and Sons, 1978.

Bloch, Marc. *The Historian's Craft.* New York: McGraw-Hill, 1964.

Braudel, Fernand. *On History.* Chicago: University of Chicago Press, 1980.

Butterfield, Herbert. *Man on His Past.* Cambridge: Cambridge University Press, 1955.

———. *The Whig Interpretation of History.* London: G. Bell, 1931.

Carr, E. H. *What is History?* New York: Random, 1967.

Collingwood, R.G. *The Idea of History.* Oxford: Clarendon Press, 1946.

Commager, Henry Steele. *The Nature and Study of History.* New York: Garland, 1984.

Conkin, Paul K. and Roland N. Stromberg. *Heritage and Challenge: The History and Theory of History.* Wheeling, IL.: Harlan Davidson, Inc., 1989.

Dray, William H. *Philosophy of History.* Englewood Cliffs, NJ: Prentice-Hall, 1964.

Fischer, David Hackett. *Historians' Fallacies: Toward a Logic of Historical Thought.* New York: Harper and Row, 1970.

Gardiner, Patrick L. *The Nature of Historical Explanation.* New York: Oxford University Press, 1952.

Gottschalk, Louis. *Understanding History.* New York: Knopf, 1969.

Gustavson, Carl G. *The Mansion of History.* New York: McGraw-Hill, 1976.

———. *A Preface to History.* New York: McGraw-Hill, 1955.

Hexter, J. H. *The History Primer.* New York: Basic Books, 1971.

Hobsbawm, Eric. *On History.* New York: The New Press, 1997.

Hughes, H. Stuart. *History as Art and as Science.* New York: Garland, 1985.

Jordanova, Ludmilla. *History in Practice.* London: Arnold, 2000.

Kitson Clark, George. *The Critical Historian.* London: Heinemann, 1967.

Marwick, Arthur. *The Nature of History.* London: Macmillan, 1970.

Meyerhoff, Hans, ed. *The Philosophy of History in Our Time.* New York: Doubleday, 1959.

Nash, Ronald H., ed. *Ideas of History.* 2 vols. New York: E. P. Dutton, 1969.

Nevins, Allan. *The Gateway to History.* Chicago: Quadrangle Books, 1963.

Norling, Bernard. *Timeless Problems in History.* Notre Dame, IN.: Univ. of Notre Dame Press, 1970.

Smith, Page. *The Historian and History*. New York: Knopf, 1964.

Tholfsen, Trygve R. *Historical Thinking*. New York: Harper and Row, 1967.

Trevelyan, G. M. *Clio, A Muse and Other Essays*. New ed. London: Longmans, Green, 1930.

Vaughn, Stephen, ed. *The Vital Past: Writings on the Uses of History*. Athens, GA.: University of Georgia Press, 1985.

Walsh, W. H. *An Introduction to Philosophy of History*. 3rd ed. rev. London: Hutchinson University Library, 1967.

Historical Methodology

Altick, Richard D. *The Scholar Adventurers*. Columbus: Ohio State University Press, 1987.

Aydelotte, William O. *Quantification in History*. Reading, MA.: Addison-Wesley, 1971.

Barzun, Jacques. *Clio and the Doctors: Psycho-History, Quanto-History and History*. Chicago: University of Chicago Press, 1974.

———, and Henry F. Graff. *The Modern Researcher*. Rev. ed. New York: Harcourt, Brace, 1985.

Benjamin, Jules R. *A Student's Guide to History*. 10th ed. New York: Bedford/St. Martin's, 2006.

Brundage, Anthony. *Going to the Sources: A Guide to Historical Research and Writing*. 4th ed. Wheeling, IL,: Harlan Davidson, Inc., 2008.

Cantor, Norman F. and Richard I. Schneider. *How to Study History*. Wheeling, IL.: Harlan Davidson, Inc., 1967.

Daniels, Robert V. *Studying History: How and Why*. 3rd ed. Englewood Cliffs, NJ: Prentice-Hall, 1981.

Davidson, James W. and Mark Lytle. *After the Fact: The Art of Historical Detection*. 4th ed. New York: McGraw, 1998.

Davis, Cullom, Kathryn Back, and Kay MacLean. *Oral History: From Tape to Type*. Chicago: American Library Association, 1977.

Dunaway, David K. and Willa K. Baum, eds. *Oral History: An Interdisciplinary Anthology*. Nashville: American Association for State and Local History, 1984.

Elton, G. R. *The Practice of History*. London: Sydney University Press, 1967.

Gray, Wood, et al. *Historian's Handbook: A Key to the Study and Writing of History*. 2nd ed. Boston: Houghton Mifflin, 1964.

Greenstein, Daniel I. *A Historian's Guide to Computing*. New York: Oxford University Press, 1994.

Handlin, Oscar. *Truth in History*. Cambridge, MA.: Harvard University Press, 1979.

The History Teacher. Long Beach, CA.: The Society for History Education. Published Quarterly.

Kyvig, David E. and Myron A. Marty. *Your Family History: A Handbook for Research and Writing*. Wheeling, IL.: Harlan Davidson, Inc., 1978.

Lichtman, Allan J. and Valerie French. *Historians and the Living Past*. Wheeling, IL.: Harlan Davidson, Inc., 1978.

Lowenthal, David. *The Past is a Foreign Country*. Cambridge: Cambridge University Press, 1985.

Marwick, Arthur. *What History Is and Why It Is Important; Primary Sources; Basic Problems of Writing History; Common Pitfalls in Historical Writing*. Bletchley, England: The Open University Press, 1970.

McMichael, Andrew. *History on the Web*. Wheeling, IL: Harlan Davidson, Inc., 2005.

Presnell, Jenny L. *The Information-Literate Historian*. New York: Oxford University Press, 2007.

Reiff, Janice L. *Structuring the Past: The Use of Computers in History*. American Historical Association, 1991.

Renier, G. J. *History: Its Purpose and Method*. Macon, GA.: Mercer University Press, 1982.

Shafer, Robert Jones, ed. *A Guide to Historical Method*. 3rd ed. Belmont, CA.: Wadsworth Publishing, 1980.

Shorter, Edward. *The Historian and the Computer*. Englewood Cliffs, NJ: Prentice-Hall, 1971.

Sitton, Thad, George L. Mehaffy, and G. L. Davis, Jr. *Oral History: A Guide for Teachers (and Others)*. Austin: University of Texas Press, 1983.

Stanford, Michael. *A Companion to the Study of History*. Oxford: Blackwell, 1994.

Stephens, Lester D. *Probing the Past: A Guide to the Study and Teaching of History*. Boston: Allyn and Bacon, 1974.

Teaching History, A Journal of Methods. Emporia, KS: Division of Social Sciences and the College of Liberal Arts and Sciences, Emporia State University. Published semi-annually.

Thompson, Paul. *The Voice of the Past: Oral History*. 2nd. ed. Oxford: Oxford University Press, 1988.

Tosh, John. *The Pursuit of History: Aims, Methods and New Directions in the Study of Modern History*. London: Longman, 1984.

Trinkle, Dennis A., Dorothy Auchter, Scott A. Merriman, and Todd E. Larson. *The History Highway: A Guide to Internet Resources*. Armonk, NY: M. E. Sharpe, 1997.

Tuchman, Barbara W. *Practicing History*. New York: Knopf, 1981.

Wineburg, Sam. *Historical Thinking and Other Unnatural Acts*. Philadelphia: Temple University Press, 2001.

Winks, Robin W., ed. *The Historian as Detective*. New York: Harper Colophon, 1970.

Historiography

Appleby, Joyce, Lynn Hunt, and Margaret Jacob. *Telling the Truth About History*. New York: W. W. Norton, 1994.

Barnes, Harry E. *A History of Historical Writing*. 2nd rev. ed. New York: Dover, 1963.

Benson, Susan P., Stephen Brier, and Roy Rosenzweig. *Presenting the Past: Essays on History and the Public*. Philadelphia: Temple University Press, 1986.

Breisach, Ernst. *Historiography: Ancient, Medieval, and Modern*. Chicago: The University of Chicago Press, 1983.

Burrow, John. *A History of Histories*. New York: Knopf, 2008.

Carnes, Mark C. ed. *Novel History: Historians and Novelists Confront America's Past (and Each Other)*. New York: Simon and Schuster, 2001

Gay, Peter, and Gerald J. Cavanaugh, eds. *Historians at Work*. 4 Vols. New York: Irvington, 1975.

Geyl, Pieter. *Debates with Historians*. New York: Meridian Books, 1958.

Gilbert, Felix, and Stephen R. Graubard, eds. *Historical Studies Today*. New York: Norton, 1972.

Gilderhus, Mark T. *History and Historians*. 6th ed. Upper Saddle River, NJ: Pearson Education, 2007.

Gooch, George Peabody. *History and Historians in the Nineteenth Century*. Rev. ed. London: Longmans, Green, 1952.

Halperin, S. William, ed. *Some Twentieth-Century Historians*. Chicago: University of Chicago Press, 1961.

Higham, John, Leonard Krieger, and Felix Gilbert. *History: The Development of Historical Studies in the United States*. Englewood Cliffs, NJ: Prentice-Hall, 1964.

Himmelfarb, Gertrude. *The New History and the Old*. Cambridge: The Belknap Press of Harvard University Press, 1987.

Kren, George M. and Leon H. Rappoport, eds. *Varieties of Psychohistory*. New York: Springer, 1976.

Lindaman, Dana, and Kyle Ward. *History Lessons: How Textbooks from Around the World Portray U.S. History*. New York: The New Press, 2004.

Noble, David W. *The End of American History*. Minneapolis: University of Minnesota Press, 1985.

Novick, Peter. *That Noble Dream*. Cambridge: Cambridge University Press, 1988.

Scott, Joan Wallach, ed. *Feminism and History*. Oxford: Oxford University Press, 1996.

Southgate, Beverley. *What is History For?* London: Routledge, 2005.

———. *Why Bother with History?* Harlow, England: Pearson Education, 2000.

Stannard, David E. *Shrinking History*. New York: Oxford University Press, 1980.

Stephens, Lester D. *Historiography: A Bibliography*. Metuchen, NJ: Scarecrow Press, 1975.

Stern, Fritz, ed. *The Varieties of History from Voltaire to the Present*. New York: Random, 1956.

Sternsher, Bernard. *Consensus, Conflict, and American Historians*. Bloomington: Indiana University Press, 1975.

Thompson, James Westfall. *A History of Historical Writing*. 2 Vols. New York: Irvington, 1942.

Tosh, John, ed. *Historians on History*. Harlow, England: Pearson Education, 2000.

Ward, Kyle. *History in the Making*. New York: The New Press, 2006.

Wilson, Norman J. *History in Crisis? Recent Directions in Historiography*, 2nd ed. Upper Saddle River, NJ: Pearson Education, 2005.

Windschuttle, Keith. *The Killing of History: How Literary Critics and Social Theorists Are Murdering Our Past.* New York: The Free Press, 1997.

Wise, Gene. *American Historical Explanations.* Minneapolis: University of Minnesota Press, 1980.

Writing Skills

Anderson, Richard. *Writing That Works.* New York: McGraw-Hill Publishing Company, 1989.

Barnes, Gregory A. *Write for Success.* Philadelphia: ISI Press, 1986.

Bennett, James D. and Lowell H. Harrison. *Writing History Papers.* Wheeling, IL.: Harlan Davidson, Inc., 1979.

Cuba, Lee. *A Short Guide to Writing about Social Science.* 2nd ed. New York: HarperCollins College Publishers, 1993.

Hacker, Diane. *A Writer's Reference.* 6th ed. Boston: Bedford/St. Martins Press, 2006.

Hashimoto, Irvin Y. *Thirteen Weeks: A Guide to Teaching College Writing.* Portsmouth: Boynton/Cook Publishers, 1991.

Meyer, Herbert E. and Jill M. Meyer. *How to Write.* Washington, D.C.: Storm King Press, 1987.

Ponsot, Marie, and Rosemary Deen. *Beat Not the Poor Desk.* Portsmouth, NH: Boynton/Cook Publishers, 1982.

Storey, William Kelleher. *Writing History: A Guide for Students.* 2nd ed. New York: Oxford University Press, 2004.

Strunk, William, Jr. and E. B. White. *The Elements of Style.* 3rd ed. New York: The Macmillan Company, 1979.

Film and History

Carnes, Mark C. *Past Imperfect: History According to the Movies.* New York: Henry Holt and Co., 1995.

Ferro, Mark. *Cinema and History.* Detroit: Wayne State University Press, 1988.

Mintz, Steven, and Randy Roberts. *Hollywood's America: United States History Through Its Films.* St. James, NY: Brandywine Press, 1993.

Monaco, James. *How to Read a Film.* Rev. ed. New York: Oxford University Press, 1981.

O'Connor, John, ed. *Image as Artifact: The Historical Analysis of Film and Television.* Malabar, FL.: Robert E. Krieger Publishing Co., 1990.

———, and Martin A. Jackson. *Teaching History with Film.* Washington, D.C.: American Historical Association, 1974.

Rollins, Peter, ed. *Hollywood as Historian: American Film in a Cultural Context.* Lexington: University Press of Kentucky, 1983.

Roquemore, Joseph. *History Goes to the Movies.* New York: Broadway Books, 1999.

Rosenstone, Robert A. *History on Film/Film on History.* Harlow, England: Pearson Education Ltd., 2006.

Short, K. R. M., ed. *Feature Films as History.* Knoxville: University of Tennessee Press, 1981.

Smith, Paul, ed. *The Historian and Film.* Cambridge: Cambridge University Press, 1976.

Toplin, Robert Brent, *History by Hollywood.* Urbana: University of Illinois Press, 1996.

INDEX

The Methods and Skills of History: A Practical Guide
Developmental editor and copy editor: Andrew J. Davidson
Production editor: Linda Gaio
Proofreader: Claudia Siler
Typesetter: Bruce Leckie
Printer: Versa Press